PARLEZ TOURISME

CERT
The State Tourism Training Agency

Authors:
Juliette Péchenart
David Pyle
Frédérique Rantz
Anne Tangy

Gill & Macmillan

Gill & Macmillan Ltd

Goldenbridge

Dublin 8

with associated companies throughout the world

© CERT — The State Tourism Training Agency 1995

© Artwork Paul Mc Elheron & Associates

0 7171 2153 4

Print origination in Ireland by Paul Mc Elheron & Associates

All rights reserved.
No part of this publication may be reproduced, copied or transmitted in any form or by any means without written permission of the publishers or else under the terms of any licence permitting limited copying issued by the Irish Copyright Licensing Agency, The Writers' Centre, Parnell Square, Dublin 1.

ACKNOWLEDGMENTS

CERT would like to thank the many people involved in the preparation of this book – its advisory and administrative staff, tourism teachers and industry consultants, and the teachers and staff in regional tourist offices who piloted draft units.

In particular CERT acknowledges:

- the support of the LINGUA programme of the European Union which partly funded the development of *Parlez Tourisme* (without which support this book would not have been possible)

- CERT's partners in this LINGUA project in France, Germany, Greece, Italy and Spain who contributed to the language needs analysis and syllabus design from which this book has been developed

- those who patiently produced the successive drafts of *Parlez Tourisme,* especially Eileen Colgan and Gerardine Prendergast

- Sheena Brown and Dorothy Kenny who compiled the glossary

- Clara Martin who prepared the *Pause Café* culture sections

- the 'voices' on the audio cassettes: Nathalie Barbier, Catherine André, Alain Bardillon, Albert Bertoux and Vincent Boulard.

Picture Credits
For permission to reproduce photographs, grateful acknowledgment is made to the following: John Topham Picture Library, Camera Press, Magnum Photos Ltd, Barnaby's Picture Library.

For assistance with illustrations, the publishers are grateful to the following:

Air France

Bord Fáilte

Catering Equipment Association with BWG Foods Caterservice

Club Med

Comité Départmental du Tourisme, Chambre de Commerce, Cahors

Comité Régional du Tourisme et des Loisirs d'Ile de France

Delphi Adventure Centre, Leenane, Co. Galway

Dublin City University

Istres Syndicat d'Initiative

La Manche - Guide Des Hôtels et Restaurants 1991 (published by Office Départmental du Tourisme de la Manche)

Le Parc International d'Expositions Paris-Nord (published by Chambre de Commerce et d'Industrie de Paris)

Les Arc (published by Office du Tourisme, Bourg St Maurice)

Nouvelles Frontières

Pierre et Vacances, Eté 93

Que Choisir July/August 1990 (published by Union Fédérale des Consommateurs)

SNCF

Syndicat d'Initiative, Bretenoux

Syndicat d'Initiative de Mende et des Gorges du Tarn

10° West, Elly Bay, Belmullet, Co. Mayo

Top Rail (published by The BLA Group Ltd)

Vacances en Irlande 1987 (published by Irish Continental Line, now Irish Ferries)

CONTENTS

Introduction	vii
Users' Guide	ix
Unit 1: Greetings and responding to greetings	1
Greetings 'À la française'	11
Unit 2: Dealing with numbers, dates, time and money	13
Time for a break?	26
Unit 3: Dealing with directions, signs and regulations	29
So near and yet so far	43
Unit 4: Using the telephone	45
Calling all travellers!	53
Test your Competence 1	55
Unit 5: Tourist information	63
Where to stay	76
Unit 6: Travel information	78
Travelling by train	94
Unit 7: Sports and leisure	98
Time on your hands	111
Unit 8: Excursions and tours	113
A trip around the parks	131
Unit 9: Conferences and fairs	134
France for business	147
Test your Competence 2	149
Grammar Summary	173
Pronunciation Guide	186
Glossary	191
Answer Keys	207

INTRODUCTION

Parlez Tourisme is a new audio language learning package for students of tourism or professionals working within the tourism industry in the following areas:

Tourist information offices
Travel agencies
Sports and leisure centres
Tour guiding
Conference centres and trade fairs

It has been designed for people with little or no French who want to communicate effectively with French-speaking visitors and upgrade their overall standard of service.
All of the activities have been designed from the point of view of people who work in the tourism industry and aim to meet their on-the-job needs.
Considerable emphasis is placed on active learning with a balance between listening and speaking skills throughout.
The course is divided into two main parts and nine units. Units 1 to 4 cover all the basic general language a professional in tourism needs. Units 5 to 9 look at specific areas of the tourism industry and introduce specialised vocabulary and interactions taking place in work situations.
Learners can monitor their progress in the **Test your Competence** sections included at the end of the first and second parts of the book.
The book should be used in conjunction with the accompanying audio cassettes.

USERS' GUIDE

The Purpose
Parlez Tourisme is an audio language learning package designed to meet the needs of students of tourism or professionals already employed in the tourism industry, whether studying alone or in a group.

The Level
Parlez Tourisme is aimed at beginners or lower intermediate students. It can also be used as a refresher course by people who have studied French at school but need a more practical and professional knowledge of the language.

The Materials
The package consists of a book and audio cassettes. A grammar summary, a pronunciation guide, a glossary and answer keys are included at the back of the book. The audio cassettes, with a tape script and English translations, are available separately.

The Components
Parlez Tourisme has nine units. The first four units include most of the general language you will need as a professional working in tourism. At the end of unit 4, you will be able to review your progress before you move on to the next five units which look at specific areas of the tourism industry: tourist information, travel information, sports and leisure, excursions and tours, conferences and fairs.

Once you have studied the first four units, you can use *Parlez Tourisme* as you wish. Depending on your area of work or study, your time and your preferences, you can tailor *Parlez Tourisme* to fit your own specific needs.

How to Use the Course

Listening passages
To start with we recommend that you read the questions that accompany each listening passage before you listen to the tape. This will focus your ears and help you to concentrate on those key words and expressions you really need to understand the passage. You can then listen to the passage as many times as you need as this will help you build up your listening skills.

All the interactions are situational and take place in various working environments with which you are probably already familiar.

How to say it
You will find there is a selection of key structures and phrases. Study them and see how the French language works. A lot of these structures and phrases are used in the **Language practice** exercises, in both listening and speaking activities, so do look back at the **How to say it** section if

you get stuck for a word or an expression.

Help!
These are vocabulary lists which we have selected and which we consider to be particularly useful. They will also be of help if you get stuck in any of the exercises.

Pause Café
A series of short articles, in English, gives you that practical information you will need to reach a better understanding of the French people you will meet in your work place, in your own country or when on holiday in France. They have been written in a humorous vein and should provide you with a well-deserved excuse for a coffee break during your study; they appear at the end of each learning unit.

At the back of the book you will find:

Grammar summary
Study some of the main aspects of French grammar if you wish to do so.

Pronunciation guide
Read about the main sounds of the French language and how they differ from English sounds.

Glossary
Check up on words you don't know.

Working on Your Own
As well as this book you will need to buy the audio cassettes. With them you will get the essential tape scripts and translations. You will notice that the audio cassettes include no pauses for your responses. So, when you are doing exercises that require your participation, remember to stop the tape each time before you answer. While you are working with this book and the audio cassettes, if you really need to do so, you can read a passage in the tape script and translations. After you have done the tasks and exercises you will be able to find out how you have done in the Answer Keys section.

After Units 4 and 9 you will find a **Test your Competence** section with which you can check your progress. Do not attempt to move on if you find you are having difficulty doing the exercises in those sections. The exercises combine the language skills most necessary in your industry, especially listening and speaking. Some of the exercises also aim at developing your reading and writing skills. You will find the answers at the back of this book.

USERS' GUIDE

There are a few things worth remembering when learning a language, particularly if you intend to study on your own.

Motivation: In order to stay motivated, you will need to define your needs and set yourself workable, realistic goals. Think about what you need French for and make a list of the situations and types of exchanges in which you are involved through your work. Try to concentrate on those when you are studying with *Parlez Tourisme*.

Little and often: People learn in different ways and at different speeds but remember that it is better to do a little every day than a lot once a month. Decide how much time you can set aside for French. Organise a regular time for practice and try to stick to it.

Practice: You will need plenty of time and practice before you feel confident in the language but remember that French visitors will really appreciate your efforts and that you don't have to be fluent to communicate. You are lucky to work in an industry where you don't need to travel to the country to practise so do not hesitate to start using your new language from the very beginning.

THROUGHOUT THIS BOOK THESE SYMBOLS ARE USED TO GUIDE YOUR STUDY :

Listen to the tape

Speak your answers

Read material for an exercise

How to say it

Special Help! Section

GREETINGS AND RESPONDING TO GREETINGS UNIT

Objectives

At the end of this unit you will be able to:

- Greet and respond to greetings

- Say who you are and what you do

- Ask somebody's name, address, telephone number, nationality

- Give your own name and details

- Spell names

- Say goodbye

1

GREETINGS AND RESPONDING TO GREETINGS

Greeting

Listening 1:

(a) Listen to the guide greeting the members of the 'Club de l'Histoire', who are travelling to Rome.

Number on the list below the names of the participants in the correct order as they are met by the guide :

```
              TRANS–VOYAGES
            LE CLUB DE L'HISTOIRE
              Voyage Paris–Rome
             Liste des Participants
```

Jean-Louis PALU ☐	Paul DUPUIS ☐
Bernard MARTIN ☐	Madame GARNIER ☐
Claire ARNOUX ☐	Chantal DUPONT ☐
Brigitte FOURNET ☐	Philippe DURAND ☐
Hervé LANCEL ☐	Isabelle HUGOT ☐

(b) Listen to the tape again as often as you find necessary and tick the following words/expressions each time you hear them:

	1	2	3	4	5	6	7	8	9	10
Bonjour										
Bienvenue										
Quel est votre nom?										
Comment vous appelez-vous?										
S'il vous plaît										

GREETINGS AND RESPONDING TO GREETINGS

How to say it

Bonjour	Monsieur/Madame/Mademoiselle	Good morning/good afternoon/hello
Bonsoir		Good evening
Bienvenue		Welcome

| Quel est votre | nom / prénom | s'il vous plaît? | What is your | name / first name | please? |

| Votre | nom / prénom | s'il vous plaît? | Your | name / first name | please? |

Comment vous appelez-vous? — What is your name?

Vous êtes	M. Martin?	Are you	Mr Martin?
	Mme Dupont?		Mrs Dupont?
	Mlle Durand?		Miss Durand?

| Je | m'appelle / suis | M. Martin / Mme Dupont / Mlle Durand | My name is / I am | Mr Martin / Mrs Dupont / Miss Durand |

Spelling

Listening 2:

Listen to the French alphabet and repeat each letter as you hear it.

A – B – C – D – E – F – G – H – I – J – K – L – M – N – O – P – Q – R – S – T – U – V – W – X – Y – Z

Listening 3:

At the Trade Fair / Au Salon

(a) Listen to the hostess at the computer trade fair giving badges to the participants.

Complete the names of the participants by filling in the missing letters.

1. P . . . C . . . . . . D
2. P . . . . . . Q . . . A . . . I . . . I
3. V A . . . . R
4. M . . . R P . . . Y
5. . . . I . . C . . . E . . .

GREETINGS AND RESPONDING TO GREETINGS

 (b)   Listen to the tape again and, on the map below, circle the countries and cities you hear.

GREETINGS AND RESPONDING TO GREETINGS

Help!

Countries/Pays	Nationalities/Nationalités
Allemagne	allemand/allemande
Angleterre	anglais/anglaise
Belgique	belge
France	français/française
Irlande	irlandais/irlandaise
Italie	italien/italienne

How to say it

Quelle est votre	nationalité?		What is your	nationality?	
	adresse?			address?	
D'où venez-vous?			Where do you come from?		
Votre	adresse	s'il vous plaît?	Your	address	please?
	nationalité			nationality	
Mon adresse	est ...		My address	is ...	
Ma nationalité			nationality		
Comment ça s'écrit?			How do you write this?		
Vous pouvez épeler?			Can you spell it?		
J'habite	Paris		I live in	Paris	
	Rome			Rome	
Voilà votre badge			There is your badge		
Merci			Thank you		
Au revoir			Goodbye		

GREETINGS AND RESPONDING TO GREETINGS

DEALING WITH NUMBERS

Listening 4:

Listen to the tape and repeat the following numbers from one to fifty.

0	zéro	20	vingt	40	quarante
1	un	21	vingt et un	41	quarante et un
2	deux	22	vingt-deux	42	quarante-deux
3	trois	23	vingt-trois	43	quarante-trois
4	quatre	24	vingt-quatre	44	quarante-quatre
5	cinq	24	vingt-cinq	45	quarante-cinq
6	six	26	vingt-six	46	quarante-six
7	sept	27	vingt-sept	47	quarante-sept
8	huit	28	vingt-huit	48	quarante-huit
9	neuf	29	vingt-neuf	49	quarante-neuf
10	dix	30	trente	50	cinquante
11	onze	31	trente et un		
12	douze	32	trente-deux		
13	treize	33	trente-trois		
14	quatorze	34	trente-quatre		
15	quinze	35	trente-cinq		
16	seize	36	trente-six		
17	dix-sept	37	trente-sept		
18	dix-huit	38	trente-huit		
19	dix-neuf	39	trente-neuf		

Listening 5:

Listen to the tape and circle the numbers you hear on the card below.

0	10	20	30	40
1	11	21	31	41
2	12	22	32	42
3	13	23	33	43
4	14	24	34	44
5	15	25	35	45
6	16	26	36	46
7	17	27	37	47
8	18	28	38	48
9	19	29	39	49

GREETINGS AND RESPONDING TO GREETINGS

Listening 6:

Tourists are looking for the telephone numbers of some car hire companies. Listen to the tape and match the telephone number with the car hire company.

1. Hertz   A. 43 05 24 29
2. Europcar   B. 49 27 25 03
3. Avis   C. 42 23 06 15
4. Budget   D. 44 07 28 20
5. Mattei   E. 48 17 02 06

Listening 7:

Listen to the Listening 3 passage again and circle the correct answers below.

1. Mrs Picard's address is:

   5
   15   avenue de l'Europe
   20

2. Mr Pasqualini's address is:

   3
   13   Piazza Rimini
   20

3. Mr Vacher's address is:

   7
   17   boulevard Gambetta
   16

4. Miss Murphy's address is:

   8
   6   Davis Street
   7

5. Mrs Fischer's address is:

   14
   18   Gartenstrasse
   8

GREETINGS AND RESPONDING TO GREETINGS

SAYING WHO YOU ARE AND WHAT YOU DO

Listening 8:

Look at the pictures below. They show people who work in various areas of the tourism industry. Now listen to the tape where those people introduce themselves and say what they do. Match the picture with the number.

Example: 1. A

2. ☐   4. ☐

3. ☐   5. ☐

GREETINGS AND RESPONDING TO GREETINGS

Help!

Professions	Professions
Guide accompagnateur/accompagnatrice	Tour escort
Agent de tourisme	Tourist information officer
Hôtesse d'accueil/Steward	Conference assistant
Animateur/animatrice	Leisure assistant
Agent de Voyages	Travel agent

Language practice

Exercise 1:

At The Reception
À La Réception

Campers are arriving and want to book in.
Take down their surnames as you hear them spelt out on the tape.

Camping de la Plage

1. . . . .   4. . . . .

2. . . . .   5. . . . .

3. . . . .   6. . . . .

Exercise 2:

Match the following French words with their English meaning.

Bonjour	Welcome
Bonsoir	Goodbye
Bienvenue	Hello
Au revoir	Thank you
Être	To be called
S'appeler	To come from
Venir de	To live
Habiter	To be
Voilà	Please
Merci	Here is
S'il vous plaît	Good evening

Note: If you are uncertain about the meaning of a word, you can check it in the glossary at the back of the book.

GREETINGS AND RESPONDING TO GREETINGS

Exercise 3:

(a) Give information about yourself, answering the questions on the tape.

(b) Now look at the identity cards below and answer the same questions as if you were Monsieur Leclerc and Madame Trigano.

1. Nom: LECLERC
    Prénom: André
    Adresse: 12 rue du Figuier
                Paris, France
    Téléphone: 43 25 16 32
    Profession: Agent de Voyages

2. Nom: TRIGANO
    Prénom: Anne
    Adresse: 30 rue Saint Blaise,
                Lyon, France
    Téléphone: 35 24 46 13
    Profession: Animatrice

Exercise 4:

You are greeting guests at the hotel reception. A guest arrives who has booked a room in advance. However, you need further information to fill out her registration form. You play the part of the receptionist.

AT THE RECEPTION

À LA RÉCEPTION

Receptionist	*Say Hello.*
Guest	Bonjour Madame.
Receptionist	*Ask her her name.*
Guest	Madame Martin.
Receptionist	*Ask her her address.*
Guest	18 avenue Parmentier, Paris.
Receptionist	*Ask her her nationality.*
Guest	Je suis française.
Receptionist	*Thank her.*

GREETINGS AND RESPONDING TO GREETINGS

GREETINGS 'A LA FRANÇAISE'

You may find the French greeting each other in various ways, some with kisses on the cheeks, others with handshakes and you may find yourself wondering what it's all about. Believe it or not, there is method in their madness!

The Handshake

The formal way of greeting someone in France is the handshake. In formal situations, introductions are always accompanied by a handshake and a polite *enchanté* to which one can reply *enchanté* as well.

The first greeting of the day can be a handshake with a friendly *bonjour* between people whose relationship is formal or between male friends.

Bises

Bises (meaning kisses) is pronounced *bees*.

Now this is where the confusion starts. How? How many? In what situation? Sometimes the French themselves are not so sure — what is sure is that the *bises* represent friendship and acceptance and do not necessarily mean that the person fancies you!

They are usually used as the greeting between young people, between adults and children and between adult men and women who are on friendly terms.

GREETINGS AND RESPONDING TO GREETINGS

How?
The most common way is for the person who wishes to start to offer their cheek. The other person may respond either by kissing the cheek or by pressing his or her cheek against that of their *bises* partner and kissing the air.
The number of kisses given depends on the region. Parisians give four — outside Paris it can be three or two.

The Place
There seems to be no limit to location. An early morning kisser will feel no guilt at causing a traffic jam on a school staircase or in the doorway of a bus or tram!

N.B. Points to remember as a professional working with tourists:

DO NOT shake hands with or give *bises* to a tourist unless he or she has initiated it.
DO NOT forget to address a tourist as *Madame, Monsieur* or *Mademoiselle* in the singular or *Mesdames, Messieurs* or *Mesdemoiselles* in the plural. If the group includes both men and women you can use *Messieurs/dames*. There is no French equivalent of Ms.

DEALING WITH NUMBERS, DATES, TIME AND MONEY UNIT 2

Objectives

At the end of this unit you will be able to:

- Give information about time and time of day

- Give information about dates

- Inform about times of services

- Give information about prices and accept payments

- Thank and respond to thanks

Pavement café in Grasse (Alpes-Maritimes)

DEALING WITH NUMBERS, DATES, TIME AND MONEY

GIVING INFORMATION ABOUT THE TIME

Listening 1:

(a) The hotel receptionist is telling tourists what time it is.
Listen and check the times on the clocks.

A. Il est 9 heures

B. Il est 9 heures et quart

C. Il est 9 heures et demie

D. Il est dix heures moins le quart

E. Il est midi

F. Il est minuit

(b) Listen to the receptionist again and repeat each time as it is given on the tape.

Listening 2:

A conference assistant is giving the time to participants.
Listen and write in the times on the clocks below.

A.

B.

C.

D.

E.

F.

DEALING WITH NUMBERS, DATES, TIME AND MONEY

Listening 3:

What is the correct time? Listen to the tape and tick the correct clock.

A. 2h00   10h00

B. 6h00   10h00

C. 7h15   5h15

D. 10h30   6h30

E. 6h45   7h45

F. midi   minuit

DEALING WITH NUMBERS, DATES, TIME AND MONEY

HOW TO SAY IT

| Quelle heure est-il,
Il est quelle heure,
Vous avez l'heure, | s'il vous plaît? | What time is it,
Have you the right time, | please? |

Il est ... **heures**
midi
minuit

It is ... o'clock
midday
midnight

Excusez-moi
Pardon

Excuse me

De rien
Je vous en prie

You are welcome

GIVING INFORMATION ABOUT TIMES OF DAY, DATES AND TIMES OF SERVICES

Listening 4:

(a) Listen to the travel agent giving her itinerary to a client. Indicate the itinerary on the map below.

AT THE TRAVEL AGENCY

À L'AGENCE DE VOYAGES

Excursion Provence-Côte d'Azur

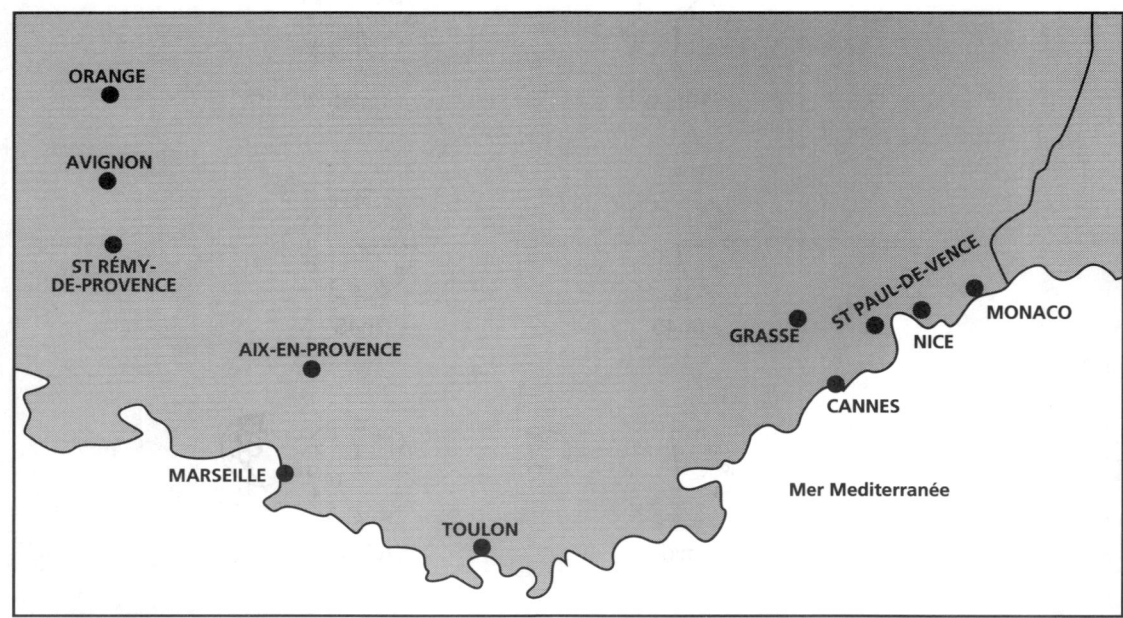

DEALING WITH NUMBERS, DATES, TIME AND MONEY

 HELP!

Jours de la semaine	Days of the week
lundi	Monday
mardi	Tuesday
mercredi	Wednesday
jeudi	Thursday
vendredi	Friday
samedi	Saturday
dimanche	Sunday

 HELP!

matin	morning
après-midi	afternoon
soir	evening

 (b) Listen again and indicate the towns visited in the programme below.

	matin	après-midi	soir
lundi		−	−
mardi		−	−
mercredi			−
jeudi		−	
vendredi			
samedi	−	−	−
dimanche		−	

Listening 5:

A businessman is checking the dates and locations of various trade fairs in France. Listen to the secretary at the National Trade Information Centre giving him the information and match the list of trade fairs below with the corresponding dates.

AT THE TRADE FAIR

AU SALON

DEALING WITH NUMBERS, DATES, TIME AND MONEY

 **HELP!**

Mois de l'année	Months of the year
janvier	January
février	February
mars	March
avril	April
mai	May
juin	June
juillet	July
août	August
septembre	September
octobre	October
novembre	November
décembre	December

1. Foire de Limoges ☐   a. 14–17 janvier
2. Foire de Lyon ☐   b. 5–8 février
3. Foire de Paris ☐   c. 12–19 mars
4. Foire de Nice ☐   d. 3–9 avril
5. Foire de Bordeaux ☐   e. 19–24 mai
6. Foire de Strasbourg ☐   f. 5–11 juin
7. Foire de Grenoble ☐   g. 23–26 juillet
8. Foire de Toulouse ☐   h. 7–14 août
9. Foire de Biarritz ☐   i. 24–28 septembre
10. Foire de Dijon ☐   j. 1–7 octobre
11. Foire de Marseille ☐   k. 6–9 novembre
12. Foire de Rennes ☐   l. 3–6 décembre

DEALING WITH NUMBERS, DATES, TIME AND MONEY

Listening 6:

The tourist information officer is giving information about opening times of tourist attractions and services.

Listen to the dialogues and fill in the missing details.

1.
Banque
Ouverte de ..... à .....
Open from   to
et de ..... à .....
and from   to
Fermée le ....
Closed on

2.
Poste
Ouverte de ..... à .....
Open from   to
Fermée le ....
Closed on

3.
Château
Ouvert de ..... à .....
Open from   to
Fermé le ....
Closed on

4.
Musée
Ouvert de ..... à .....
Open from   to
Fermé le ....
Closed on

HELP!

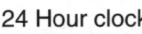

24 Hour clock

Most timetables use the 24 hour clock.
Here is a table of equivalent times.

1.00 p.m.	= 13 heures (treize heures)
2.00 p.m.	= 14 heures (quatorze heures)
3.00 p.m.	= 15 heures (quinze heures)
4.00 p.m.	= 16 heures (seize heures)
5.00 p.m.	= 17 heures (dix-sept heures)
6.00 p.m.	= 18 heures (dix-huit heures)
7.00 p.m.	= 19 heures (dix-neuf heures)
8.00 p.m.	= 20 heures (vingt heures)
9.00 p.m.	= 21 heures (vingt et une heures)
10.00 p.m.	= 22 heures (vingt-deux heures)
11.00 p.m.	= 23 heures (vingt-trois heures)
12.00 midnight	= minuit

DEALING WITH NUMBERS, DATES, TIME AND MONEY

How to say it

| La banque
Le musée | ouvre
ferme | à ... heures | The bank
The museum | opens
closes | at ... o'clock |

| Le château est ouvert
La poste est fermée | de ... heures à ... heures | The castle is open
The post office is closed | from ... o'clock to ... o'clock |

| Le musée est ouvert
La banque est fermée | le dimanche
en août
aujourd'hui
demain | The museum is open
The bank is closed | on Sundays
in August
today
tomorrow |

| Je peux vous aider?
Vous désirez? | | Can I help you? | |

Giving information about prices and accepting payment

Listening 7:

(a) Listen to the tape and repeat the following numbers from fifty to three thousand:

50	cinquante	70	soixante-dix	90	quatre-vingt-dix
51	cinquante et un	71	soixante et onze	91	quatre-vingt-onze
52	cinquante-deux	72	soixante-douze	92	quatre-vingt-douze
53	cinquante-trois	73	soixante-treize	93	quatre-vingt-treize
54	cinquante-quatre	74	soixante-quatorze	94	quatre-vingt-quatorze
55	cinquante-cinq	75	soixante-quinze	95	quatre-vingt-quinze
56	cinquante-six	76	soixante-seize	96	quatre-vingt-seize
57	cinquante-sept	77	soixante-dix-sept	97	quatre-vingt-dix-sept
58	cinquante-huit	78	soixante-dix-huit	98	quatre-vingt-dix-huit
59	cinquante-neuf	79	soixante-dix-neuf	99	quatre-vingt-dix-neuf
60	soixante	80	quatre-vingts	100	cent
61	soixante et un	81	quatre-vingt-un	200	deux cents
62	soixante-deux	82	quatre-vingt-deux	300	trois cents
63	soixante-trois	83	quatre-vingt-trois	400	quatre cents
64	soixante-quatre	84	quatre-vingt-quatre	500	cinq cents
65	soixante-cinq	85	quatre-vingt-cinq	600	six cents
66	soixante-six	86	quatre-vingt-six	700	sept cents
67	soixante-sept	87	quatre-vingt-sept	800	huit cents
68	soixante-huit	88	quatre-vingt-huit	900	neuf cents
69	soixante-neuf	89	quatre-vingt-neuf	1000	mille
				2000	deux mille
				3000	trois mille

DEALING WITH NUMBERS, DATES, TIME AND MONEY

(b) Now, try to say, and then listen and repeat the large numbers below:
2850   7060
1994   1956

Listening 8:

How much money do these guests want to change?
Listen to the tape and write down the amounts.

AT THE SHOPS

DANS LES MAGASINS

1. $ = ...   2. £ = ...
3. DM = ...   4. SF = ...
5. ¥(Yen) = ...   6. BF = ...

Listening 9:

(a) Listen to tourists asking the price of goods in a duty-free shop and fill in the price of each object. Remember, instead of a decimal point, French people use a comma *(une virgule)*.

a. ....   b ....
c ....   d ....
e ....   f ....

(b) Listen to the tourists on the tape again and tick how they are going to pay.

	whisky whiskey	chocolats chocolates	vodka vodka	parfum perfume	cigarettes cigarettes	champagne champagne
en espèces in cash						
par chèque by cheque						
par carte de crédit by credit card						

DEALING WITH NUMBERS, DATES, TIME AND MONEY

 HOW TO SAY IT

Combien coûte	ce parfum?	How much is	this perfume?
Ça coûte	combien	un paquet de cigarettes?		a packet of cigarettes?
C'est			
Ça fait			

Ça coûte | ... francs   It costs | ... francs
C'est   It is
Ça fait

Comment payez-vous?
Vous payez comment?   How are you going to pay?

DEALING WITH NUMBERS, DATES, TIME AND MONEY

LANGUAGE PRACTICE

Exercise 1: Word Search

Hidden in this square are all seven days of the week and twelve months of the year. They read from left to right and from top to bottom.

A	V	R	I	L	M	O	N	T	A	F	E	V	H	O	M
R	O	T	O	M	O	N	T	A	E	E	E	E	M	A	A
S	D	E	C	E	M	B	R	E	T	V	E	N	E	T	I
J	K	I	F	K	I	L	O	G	I	R	P	D	R	M	S
U	L	L	R	J	U	I	N	H	T	I	H	R	A	A	R
I	O	U	A	P	L	A	N	I	R	E	A	E	R	R	M
L	M	N	T	R	U	M	M	A	O	R	N	D	C	D	O
L	A	D	O	N	B	O	R	D	D	P	W	I	Z	I	T
E	T	I	P	D	I	M	A	N	C	H	E	A	T	A	S
T	R	V	C	E	R	O	N	F	G	H	I	J	M	V	A
A	T	T	E	N	T	O	C	T	O	B	R	E	N	O	M
L	M	A	R	S	U	L	U	P	E	R	E	S	F	B	E
B	O	L	D	E	N	O	V	E	M	B	R	E	H	L	D
C	O	M	M	U	N	E	F	O	N	O	G	R	A	M	I
J	A	N	V	I	E	R	G	A	N	T	I	E	R	E	S
Z	Y	L	O	P	H	O	N	E	S	A	O	U	T	C	D
O	M	E	R	C	R	E	D	I	V	R	Z	M	E	O	Z
N	R	X	A	B	C	S	W	M	T	O	J	E	U	D	I
T	A	S	E	P	T	E	M	B	R	E	X	L	V	S	O

DEALING WITH NUMBERS, DATES, TIME AND MONEY

TOURIST INFORMATION
INFORMATIONS

Exercise 2:

You are working at the tourist information desk.

(a) Look at the signs below and practise giving information about the following places:

Example: Le musée national est ouvert de 10h à 17h. Il est fermé le mardi.

1.
```
National Museum
10.00 a.m. – 5.00 p.m.
Closed on Tuesdays
```

2.
```
International Hotel
Open March–November
Closed December/January/February
```

3.
```
Bank
Open 9.00 a.m. – 12.30 p.m.
2.00 p.m. – 5.30 p.m.
Closed on Saturdays
```

4.
```
Botanic Gardens
10.00 a.m. – 6.00 p.m.
Closed in December
```

(b) Listen to the questions on the tape and give the tourist the information required.
Example: Q: À quelle heure ouvre le jardin botanique?
          A: Le jardin botanique ouvre à 10h.

Exercise 3:

You are working in a duty-free shop. Tell tourists how much these items cost:

Example: a)   Ça coûte deux cents francs

AT THE SHOPS
DANS LES MAGASINS

a) 200,00F

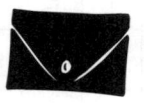
b) 350,00F

c) 45,00F

d) 15,00F

DEALING WITH NUMBERS, DATES, TIME AND MONEY

 e) 130,00F    f) 725,00F

 g) 23,00F    h) 73,00F

Exercise 4:

You are working in a tourist office. A visitor from France comes looking for information.

 Listen to the visitor and answer the questions as prompted below.

 You play the part of the assistant.

Visitor	Bonjour.
Assistant	*Greet the visitor and offer help.*
Visitor	Est-ce que le musée est ouvert aujourd'hui, s'il vous plaît?
Assistant	*Say that the museum is closed today.*
Visitor	Il est ouvert quand?
Assistant	*Say that the museum is open Tuesday to Sunday from 10.00 a.m. until 5.00 p.m.*
Visitor	Avez-vous un guide pour le musée?
Assistant	*Say yes, and that it costs two pounds.*
Visitor	Je vais en prendre un. Voilà.
Assistant	*Thank the visitor.*
Visitor	Merci bien.
Assistant	*Say goodbye to the visitor.*

DEALING WITH NUMBERS, DATES, TIME AND MONEY

TIME FOR A BREAK?

The French are hard-working people but nonetheless find the time to relax; the importance of knowing when to stop work is reflected in the opening and closing times of shops, banks and offices and in the number of mini-breaks which punctuate the working year.

Les Heures d'Ouverture (Opening times)
Les Banques (Banks)
These are usually *ouvertes* (open) from 8.00 or 9.00 a.m. to noon and from 2.00 to 6.00 p.m. from Monday to Friday, except on bank holidays of course! Outside Paris, in the provinces, some banks open on Saturday mornings.

Les Magasins (Shops)
Paris opening times are from 8.30 or 9.00 a.m. until 7.00 p.m. Shops in Paris usually remain open at lunchtime. However, outside Paris the two or even three-hour lunch break is something of an institution particularly in the South of France where midday temperatures in summer can keep even the most enthusiastic shopper from venturing out. It is worth while checking the times and *les jours d'ouverture* (opening days) on the entrance door. Don't be surprised if you see *fermé le lundi* (closed on Mondays) as some shops may take their weekends on Sundays and Mondays.

Fortunately however, if you are in great distress, you will almost certainly find a *centre commercial* or shopping centre which stays open through lunchtime and closes as late as 9.00 or 10.00 p.m.

Fêtes et Jours Fériés (Feast days and public holidays)

A look at a French calendar may confuse you until you realise that the French celebrate not only *les anniversaires* (birthdays) but also *les fêtes* (feast days) of the saints after whom they are named. For example someone called Marc would celebrate his *fête* on 25 April as well as his birthday whenever it is.

1994 JANVIER ☉ 7h46 à 16h03	FÉVRIER ☉ 7h23 à 16h46	MARS ☉ 6h35 à 17h32	AVRIL ☉ 5h30 à 18h20	MAI ☉ 4h32 à 19h04	JUIN 1994 ☉ 3h54 à 19h44
1 S JOUR de l'AN	1 M S°Ella	1 M S. Aubin	1 V S. Hugues	1 D FÊTE du TRAVAIL	1 M S. Justin ☾
2 D Epiphanie	2 M Présentation	2 M S. Charles le B.	2 S S°Sandrine	2 L S Boris ☾	2 J S°Blandine
3 L S°Geneviève	3 J S Blaise ☾	3 J S. Guénolé	3 D PAQUES ☾	3 M SS. Phil., Jacq.	3 V S. Kévin
4 M S. Odilon	4 V S°Véronique	4 V S. Casimir ☾	4 L S. Isidore	4 M S. Sylvain	4 S S°Clotilde
5 M S. Édouard ☾	5 S S°Agathe	5 S S. Olive	5 M S°Irène	5 J S°Judith	5 D Fête Dieu
6 J S. Mélanie	6 D S. Gaston	6 D S°Colette	6 M S. Marcellin	6 V S°Prudence	6 L S. Norbert
7 V S. Raymond	7 L S°Eugénie	7 L S°Félicité	7 J S. J.-B. de la S.	7 S S°Gisèle	7 M S. Gilbert
8 S S. Lucien	8 M S°Jacqueline	8 M S. Jean de D.	8 V S°Julie	8 D VICT.1945/F. J.-d'Arc	8 M S. Médard
9 D S°Alix	9 M S°Apolline	9 M S°Françoise	9 S S. Gautier	9 L S. Pacôme	9 J S°Diane ●
10 L S. Guillaume	10 J S. Arnaud ●	10 J S. Vivien	10 D S. Fulbert	10 M S°Solange ●	10 V S. Landry
11 M S. Paulin ●	11 V N.-D. Lourdes	11 V S°Rosine	11 L S. Stanislas ●	11 M S°Estelle	11 S S. Barnabé
12 M S°Tatiana	12 S S. Félix	12 S S°Justine	12 M S. Jules	12 J ASCENSION	12 D S. Guy
13 J S°Yvette	13 D S°Béatrice	13 D S. Rodrigue	13 M S°Ida	13 V S°Rolande	13 L S. Antoine de P.
14 V S°Nina	14 L S. Valentin	14 L S°Mathilde	14 J S. Maxime	14 S S. Matthias	14 M S. Elisée
15 S S. Rémi	15 M Mardi-Gras	15 M S°Louise	15 V S. Paterne	15 D S°Denise	15 M S°Germaine
16 D S. Marcel	16 M Cendres	16 M S°Bénédicte	16 S S. Benoît-J.	16 L S. Honoré	16 J S. J.F. Régis D
17 L S°Roseline	17 J S. Alexis	17 J S. Patrice	17 D S. Anicet	17 M S. Pascal	17 V S. Hervé
18 M S°Prisca	18 V S°Bernadette D	18 V S. Cyrille	18 L S. Parfait	18 M S. Eric D	18 S S. Léonce
19 M S. Marius D	19 S S. Gabin	19 S S. Joseph	19 M S°Emma D	19 J S. Yves	19 D S. Romuald
20 J S. Sébastien	20 D Carême	20 D PRINTEMPS D	20 M S°Odette	20 V S. Bernardin	20 L S. Silvère
21 V S°Agnès	21 L S. P. Damien	21 L S°Clémence	21 J S. Anselme	21 S S. Constantin	21 M ÉTÉ
22 S S. Vincent	22 M S°Isabelle	22 M S°Léa	22 V S. Alexandre	22 D PENTECÔTE	22 M S. Alban
23 D S. Barnard	23 M S. Lazare	23 M S. Victorien	23 S S. Georges	23 L S. Didier	23 J S°Audrey ☾
24 L S. Fr. de Sales	24 J S. Modeste	24 J S°Cath. de Su.	24 D Jour du Souvenir	24 M S. Donatien	24 V S. Jean-Bapt.
25 M Conv. S. Paul	25 V S. Roméo	25 V Annonciation	25 L S. Marc ☾	25 M S°Sophie ☾	25 S S. Prosper
26 M S°Paule	26 S S. Nestor ☾	26 S S°Larissa	26 M S°Alida	26 J S. Bérenger	26 D S. Anthelme
27 J S°Angèle ☾	27 D S°Honorine	27 D Rameaux	27 M S°Zita	27 V S. Augustin	27 L S. Fernand
28 V S. Th. d'Aquin	28 L S. Romain	28 L S. Gontran	28 J S°Valérie	28 S S. Germain	28 M S°Irénée
29 S S. Gildas		29 M S°Gwladys	29 V S°Cath. de Si.	29 D Fête des Mères	29 M SS. Pierre, Paul
30 D S°Martine	Epacte 17 / Lettre dominicale B	30 M S. Amédée	30 S S. Robert	30 L S. Ferdinand	30 J S. Martial ☾
31 L S°Marcelle	Cycle solaire 15 / Nbre d'or 19 Indiction romaine 2	31 J S. Benjamin		31 M Visitation	

26

DEALING WITH NUMBERS, DATES, TIME AND MONEY

Also included on the calendar are the various *jours fériés* or public holidays many of which are religious feast days:

1er janvier	*Le Jour de l'An* (New Year's Day)
mars–avril	*Pâques* (Easter)
1er mai	*La fête du travail* (Labour Day)
8 mai	*Armistice 1945* (the end of World War II)
avril–mai	*Ascension* (Feast of the Ascension)
mai–juin	*Pentecôte* (Whit — seventh Sunday after Easter)
14 juillet	*Fête Nationale* (Bastille Day)
15 août	*Assomption* (Feast of the Assumption)
1er novembre	*Toussaint* (All Saints' Day)
11 novembre	*Armistice 1918* (end of World War I)
25 décembre	*Noël* (Christmas Day)

Faire le pont

To make a proper mini-holiday the French are often given some free days to join the *jour férié* (public holiday) to the weekend. This is known as *faire le pont* (making a bridge). In some companies, employees must take the extra days from their annual leave. Needless to say the chance to *faire le pont* is not only the privilege of builders and engineers, anyone can do it!

DEALING WITH NUMBERS, DATES, TIME AND MONEY

Market in Plessey-le-Roi, near Paris

Les Grandes Vacances

If you visit Paris in August, you may find a large number of foreign tourists walking the streets and mixing with not very many natives. This is probably because Parisians have fled the city for the sunnier climes of the South of France or the mountains: they traditionally take the month of August off. Of course services are maintained but you may need to walk some distance to find an open *boulangerie* where you can buy your croissants!

C'est combien s'il vous plaît? (How much is it please?)
When you finally find that boulangerie you may discover that you have another problem to deal with: payment and how to understand prices!

Sixty-thirteen francs, four twenties and fifteen is normally how a French person says seventy three francs, ninety five! So learning to count *à la française* is great fun.

Of course not all French-speaking people live in France. Your knowledge of French will be valuable in other countries too, such as Belgium and Switzerland. People there will understand you, but you will find they have their own way of saying some things *à la belge* or *à la suisse* (in the Belgian or Swiss way). Take the way they count. You may well hear the Belgian French or Swiss French use *septante* instead of *soixante-dix, octante* instead of *quatre-vingts* and *nonante* instead of *quatre-vingt-dix.* So you have:

Septante-sept   77
Octante-trois   83
Nonante-six   96

By the way, remember that French numbers are written differently from those in English-speaking countries. In France, 1,000 is written as 1.000. The decimal point is a comma, not a full stop; so don't have heart failure if the price of something you buy is 60,00F!

DEALING WITH DIRECTIONS, SIGNS AND REGULATIONS UNIT 3

Objectives

At the end of this unit you will be able to:

- Give directions

- Express distances

- Say how to get there

- Explain signs and notices

- Explain regulations

- Request people to comply with regulations

Entrance to the Paris métro at Strasbourg-St Denis station

DEALING WITH DIRECTIONS, SIGNS AND REGULATIONS

GIVING DIRECTIONS OUTDOORS AND INDOORS

Listening 1:

(a) The hostess at the tourist office's information desk is giving directions to tourists.

 Listen to the first three dialogues and follow the directions and arrows on the maps below.

    A. L'office du tourisme   B. La poste
    C. La banque   D. Le musée
    E. La gare   F. La pharmacie
    G. L'hôtel   H. L'agence de voyages
    I. La piscine

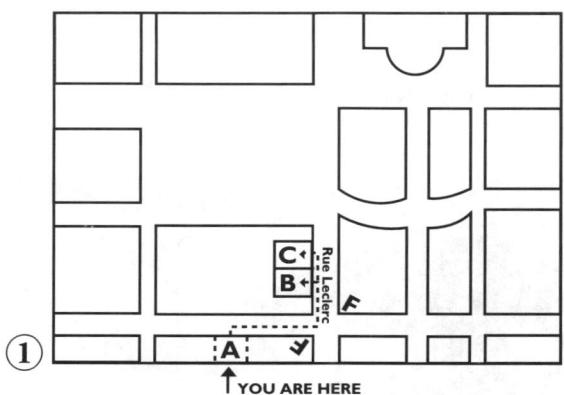

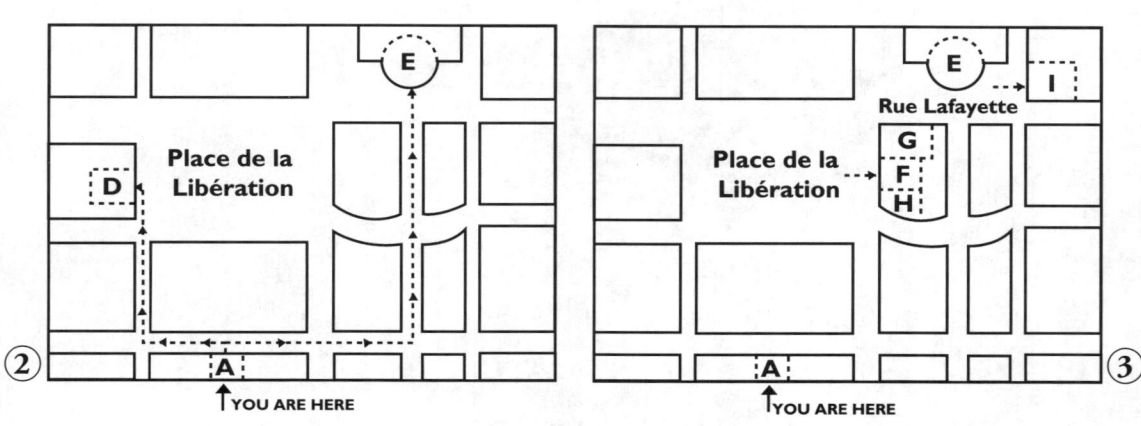

DEALING WITH DIRECTIONS, SIGNS AND REGULATIONS

HELP!

premier/première	first
deuxième	second
troisième	third
quatrième	fourth

à gauche	to the left
à droite	to the right
tout droit	straight on

(b) Now listen to the next three dialogues, and indicate on the maps below the directions given and the letters corresponding to the buildings.

- J. Le cinéma
- K. L'église
- L. Le restaurant
- M. Le café
- N. La boulangerie
- O. Le supermarché

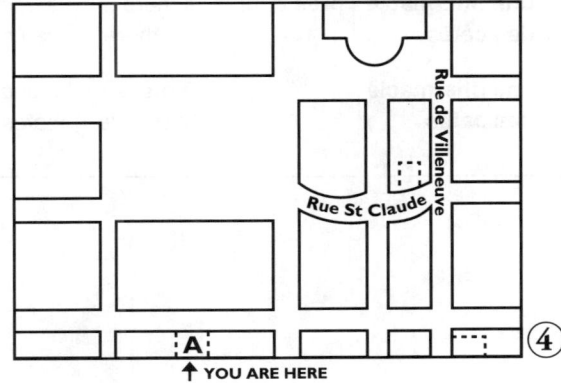

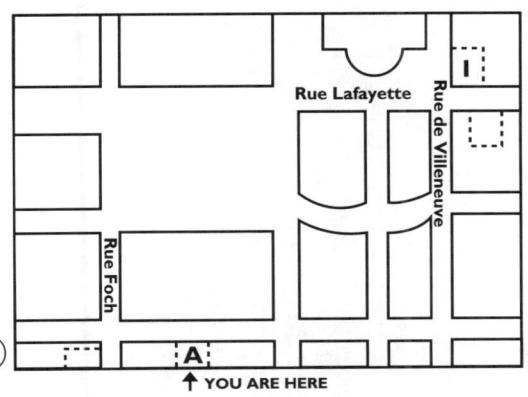

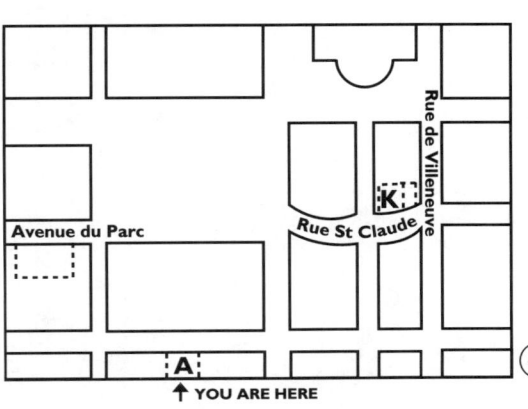

DEALING WITH DIRECTIONS, SIGNS AND REGULATIONS 3

How to say it

Où	est	le musée?		Where is	the museum?	
		la gare?			the railway station?	
	se trouve	le cinéma?			the cinema?	
		la pharmacie?			the chemist?	

Où sont		les toilettes?		Where are	the toilets?	

Pour aller	à	la piscine?		How do I get to	the swimming pool?	
		la poste?			the post office?	
	au	cinéma?			the cinema?	
		musée?			the museum?	

Prenez	à	gauche	au	cinéma	Turn	left	at the	cinema
Tournez		droite		feu rouge		right		traffic lights

Prenez la	première	rue	à gauche	Take the	first street on the left
	deuxième		à droite		second on the right

Continuez	tout droit		Continue	straight on
Allez			Go	

Est-ce qu'il y a	une pharmacie	près d'ici?	Is there	a chemist	nearby?
	des cafés		Are there	cafés	

Il y a	une pharmacie		There is	a chemist
	des cafés		There are	cafés

DEALING WITH DIRECTIONS, SIGNS AND REGULATIONS **3**

Listening 2:

Listen to a guide telling his group of tourists how to find various facilities in the Galerie Nationale. Locate the facilities and departments on the floor plans below and then indicate the order in which they are mentioned in the boxes below.

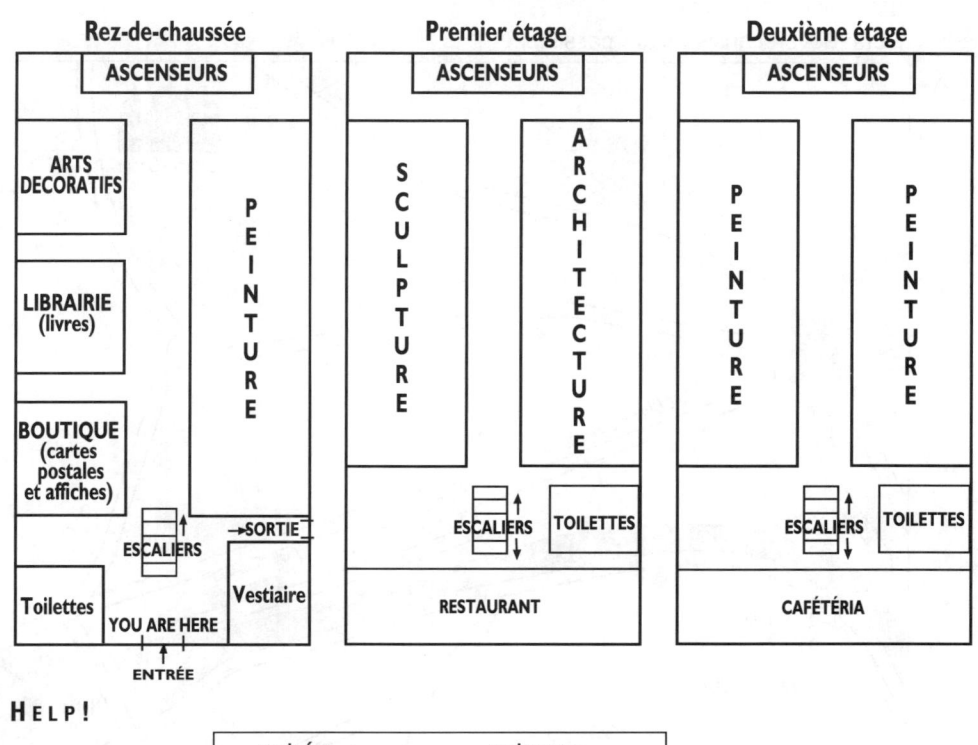

HELP!

entrée	entrance
sortie	exit
toilettes	toilets
librairie	bookshop
vestiaire	cloakroom
escaliers	stairs
ascenseurs	lifts

les toilettes ☐   les escaliers ☐

la cafétéria ☐   les ascenseurs ☐

le vestiaire ☐   le restaurant ☐

la boutique ☐   la librairie ☐

DEALING WITH DIRECTIONS, SIGNS AND REGULATIONS

SAYING HOW TO GET SOMEWHERE, EXPRESSING DISTANCES

Listening 3:

Listen to the hostess at the tourist information kiosk at the museum Centre Georges Pompidou in Paris directing tourists to various places. Listen to the dialogues and tick the appropriate mode(s) of transport to get to each monument.
Note: Several answers are possible.

AT THE MUSEUM / AU MUSÉE

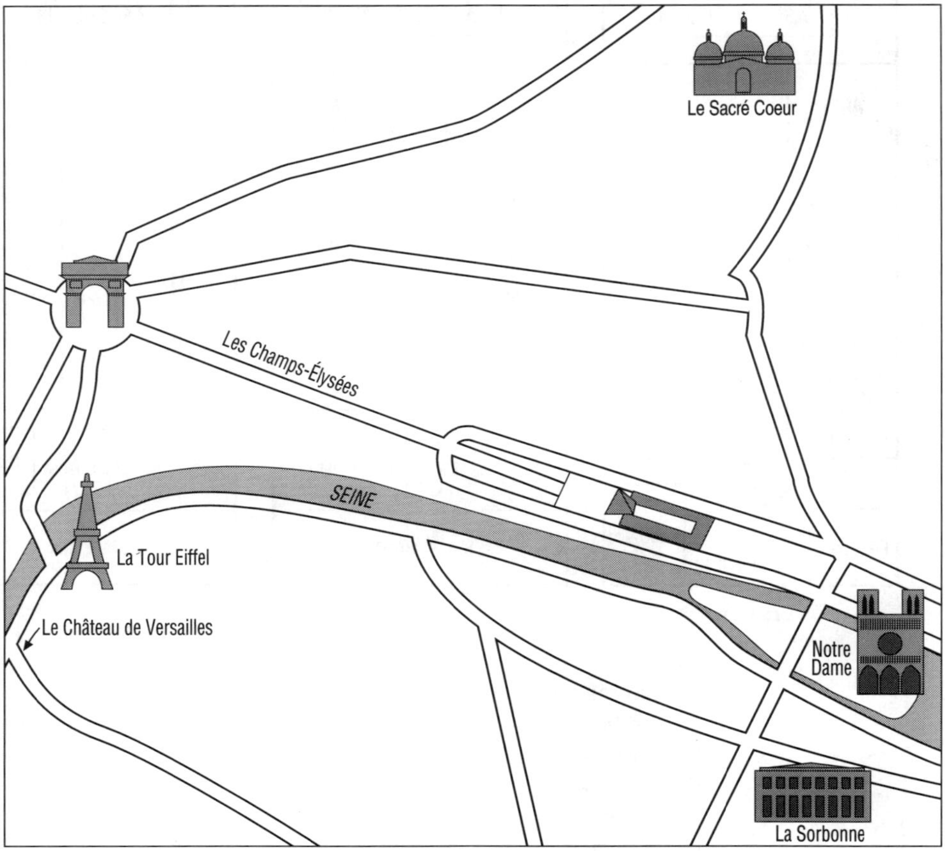

	À pied	Métro	Autobus/Bus	Train	Taxi	Voiture/Auto
Notre-Dame						
La Sorbonne						
Le Sacré-Coeur						
La Tour Eiffel						
Les Champs-Élysées						
Le Château de Versailles						

DEALING WITH DIRECTIONS, SIGNS AND REGULATIONS

Listening 4:

The information officer at the tourist office in Tours is giving information about the location of some *châteaux* (castles) and towns in the Loire Valley. Listen to her on the tape and fill in the distances and directions on the grid below.

	Distance: km	Direction
Châteaux:		
Chenonceaux (example)	30	Est
Montrichard		
Villandry		
Ussé		
Chinon		
Villes/Towns:		
Angers		
Le Mans		
Poitiers		
Camping/Campsite:		
Municipal		

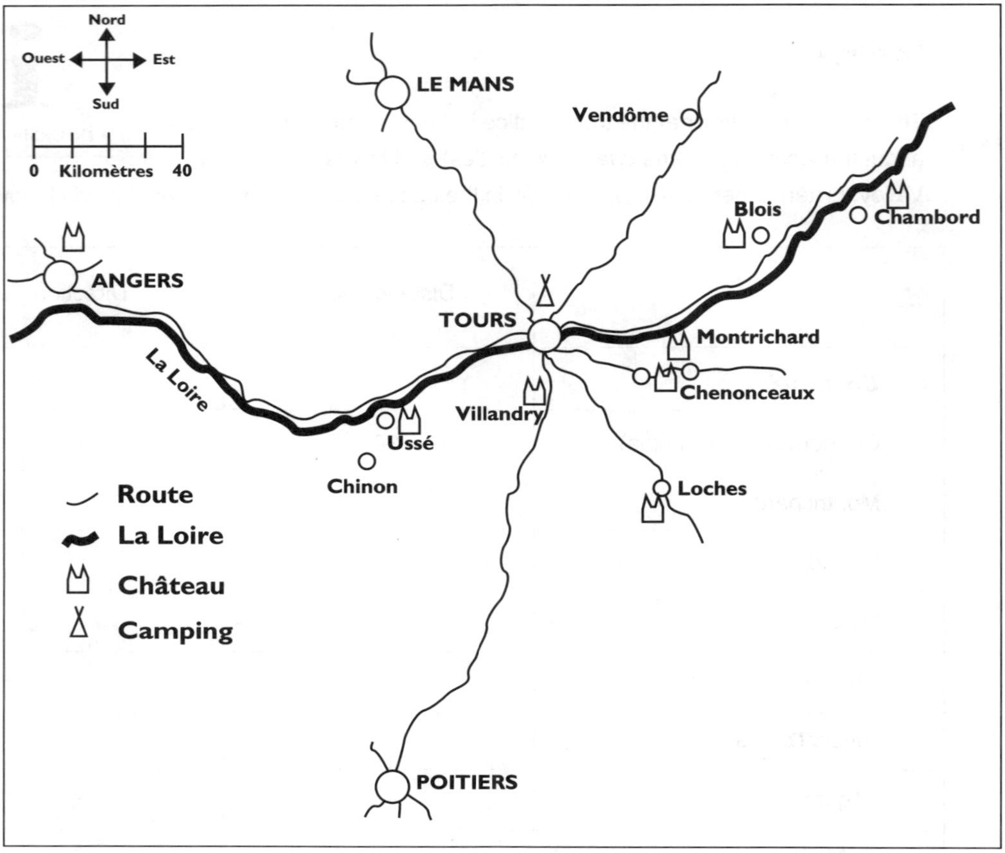

DEALING WITH DIRECTIONS, SIGNS AND REGULATIONS

HOW TO SAY IT

| C' | est | loin | | It | is | far | |
| Le château | | près | | The castle | | near | |

| C' | est | à | cinq | minutes | It | is | five | minutes | away |
| La ville | | | | kilomètres | The town | | | kilometres | |

| C'est | | à combien de | minutes? | How many | minutes | is it from | here? |
| Le camping est | | | kilomètres? | | kilometres | | the campsite? |

REQUESTING PEOPLE TO COMPLY WITH REGULATIONS

Listening 5:

Listen to the leisure assistant explaining the meaning of the various signs below, then match the English signs with their French equivalents. The order of the French words has been changed.

DEALING WITH DIRECTIONS, SIGNS AND REGULATIONS

1.	Closed	a.	Entrée
2.	Open	b.	Sortie
3.	Entrance	c.	Fermé
4.	Exit	d.	Sortie de secours
5.	Emergency exit	e.	Ouvert
6.	Private	f.	Privé
7.	Out of order	g.	Occupé
8.	Engaged	h.	Toilettes-dames
9.	Ladies	i.	Toilettes-messieurs
10.	Gentlemen	j.	Hors service
11.	Cashier	k.	Caisse
12.	Showers	l.	Vestiaire
13.	Cloakroom	m.	Entrée interdite
14.	No entry	n.	Douches

Listening 6:

 (a) Listen to the sports centre attendants requesting customers to comply with regulations and look at the corresponding signs below.

1.

2.

3.

4.

5.

6.

(b) Now, listen to the sports centre attendants requesting customers to comply with regulations and tick the corresponding sign in each case.

DEALING WITH DIRECTIONS, SIGNS AND REGULATIONS   3

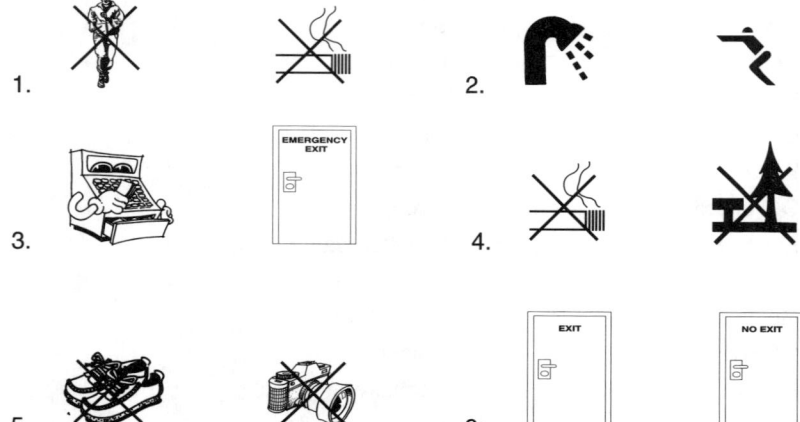

1.
2.
3.
4.
5.
6.

How to say it

Il faut	un bonnet de bain prendre une douche	You must	wear a swimming cap have a shower
La douche Le bonnet de bain	est obligatoire	Shower Swimming cap	obligatory
Il ne faut pas	fumer courir	Smoking Running	is forbidden
Pas de	chaussures, cigarettes,	s'il vous plaît	No	shoes cigarettes	please
Qu'est-ce que ça veut dire?		What does it mean?	
Ça veut dire toilettes hommes		It means gents' toilets	

DEALING WITH DIRECTIONS, SIGNS AND REGULATIONS

3

LANGUAGE PRACTICE

Exercise 1:

You are working at the information desk of the railway station (see map below).

Listen on the tape to tourists asking where various places are and reply.

A.	L'office du tourisme	F.	La pharmacie	K.	L'église
B.	La poste	G.	L'hôtel	L.	Le restaurant
C.	La banque	H.	L'agence de voyages	M.	Le café
D.	Le musée	I.	La piscine	N.	La boulangerie
E.	La gare	J.	Le cinéma	O.	Le supermarché

DEALING WITH DIRECTIONS, SIGNS AND REGULATIONS 3

(a) Look carefully at the map below and say which building is being referred to:

Note: You are standing in the middle of place de l'Horloge facing the cinema.

1. C'est à droite du café: ....
2. C'est entre la pharmacie et le supermarché: ....
3. C'est à côté du cinéma, à droite : ....
4. C'est entre la rue de la République et la rue de Paris: ....
5. C'est entre l'église et la poste: ....

(b) Complete the following sentences.

1. Le restaurant est .... du cinéma.
2. Le supermarché est .... de la boulangerie.
3. La pharmacie est .... de la boulangerie.
4. L'église est .... du café.
5. La poste est .... du café.

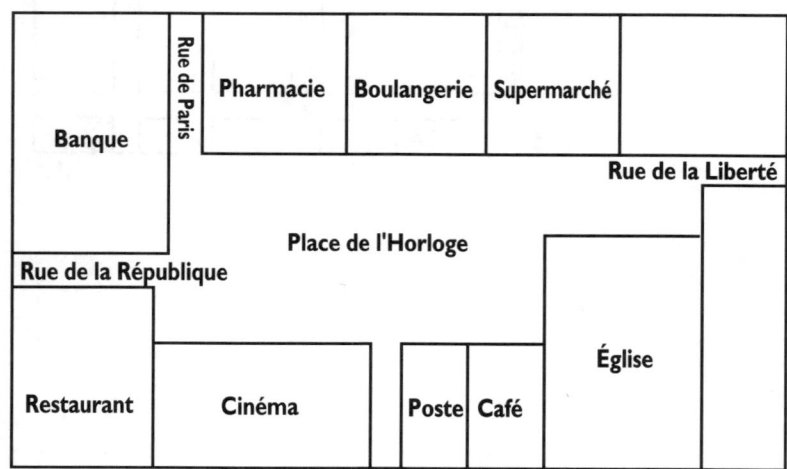

Exercise 3:

You are working as a guide in the *Galerie Nationale* (see map Listening 2, page 33).

Listen to the tape and reply to the questions asked by tourists.

AT THE GALLERY

À LA GALERIE

DEALING WITH DIRECTIONS, SIGNS AND REGULATIONS

Exercise 4:

You are working in a tourist office. Look at the document below and tell tourists how many kilometres each city is from the ski resort of La Rosière.

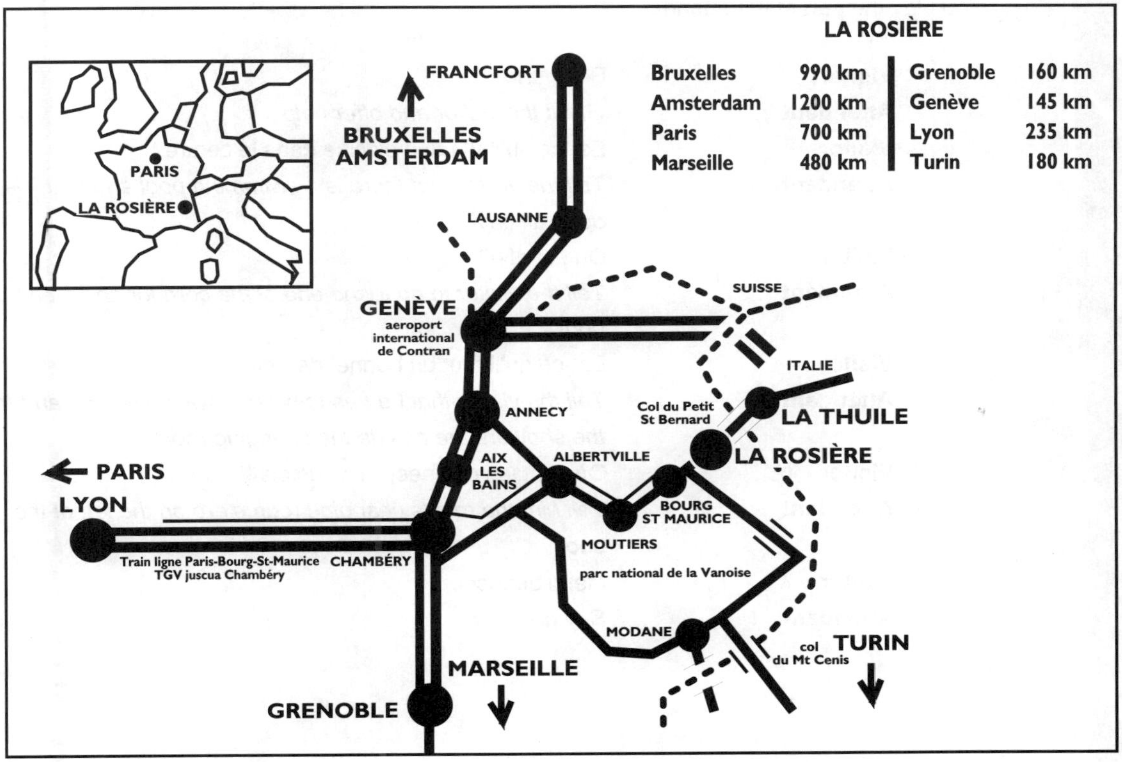

Exercise 5:

Look at the following signs and explain in French what they mean.

Example 1: Ça veut dire 'interdit de fumer'.

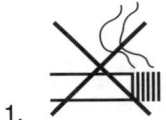   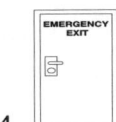

1.   2.   3.   4.

DEALING WITH DIRECTIONS, SIGNS AND REGULATIONS

Exercise 6:

You are working as an attendant in a leisure centre.
A French person arrives at the reception desk.
Listen to him and answer the questions on the tape as prompted below.
You play the part of the attendant.

Visitor	Bonjour.
Attendant	*Greet the visitor and offer help.*
Visitor	Est-ce qu'il y a une piscine dans le centre?
Attendant	*Tell the visitor that there is a swimming pool and that it is open all day.*
Visitor	Où est-elle?
Attendant	*Tell the visitor to go to the end of the corridor and then turn right.*
Visitor	Est-ce qu'il faut un bonnet de bain?
Attendant	*Tell the visitor that he has to wear a swimming cap and that the showers are beside the changing rooms.*
Visitor	Où sont les cabines, s'il vous plaît?
Attendant	*Tell him the men's changing rooms are on the left of the pool.*
Visitor	Merci beaucoup.
Attendant	*Say goodbye.*

DEALING WITH DIRECTIONS, SIGNS AND REGULATIONS   3

SO NEAR AND YET SO FAR

With the exception of those tourists who have chosen to travel to Paris by rail, some visitors to France may have some difficulty in getting in to the nation's capital. The following tips may be of use.

Arriving by air

Orly airport to the south of Paris and Charles de Gaulle, also known as Roissy, north of the city, are located at some distance from the centre so a taxi fare may leave your pocket lighter than you would like! The alternatives are less expensive but still efficient, although you may carry your baggage and use your feet a little more!

Charles de Gaulle/Roissy airport, Paris

One possibility is to take *la navette,* the shuttle bus which runs from the airport to points from which you can take another bus or a *métro* (underground train).

Another way to get to the city is by the RER (pronounced err euh err) which is a rapid train system serving the outskirts of Paris including the airports. Tickets are available in the RER station at the airport. This, too, can get you to the local bus and *métro* networks. In less than an hour you will be in central Paris.

Traffic in the Champs-Élysées, Paris

DEALING WITH DIRECTIONS, SIGNS AND REGULATIONS   3

Arriving by rail

When you arrive by rail you will be introduced quickly to the variety and sophistication of the Paris transport system. Access to the *métro* is usually clearly marked. Tickets are to be had at the kiosk at the entry to the *métro* and are sold individually or in a *carnet* (a book of ten) which is cheaper, around 40 francs, or a daily ticket may meet your needs.

If you plan to stay a week or longer it may be worthwhile getting a *carte orange* which gives you unlimited travel on buses and the *métro.* You can buy one for a week or a month.

Moving around the *métro*

The *métro* lines are identified by the terminus at each end of the line. You should follow the sign in the station that says *Direction.* Sometimes you may need to take several trains to get to your destination. This means you will need to look for the sign saying *Correspondance* or connection, where you can change lines.

Some stations have helpful illuminating wall maps which allow you to select your destination and then light your route on the map. Otherwise do avail of a free *métro* map which is available at the ticket kiosk at the entrance to the station.

Remember that if you get lost and take the wrong train, there is no extra charge! You can move around in the *métro* all day for the price of one ticket. Once you leave the *métro* system of course you lose this privilege!

Métro ticket

Finally, the last *métro* leaves the terminus at 12.45 a.m. and it does leave on time!

Drivers beware!

If you intend to approach Paris from the outside, you will have to encounter what is, to foreign drivers, the somewhat hectic *périphérique* or ring-road. This is a motorway with four lanes in each direction and an endless number of *sorties* (exits). It is easy to miss your exit point, so keep your eyes peeled, otherwise you may risk getting lost finding your way back or having to do another circuit of Paris. A full tank of petrol is advisable!

By the way, if you have to ask directions, don't expect anyone to tell you how many miles you have to go. The French only use kilometres.

USING THE TELEPHONE

UNIT 4

Objectives

At the end of this unit you will be able to:

- Receive a telephone call

- Put someone through

- Ask for someone to hold on

- Apologise

- Ask for somebody's name and telephone number

- Say you do not understand

- Ask for repetition and/or slower delivery

USING THE TELEPHONE

Receiving a simple telephone call

Listening 1:

Listen to the four telephone conversations on the tape, then look at their scripts which follow and put the lines in the correct order.

1. a) Monsieur Martin? Oui, ne quittez pas, s'il vous plaît.
   b) Hôtel de la Gare, bonjour!
   c) Merci.
   d) Bonjour, je voudrais parler à Monsieur Martin, s'il vous plaît.

2. a) Allô, c'est l'hôtel du Midi?
   b) Je voudrais parler à Madame Dufour, s'il vous plaît.
   c) Allô.
   d) Madame Dufour, un instant, s'il vous plaît.
   e) Oui Madame, je peux vous aider?

3. a) La 612, oui Monsieur, ne quittez pas, s'il vous plaît.
   b) Hôtel Saint Pierre, bonsoir!
   c) Bonsoir, la chambre 612, s'il vous plaît.

4. a) La 312, oui Madame, un instant, s'il vous plaît.
   b) Allô?
   c) Oui, la 312, s'il vous plaît.
   d) Oui, Hôtel de France, bonjour, puis-je vous aider?

Listening 2:

Listen to the four telephone conversations on the tape and fill in the information below.

Hôtel Norotel Call for: Room number:	**Hôtel Bonsaï** Call for: Room number:
Hôtel Neptune Call for: Room number:	**Hôtel de la Poste** Call for: Room number:

USING THE TELEPHONE

How to say it

Allô!			Hello!		
Hôtel Bonsaï	bonjour!		Hotel Bonsai	good morning!	
Hôtel Neptune	bonsoir!		Hotel Neptune	good evening!	
Ne quittez pas,	s'il vous plaît		Hold on,	please	
Un instant,			One minute,		
Je vous	la / le	passe	I'll transfer you to	her / him	
Je vous passe	la chambre		I'll put you through to	the room	
	le poste			the extension	
	M. Martin			Mr Martin	
	la communication		I'll put you through		
Pardon	vous pouvez	répéter?	Sorry, could you	repeat that?	
Excusez-moi		répéter plus lentement?		repeat that more slowly?	
		épeler?		spell it?	
Comment ça s'écrit?			How do you spell it?		
Je ne comprends pas			I don't understand		
Je voudrais	parler à	Monsieur Martin	I'd like to	speak to	Mr Martin
Pourrais-je		Annette?	Could I		Annette?
C'est	l'hôtel Neptune?		Is this	the hotel Neptune?	
	la chambre 18 ?			room 18?	
La chambre	312	s'il vous plaît	Room	312	please
Le poste	25		Extension	25	

Taking simple messages

Listening 3:

(a) Listen to the telephone conversation and answer the following questions:

1. The caller is phoning

        a) an hotel
        b) a travel agency
        c) a bank

2. The caller wants to speak to

        a) Mireille
        b) Martine
        c) Michelle

USING THE TELEPHONE

3. The person being called is
   a) out of the office
   b) at a meeting
   c) on the phone

4. The caller will
   a) hold the line
   b) leave a message
   c) call back

5. What is the caller's name?...

6. Complete the caller's telephone number: 3 ...   ... 5 ...   .

7. Why does the telephone operator ask the caller to speak louder?

....

(b) Listen to the conversation again and fill in the form below.

Fiche Téléphonique
Telephone Message

Pour: ....
To:

De: ....
From:

Téléphone: ....
Telephone:

a téléphoné / phoned □	prière de rappeler / please call back □
rappellera / will phone back □	

USING THE TELEPHONE

How to say it

Boomerang Voyages, **Trans-Voyages**	j'écoute!		Boomerang Voyages Trans-Voyages	speaking!
Je regrette	la ligne est occupée ça ne répond pas		I'm sorry	the line is engaged there is no answer
Voulez-vous	patienter? laisser un message?		Do you want to	hold on? leave a message?
Je n'entends pas bien			I can't hear very well	
La ligne est mauvaise			The line is bad	
Vous pouvez parler plus fort?			Can you speak louder?	
Est-ce qu'il peut	vous me	rappeler?	Can he call	you me	back?

Receiving a telephone call

At The Switchboard
Au Standard

Listening 4:

(a) Listen to the four telephone conversations and match the following information according to what you hear.

1. Salon du Tourisme   a) c'est occupé
2. Salon de l'Automobile   b) ça ne répond pas
3. Salon du Meuble   c) en réunion
4. Salon de l'Informatique   d) je vous la passe

(b) Listen to the conversations again and complete the information grid below.

Salon Trade Fair	De From	Pour To	Contact établi Contact made	Message Message
Tourisme	– –		non	
Automobile		Mme Ricard		
Meuble	– –			rappellera
Informatique		M. Martin		

USING THE TELEPHONE

HOW TO SAY IT

Ça ne répond pas	There is no answer
C'est de la part de qui?	May I say who is speaking?
C'est occupé	It's engaged
Monsieur Martin est en réunion	Mr Martin is at a meeting
Le directeur	The manager

LANGUAGE PRACTICE

Exercise 1:

Complete the crossword below by filling in the missing words in the following telephone conversation:

– *Hôtel de la Plage, bonsoir!*
– *Bonsoir, je voudrais (1) . . . . . à Mlle Laplanche, s'il vous plaît.*
– *Un (2) . . . . s'il vous plaît . . . Je regrette, Madame, c'est (3) . . . Voulez-vous (4) . . . . ?*
– *Non, passez-moi la chambre 203.*
– *Certainement, ne (5) . . . . . . pas. Je vous la (6) . . . . .*

USING THE TELEPHONE

Exercise 2:

 Listen.

– Je voudrais parler à Monsieur Parot.
– *Un instant, je vous **le** passe.*

– Pourrais-je parler à Madame Durand?
– *Ne quittez pas, je vous **la** passe.*

 Now, to answer the callers on the tape use the expressions above, writing your answers below.

1. Je voudrais parler à Monsieur Durand.

....

2. Monsieur Lemarchand, s'il vous plaît.

....

3. Le poste 197, s'il vous plaît.

....

4. Pourrais-je parler à Madame Legris?

....

5. Madame Caron, s'il vous plaît.

....

6. La chambre 215, s'il vous plaît.

....

USING THE TELEPHONE

Exercise 3:

Put the lines of the following conversation in the right order:

1) C'est de la part de qui?
2) Non, je rappellerai, merci.
3) Voyages Aventures, bonjour!
4) Mlle Robin.
5) D'accord, au revoir.
6) Ne quittez pas, s'il vous plaît . . . Je regrette, c'est occupé, vous voulez patienter?
7) Au revoir.
8) Bonjour, je voudrais parler à Jean-Marc, s'il vous plaît.

Exercise 4:

You are working in the Boomerang Voyages travel agency when the phone rings. Listen to the caller and answer the questions as prompted below. You play the part of the switchboard operator.

Caller	Allô, Boomerang Voyages?
Operator	*Answer the phone in French.*
Caller	Bonjour, j'aimerais avoir des informations sur les voyages organisés sur la Côte d'Azur, s'il vous plaît.
Operator	*Say that you do not understand and ask him to repeat more slowly.*
Caller	Oui, je voudrais des informations sur les voyages organisés sur la Côte d'Azur.
Operator	*Apologise and say you do not understand.*
Caller	Je pourrais parler au directeur, s'il vous plaît?
Operator	*Ask him to hold on . . . Say that there is no answer and ask him if he would like to leave a message.*
Caller	Oui, dites-lui de me rappeler.
Operator	*Ask him what his name is.*
Caller	Je m'appelle Monsieur Durand.
Operator	*Ask him what his telephone number is.*
Caller	C'est le 43 25 32 56.
Operator	*Thank him and take your leave.*
Caller	Au revoir.

USING THE TELEPHONE

 CALLING ALL TRAVELLERS!

France can boast one of the most sophisticated systems of telecommunications in the world although this may not be always obvious to the person in the street looking for a coinbox telephone in working order. The invention of the *télécarte* or telephone card has solved that problem and now most public phones are card-operated. The *télécarte* can be bought in *la poste* (the post office), at *un kiosque à journaux* (a newspaper kiosk) or *un tabac* (more like a newsagent's shop). It can come with 50 or 120 units.

Finding the number

All telephone numbers have eight digits. The first two are the area code which is always used, even for local calls. The codes for dialling inside and outside France are:
Within France:

    From Paris to the provinces   16 + number
    From the provinces to Paris   16 + 1 + number (8 digits)
    Within the provinces   Dial the eight digit number

Calling internationally from France:
    Dial 19 + the country code + the area code without the first zero + number.

From Ireland or Britain to Paris: 00 + 33 + 1 + number
From Ireland or Britain to French provinces: 00 + 33 + number

Paying for the call

If you are a tourist in distress it is important to know that the reverse charge call facility applies only to international calls known in France as *appeler en PCV (Paiement Contre Vérification)*.
If you are making a normal call you may be glad to know when best to avoid. The *télécarte* sometimes shows time bands and the reductions in charges available.

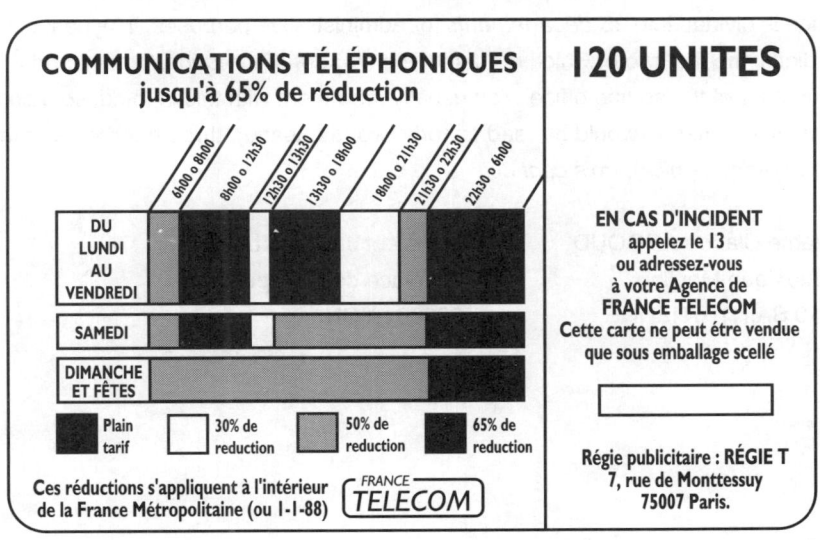

USING THE TELEPHONE

Finding the number

The French telephone directory is often called *le Bottin* and there are a large number of directories to cover all of France. If you want a local number you ask for the *annuaire* or directory for that area, call *renseignements* (directory enquiries) or consult *le minitel* in a post office.

Le Minitel

If you have access to a *minitel*, which is among other things a computerised telephone directory, you will not have to go hunting at the post office for directories, you can find all the information you need on screen. Around five million French homes have one and those who avail of all of its services (by paying the appropriate fee) can virtually become hermits in their own homes: you can do your weekly shopping, sort out your bank account, get legal advice, avail of help for your homework if you are a schoolgoer and even make new friends. Many advertisements for services carry a *minitel* number. If however you are disturbed by all of this high technology, and decide to opt for the safer if less interesting pen and paper, you may find yourself once again wrestling with digits in the form of postal codes!

Les codes postaux

France is divided into 95 *départements* for administrative purposes. The post code contains five digits, the first two of which represent the number of the *département*, and the other three the number of the sorting office. You usually read them with this in mind, so a code such as 42310 Saint Etienne would be read as forty two (thousand), three hundred and ten or *quarante-deux (mille), trois cent dix*.

Madame Claude ARGOUD
14, rue Jean Moulin
42310 SAINT-ETIENNE

Monsieur Jacques LACHOT
20, place de la République
69006 LYON

TEST YOUR COMPETENCE 1

Exercise 1:

At The Travel Agency
À L'Agence de Voyages

You are working in a travel agency. Listen to clients giving you their names on the telephone and tick which way they spell their names in the grid below:

Durant	☐	Durand	☐
Petel	☐	Paitel	☐
Delort	☐	Delors	☐
Quedec	☐	Kedec	☐
Fournet	☐	Fourney	☐

Exercise 2:

You are working at the cloakroom desk in a museum. Listen on the tape to tourists asking for their coats. What is the number each asks for?

At the Museum
Au Musée

1. 62   66   72   78   82   92
2. 82   84   94   98   103   106
3. 111   112   122   134   147   153
4. 245   256   283   297   310   325
5. 462   467   470   485   495   501
6. 525   527   533   546   559   570

Exercise 3:

You are working at the reception desk in an hotel. Guests are ringing the reception desk to arrange their morning calls.
Listen to the dialogues on the tape and fill in the grid below.

At The Reception
À La Réception

55

TEST YOUR COMPETENCE 1

Guest	Room Number	Call Time
1	....	....
2	....	....
3	....	....
4	....	....

Exercise 4:

Listen to the announcements made over the loudspeaker in a car ferry and write down when the following services are available.

1. La cafétéria est ouverte de . . . . . . à . . . . pour le petit déjeuner.
2. Le bureau de change ouvre à . . . .
3. La boutique hors taxes est ouverte de . . . . à . . . .
4. Le restaurant est ouvert de . . . . . . à . . . . . . pour le déjeuner.
5. La discothèque ferme à . . . .
6. Le bar ferme à . . . .

Exercise 5:

(a) Listen to the tourist information officer giving a customer the prices of various day trips available from Paris and circle the correct price for each tour.

1.	Les cimetières de Paris	130F	160F	170F
2.	Le château de Versailles	218F	378F	280F
3.	La cathédrale de Chartres	310F	370F	390F
4.	Les plages de Normandie	420F	404F	480F
5.	La Champagne et ses caves	405F	415F	450F
6.	Les châteaux de la Loire	414F	440F	480F

TEST YOUR COMPETENCE 1

   (b)   Now you give the following prices to a tourist:

Weekends Tourisme SNCF (au départ de Paris — prix par personne)

Luxembourg	1485F
Amsterdam	1695F
Vienne	1775F
Rome	2315F
Budapest	2810F
Genève	1182F

Example: Le weekend à Luxembourg coûte 1485F.

Exercise 6:

Listen to the dialogues you hear in a tourist office. Three tourists have come in looking for directions.

Look at the map below while listening to the tape and fill in the place each tourist wants to go to and what letter on the map marks its location.

Place	Letter
1	....
2	....
3	....

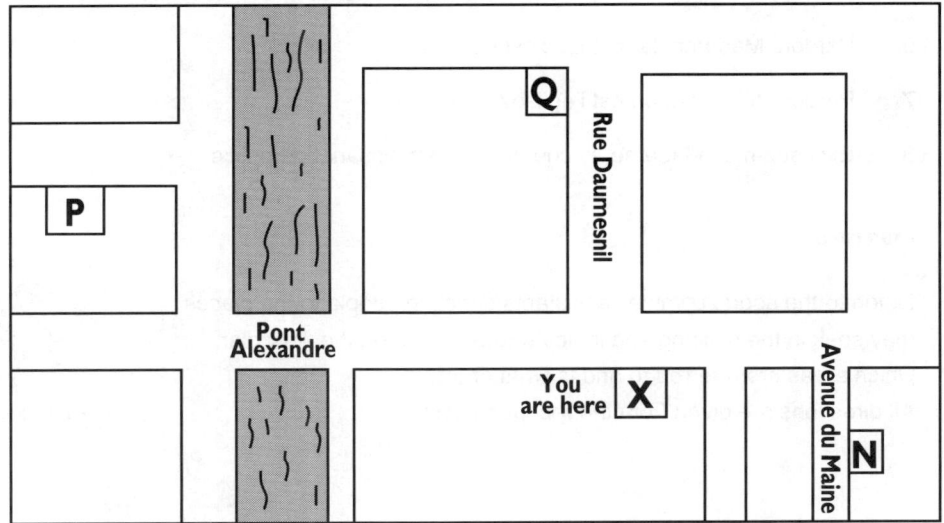

TEST YOUR COMPETENCE 1

Exercise 7:

You are working in a tourist office. Tourists come in enquiring about various places in the town. Look at the map below and give them the directions they require.

TOURIST INFORMATION

INFORMATIONS

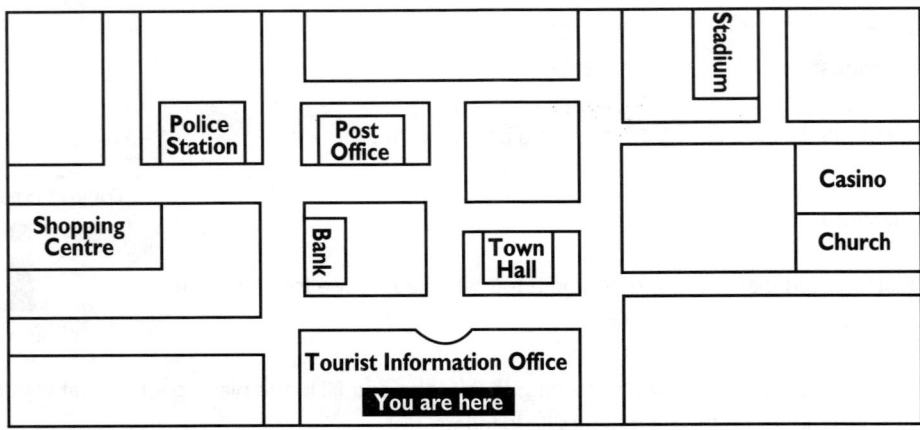

1. Pardon, Madame, pouvez-vous me dire où est la banque?

2. Pardon, Madame, pouvez-vous me dire où se trouve le casino?

3. Pardon, Madame, où se trouve le bureau de poste?

4. Excusez-moi, Madame, où se trouve le stade?

5. Excusez-moi, Madame, pouvez-vous me dire où se trouve le centre commercial?

6. Pardon, Madame, la mairie, c'est où?

7. Pardon, Madame, où est l'église?

8. Excusez-moi, Madame, je cherche le commissariat de police.

Exercise 8:

Listen to the sports complex assistants directing people to the places they seek in the building and indicate with arrows on the floor plan which areas are referred to and in what order.
All directions are given from the reception desk.

AT THE LEISURE CENTRE

AU CENTRE DE LOISIRS

TEST YOUR COMPETENCE 1

Help!

terrain de squash	squash court
salle de sport	hall
salle de gymnastique	gymnasium
salle de réunions	meeting room
vestiaires des équipes	team changing rooms
vestiaires femmes	women's changing rooms
vestiaires hommes	men's changing rooms
premiers secours	first aid
galerie des spectateurs	viewing gallery

TEST YOUR COMPETENCE 1

Exercise 9:

(a) Match the following symbols with the corresponding sentences in French.

1.    A. Il est interdit de fumer.
   Il ne faut pas fumer.

2.    B. Il est interdit de courir.
   Il ne faut pas courir.

3.    C. Pas de parapluie, s'il vous plaît.

4.    D. Le bonnet est obligatoire.
   Il faut porter un bonnet.

5.    E. La douche est obligatoire.
   Il faut prendre une douche.

6.    F. Il est interdit de photographier.
   Il ne faut pas photographier.

 (b) Then cover the sentences above (right-hand side of page) and give the instruction corresponding to each symbol.

Exercise 10:

Tourists in a travel agency are booking flights to various destinations.

 Listen to the travel agent giving them the details of their dates of departure, times of departure and arrival, fares for the return flight. Then for each tourist circle the correct information on the computer screen.

At The Travel Agency

À L'Agence de Voyages

60

TEST YOUR COMPETENCE 1

1. Paris – Londres

Date	Départ / Departure	Arrivée / Arrival	Tarif en francs (aller-retour) / Return fare (francs)
10/10	07.30	07.40	980
11/10	07.40	07.50	920
12/10	07.40	07.50	920

2. Paris – Luxembourg

Date	Départ / Departure	Arrivée / Arrival	Tarif en francs (aller-retour) / Return fare (francs)
3/6	09.10	10.10	990
6/6	12.20	13.20	860
9/6	17.10	18.10	860

3. Paris – Venise

Date	Départ / Departure	Arrivée / Arrival	Tarif en francs (aller-retour) / Return fare (francs)
8/9	10.10	11.50	2350
11/9	10.20	12.00	2350
13/9	16.20	18.00	1810

4. Paris – Nice

Date	Départ / Departure	Arrivée / Arrival	Tarif en francs (aller-retour) / Return fare (francs)
12/4	17.55	19.15	790
13/4	18.05	19.35	770
14/4	19.55	21.15	1040

TEST YOUR COMPETENCE 1

Exercise 11:

Use the map below to direct tourists between the following places.

1. From the *Syndicat d'Initiative* (tourist office) to the cathedral *(la cathédrale)*.

2. From the cathedral to the museum *(le musée)*.

3. From the museum to the Notre-Dame fountain *(la fontaine)*.

4. From the Notre-Dame fountain to the Notre-Dame bridge *(le pont)*.

5. From the Notre-Dame bridge to the town hall *(l'hôtel de ville)*.

6. From the town hall to the campsite *(le camping)*.

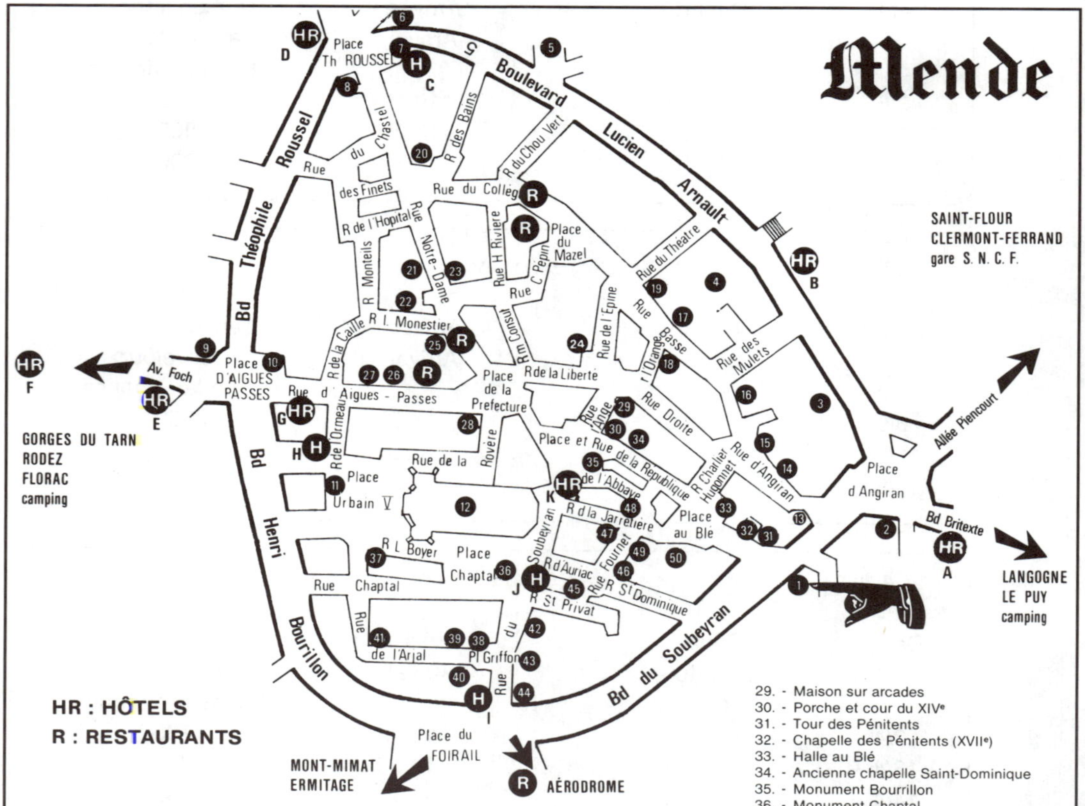

Mende

HR : HÔTELS
R : RESTAURANTS

1. - Syndicat d'Initiative (TSI-OT)
2. - Hôtel de ville (XVIII°)
3. - Maison du XVIII°
4. - Vestiges des remparts
5. - Pont Notre-Dame (XIV°)
6. - Buste de Th. Roussel et croix du XVI°
7. - Vestiges des remparts
8. - Porte du Chastel
9. - Maison classique du XIX°
10. - Fontaine d'Aigues-Passes
11. - Statue d'Urbain V
12. - Cathédrale
13. - Porte d'Angiran
14. - Hôtel de l'Orange (XVII°)
15. - Calquière, ancien lavoir
16. - Maison du XVIII°
17. - Passage couvert
18. - Maison du XVII°, salle des Gardes
19. - Maison du XVIII°
20. - Croix du Chastel
21. - Maison et cour du XIII°
22. - Fontaine Notre-Dame
23. - Passage couvert
24. - Musée
25. - Cour et escalier Renaissance
26. - Vieille porte
27. - Façade et piéta du XVI°
28. - Préfecture
29. - Maison sur arcades
30. - Porche et cour du XIV°
31. - Tour des Pénitents
32. - Chapelle des Pénitents (XVII°)
33. - Halle au Blé
34. - Ancienne chapelle Saint-Dominique
35. - Monument Bourrillon
36. - Monument Chaptal
37. - Archives départementale
38. - Fontaine du Griffon
39. - Porte du XVII°
40. - Maison du XVII°
41. - Fenêtres à meneaux
42. - Maison du XVI°
43. - Porte du XVII°
44. - Maison du XVI°
45. - Porte du XVII°
46. - Maison à encorbellement
47. - Vierge du XVII°
48. - Auvent sculpté
49. - Porche du XVII°
50. - Porche, hôtel du XVII°

TOURIST INFORMATION UNIT

Objectives

At the end of this unit you will be able to:

- Greet and offer help

- Inform and advise about local tourist attractions

- Give and sell information and publicity material

- Describe attractions and craft items

- Make reservations for tourist events, restaurants and hotels

- Give information about prices

TOURIST INFORMATION   5

Informing and advising tourists

Listening 1:

 Listen to the tourist information officer giving information to a tourist about attractions and places of interest in the French town of Istres. Tick on the list on p.65 the places mentioned in the dialogue:

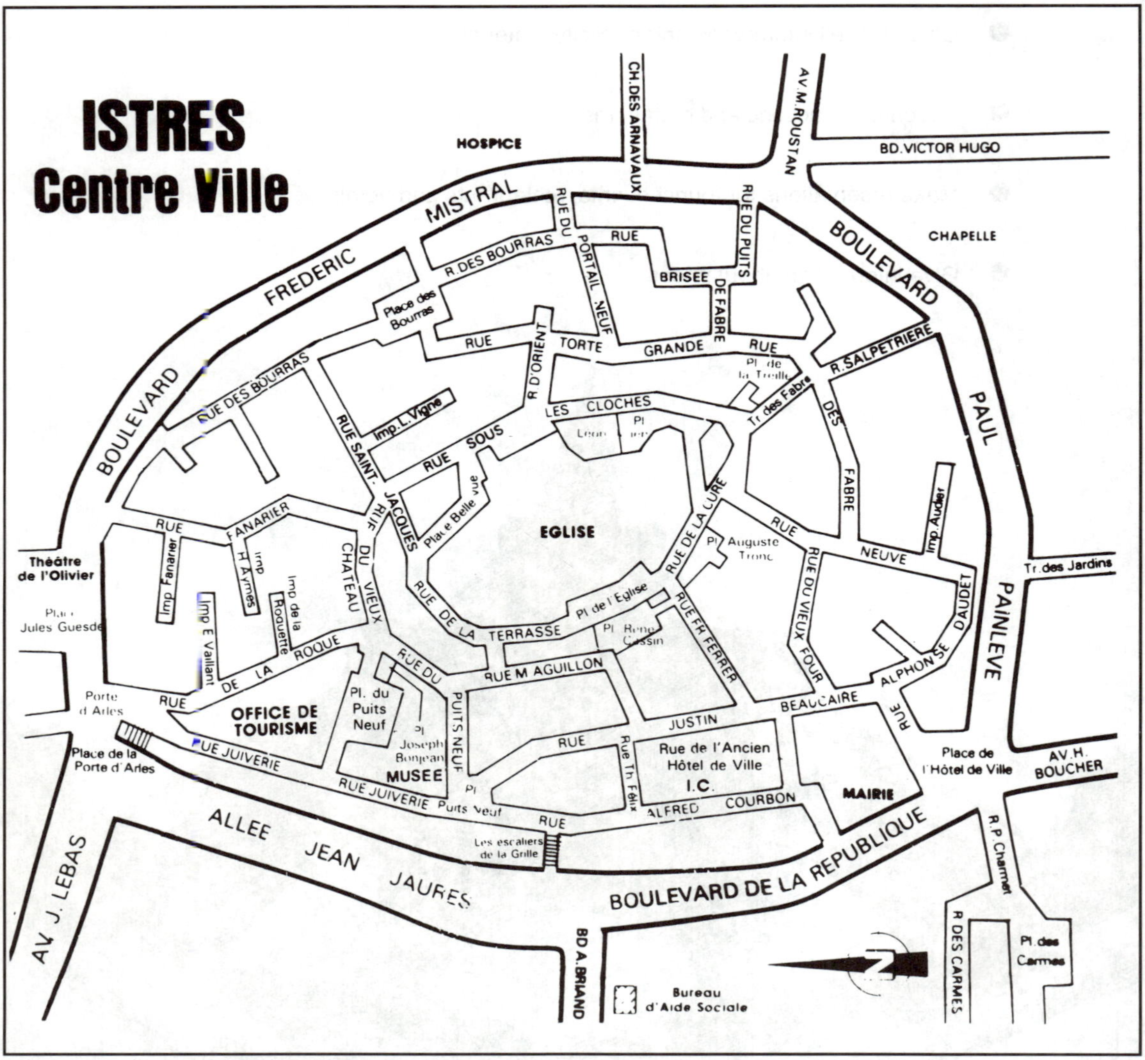

TOURIST INFORMATION 5

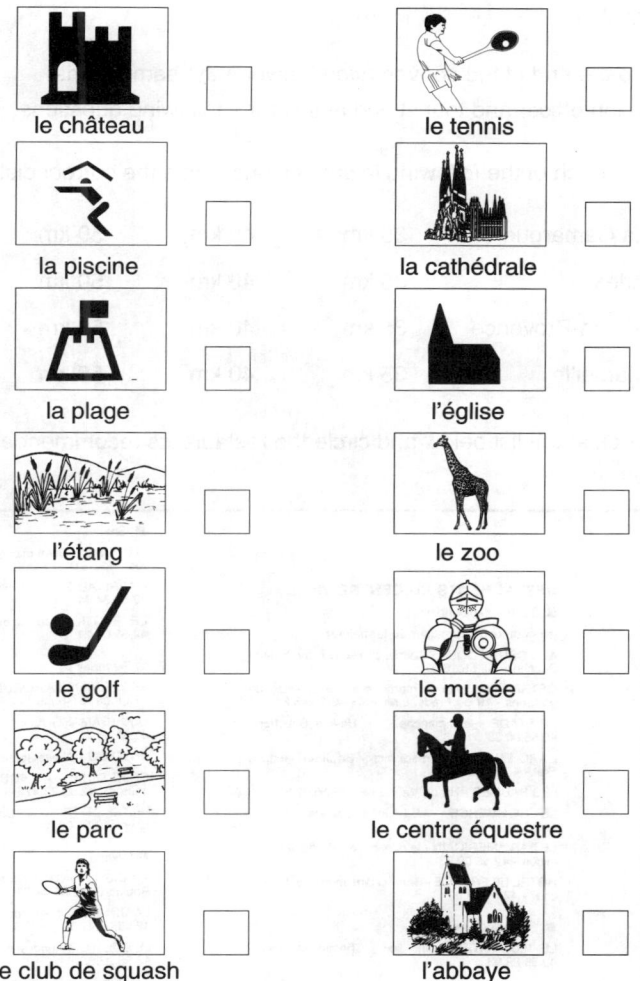

TOURIST INFORMATION

Listening 2:

Listen to the end of the conversation between the same tourist information officer and tourist and answer the following questions.

1. For each of the following towns/regions, circle the correct distance from Istres:

La Camargue	35 km	40 km	50 km
Arles	35 km	40 km	50 km
Aix-en-Provence	35 km	40 km	50 km
Marseille	35 km	40 km	50 km

2. Look at the list below and circle the restaurants recommended by the tourist information officer.

   RESTAURANTS DU CENTRE VILLE

   ■ Cuisine traditionnelle.
   (Nom du restaurant, jour de fermeture).
   AUX DEUX TOQUES - dimanche soir, 7 av. Hélène Boucher - 42.55.16.01
   OSTREION - lundi et mardi midi - Spécialités de poissons - 19 Bd Frédéric Mistral - 42.55.45.21
   LE STADE - le dimanche - av. Hélène Boucher - 42.55.00.38
   L'ARC EN CIEL - samedi midi - Bd Jean Jacques Prat - 42.55.02.55
   LES BAUMES - Bd de Vauranne - 42.56.02.63
   LE COMMERCE - Bd Jean Jacques Prat - 42.55.01.11
   LE BAR AMERICAIN - le dimanche - Bd de la République - 42.55.09.73
   HOTEL DE FRANCE - Sam. et dim. midi - Av. H.Boucher - 42.55.00.02

   ■ Spécialités italiennes
   LE 1000 PATES - dim. soir - Chemin de Tivoli - 42.55.28.93

   ■ Snacks
   O'COURS - ouvert midi et en semaine - Allées J.Jaurès - 42.55.01.19
   L'ABRIVADO - le lundi - Place Ste-Catherine - 42.56.34.41
   LE BISTRO - le lundi - Allées Jean Jaurès - 42.55.00.21

   ■ Pizzerias
   PIZZERIA DE LA ROQUE - le lundi soir et mardi midi - Rue de la Roque - 42.56.31.72
   LOU CAMARGUE - 1 rue Justin Beaucaire - 42.55.46.44
   ANTONIO - Allées Jean Jaures - 42.55.46.79
   CHEZ ROSE - AU FOURNIL - 29 bis Allées Jean Jaurès - 42.55.23.47
   HOTEL DE FRANCE - Sam. et dim. midi - Av. H.Boucher - 42.55.00.02

   ■ Orientaux
   XUANG - HONG - lundi et sam. midi - 11 av. Marcel Roustan - 42.56.43.75
   LA JONQUE II - lundi - 11 Bd Frédéric Mistral - 42.56.09.47
   LE BOL D'OR - lundi et mar. midi - Rue Abel Aubrun - 42.56.23.85
   L'HIRONDELLE - jeudi et sam. midi - Bd Frédéric Mistral - 42.55.36.91

   ■ Crêperies
   LA TABLE DE LILIA - midi et lundi - 2bis Av. Adam de Craponne - 42.55.15.56
   LA GOURMANDINE - midi et dim. - 16 rue sous les Cloches - 42.56.51.95

3. What does the tourist ask for?

   a) A leaflet   b) A map   c) A guide book

4. Does he have to pay for it?

   Yes ☐   No ☐

TOURIST INFORMATION 5

How to say it

Il y a	le château		There	is the castle	
	des musées.			are museums	
Il n'y a pas de	château		There is no castle		
	musées		There are no museums		
Nous avons	un golf		We have	a golf course	
	une piscine			a swimming pool	
Vous pouvez	faire du sport		You can	practise a sport	
	visiter Arles			visit Arles	
Je vous	conseille	le restaurant	I recommend	the restaurant	
	recommande	l'église		the church	
Voilà	une carte		There is	a map	
	un dépliant			a leaflet	
C'est gratuit			It is free		
Il y a	un club de squash?		Is there a squash club?		
	des courts de tennis?		Are there tennis courts?		
Qu'est-ce qu'il y a	à voir d'intéressant?		What is there that is interesting	to see?	
	à faire			to do?	
	à visiter			to visit?	
On peut	faire du sport?		Can one	practise sport?	
	visiter l'église?			visit the church?	
Vous pouvez me conseiller	un restaurant?		Can you recommend	a restaurant?	
	un hôtel?			an hotel?	
Est-ce que vous avez	une carte?		Have you	a map?	
	un dépliant?			a leaflet?	

Describing attractions and craft items

TOURIST INFORMATION

i

INFORMATIONS

Listening 3:

(a) Listen to the tourist information officer in the local tourist office giving information about some places of interest to a tourist.

Match the following places with their descriptions:

1. L'église
2. Le musée
3. Le château
4. Le site archéologique

a. très intéressant
b. de style roman provençal
c. à ne pas manquer
d. magnifique

67

TOURIST INFORMATION

(b) Listen again and fill in the grid below:

	jours d'ouverture opening days	heures d'ouverture opening hours
Église		
Musée		
Château		
Site archéologique		

Listening 4:

(a) Listen to the shop assistant explaining to the tourist the various souvenirs, food and craft items of the Provence region.
Circle the items **not** mentioned by the shop assistant:

AT THE SHOPS
DANS LES MAGASINS

vins

parfums

cardigans

cristal

chocolats

pastis

foulards

bijoux

fleurs séchées

poterie

huile d'olive

cigares

TOURIST INFORMATION 5

(b) Listen to the dialogue again and this time, tick the statements below as indicated:

	True	False
1. The local wine is red only		
2. The scarves are made of cotton		
3. The customer buys olive oil		
4. The total bill comes to 105F		
5. The customer wants to pay by credit card		

How to say it

Vous avez	l'église ..... le château	You have	the church ..... the castle .....
Le musée La visite	est à ne pas manquer	The museum The visit	is not to be missed
Vous voulez	un paquet cadeau? des savons?	Do you want	gift wrapping? soaps?
Bon séjour		Have a nice stay	
Le foulard coûte Les savons coûtent	combien?	How much	is the scarf? are the soaps?

MAKING RESERVATIONS AND INFORMING ABOUT PRICES

Listening 5:

(a) Listen to the tourist information officer making a reservation for a hotel room and complete the booking form below.

TOURIST INFORMATION

INFORMATIONS

Fiche de réservation

Hôtel: Le Hérel, Granville

Nombre de personnes: ....

Nombre de nuits: ....

Type de chambre: ....

Nom du client: ....

TOURIST INFORMATION

A4 - GRANVILLE
** LE HEREL - Port de Plaisance - Promenade du Dr-Lavat - Tél. 33 90 48 08 - Télex 772319 - Fax 33 90 75 95 (M. MERCIER)
43 ch. 190/300 F - Petit déj. 32 F - Ouvert T.A. - Parking - Vue sur mer et port - Tél. et Tv ds les ch. - H - Animaux admis - Change.

(b) Listen again and answer the following questions:

1. How much is the room?
   a) 300F
   b) 30F
   c) 240F

2. Is breakfast included in the price?
   Yes ☐   No ☐

3. What category does the hôtel Le Hérel belong to? Circle the correct answer.
   *   **   ***   ****

4. What does the sum of 30F refer to?
   ....

Listening 6:

(a) Listen to the hotel receptionist making a reservation for a show in a cabaret and tick the statements in the appropriate columns.

AT THE RECEPTION
À LA RÉCEPTION

	True	False
1. The customer wants a reservation for the show only		
2. The show is more expensive on Fridays and Saturdays		
3. There is a 15% discount for students		
4. The customer wants to make a group booking		
5. He wants to go to the early show		
6. He wants to pay by credit card		

TOURIST INFORMATION 5

 (b) Listen again and fill in the missing information below:

```
Name of customer:     ..........................
Date for booking:     ..........................
Amount paid:          ..........................
Method of payment:    ..........................
```

How to say it:

C'est pour combien de	personnes?	How many people	is it for?
	temps?	How long	
C'est pour	quelle date?	What date	is it for?
	quand?	When	
Je peux	réserver une chambre?	Can I	book a room?
	faire une réservation?		make a reservation?
	faire un chèque?		write a cheque?
Je voudrais	faire une réservation	I would like	to make a reservation
	réserver une chambre		to book a room

Language practice

Exercise 1:

a) Match the following words with the corresponding picture:

1. Un château   a.

2. Une église   b.

3. Un musée   c.

4. Une piscine   d.

5. Un centre équestre   e.

TOURIST INFORMATION

b) Complete the following table from this list of French terms.

Une carte, un plan, gratuit, très belle, tous les jours, une brochure, avec salle de bains, une chambre, un dépliant, une réduction, un spectacle, une pièce d'identité.

free (example)	gratuit
every day	
a brochure	
a street map or a floor plan	
a bedroom	
very beautiful	
a discount	
a map	
with bath	
identification	
a leaflet	
a show	

Note: If you are uncertain about the meaning of a word, you can check it in the glossary at the back of the book.

Exercise 2:

Listen to the cues on the tape and build up sentences as in these examples:

Le musée .... très intéressant
Le musée **est** très intéressant

Les boutiques ... pittoresques
Les boutiques **sont** très pittoresques

1. L'église .... de style roman

2. Le château .... impressionnant

3. Les chambres .... confortables

4. Le restaurant .... bien situé

5. Le foulard .... en coton

TOURIST INFORMATION 5

Exercise 3:

Listen to the cues on the tape and use the signs below to give information on what is available at this campsite as shown in these examples:

Casino/casino — Il y a **un** casino (example)

Douche**s** chaude**s**/hot showers — Il y a **des** douches chaudes (example)

Centre équestre/riding centre — ....

Tennis/tennis — ....

Golf/golf — ....

Plage/beach — ....

Rivière/river — ....

Jeux pour enfants/playground — ....

Bar/bar — ....

Restaurant/restaurant — ....

Machines à laver/launderette — ....

TOURIST INFORMATION

Exercise 4:

You are working as a tourist information officer in France. A tourist comes in to book a hotel room in Montmartin-sur-mer. Based on the extract below, you give him or her as much information as possible on the Hôtel du Bon Vieux Temps.

A4 - MONTMARTIN-SUR-MER
** HOTEL DU BON VIEUX TEMPS - Tél. 33 47 54 44 - Fax 33 46 27 12 (M. BOURBONNAIS) 20 ch. 130/220 F - Petit déj. 22 F - P 298/390 F - 1/2 P 240/329 F - Menus 58/200 F + Carte - Restaurant 100 couverts - Ouvert T.A. - Fermé dimanche soir du 1/11 au 1/05 - Parking - Tél. ds les ch. - Animaux admis - Change.

Liste des abréviations
Abbreviations

ch:	chambres/rooms
Petit déj.:	petit déjeuner/breakfast
P:	pension/full-board
½P:	demi pension/half-board
T.A.:	toute l'année/all year round
Rest.:	restaurant
Tel.:	téléphone
TV:	télévision
ds:	dans/in

TOURIST INFORMATION

Exercise 5:

You are working in a tourist information office in Dublin when a French visitor asks you for information. Listen to the visitor and answer the questions as prompted below.

Visitor	Bonjour.
TI Officer	*Greet the visitor and offer help.*
Visitor	Vous avez un plan de la ville, s'il vous plaît?
TI Officer	*Give the visitor a map and say that it is free.*
Visitor	Merci, je suis ici pour trois jours. Qu'est-ce qu'il y a à faire d'intéressant?
TI Officer	*Tell the visitor that there is a city tour every morning at 10 a.m. There are also excursions to the monastic site in Glendalough and to the mediaeval town of Kilkenny.*
Visitor	Oui, combien coûte l'excursion à Glendalough?
TI Officer	*Tell the visitor that the trip to Glendalough costs £11 and ask if he/she wants to book for the tour.*
Visitor	Oui, j'aimerais deux billets, s'il vous plaît.
TI Officer	*Say that two tickets cost £22 and ask when he/she wants to go on the tour.*
Visitor	Demain si c'est possible.
TI Officer	*Say yes, give the visitor the tickets and wish him/her a pleasant stay.*

TOURIST INFORMATION

WHERE TO STAY

When deciding where to stay you will certainly be impressed by the range of accommodation on offer in France. If you have not had time to book in advance, *hébergement* (accommodation) may be arranged from the airport or railway station when you arrive.

Les hôtels

France's tourist class hotels are not classified alphabetically. A system of *étoiles* (stars) is used. At the lower end of the scale a no-star hotel (yes there is such a thing), *un hôtel sans étoile*, offers basic accommodation; bathroom and WC are usually shared with other guests. In France hotels are not obliged to have a restaurant so this makes for some quite cheap accommodation at the bottom of the range.

The highest grade for an hotel is *quatre étoiles luxe;* there are no five-star hotels in France. Believe it or not, one of the factors taken into account when grading the hotel is the ability of the staff to speak foreign languages.

Hôtel de la Côte d'Or, Saulieu

Attention!

Remember that you pay per room in French hotels rather than per person, so the more the merrier when it comes to paying the bill!

Remember also that the price they quote you on arrival does not include *le petit déjeuner* (breakfast) so be sure to clear this one up when you arrive. Don't be disappointed if the breakfast is a bit too continental for you: the *croissant* and *café au lait* keep the French nation functioning until midday so you can get used to it even if you're a traditional breakfast person!

The alternatives

If you decide that luxury hotels are not your idea of an authentic holiday experience, there are many other options:

Un gîte — privately-owned self-catering accommodation in a rural area. Gîtes are classified by *épis* (ears of corn) rather than *étoiles*. Maximum 3 *épis*.

TOURIST INFORMATION

Une chambre d'hôte — The equivalent of a bed and breakfast. The accommodation is *chez l'habitant* (in the home of a local person). Breakfast is included in the price.

Une auberge de jeunesse — youth hostel, which is not confined to youth. Standards are good and it is very cheap to stay.

Un camping — campsites are organised so they are usually clean and well equipped. Some are on farms; this gives you the chance to sample the produce.

La belle étoile

This is multi-star accommodation which is available free of charge under bridges, in public parks and on beaches.

The parks may offer guests a free shower around 5.00 a.m when the lawn sprinklers come on. So if you do choose to sleep *à la belle étoile* (under the stars) be very careful where you pick your spot!

TRAVEL INFORMATION

UNIT 6

Objectives

At the end of this unit you will be able to:

- Greet and offer help

- Advise on and make travel arrangements

- Give information about departure and arrival times and the duration of journeys

- Describe the locations of airports, stations, ferry terminals and give directions to them

- Sell and book package tours and individual travel

- Issue travel documents such as plane, train and ferry tickets

TGV train at Lac-le-Bourget, near Aix-les-Bains

TRAVEL INFORMATION

**ADVISING ON AND MAKING TRAVEL ARRANGEMENTS
DESCRIBING THE LOCATIONS OF STATIONS AND FERRY
TERMINALS**

At The Travel Agency
À l'Agence de Voyages

Listening 1:

(a) Listen to the travel information officer providing information to a customer about the various travel options between France and Ireland.

Indicate on the map below the various possible ferry crossings between France and Ireland which are mentioned.

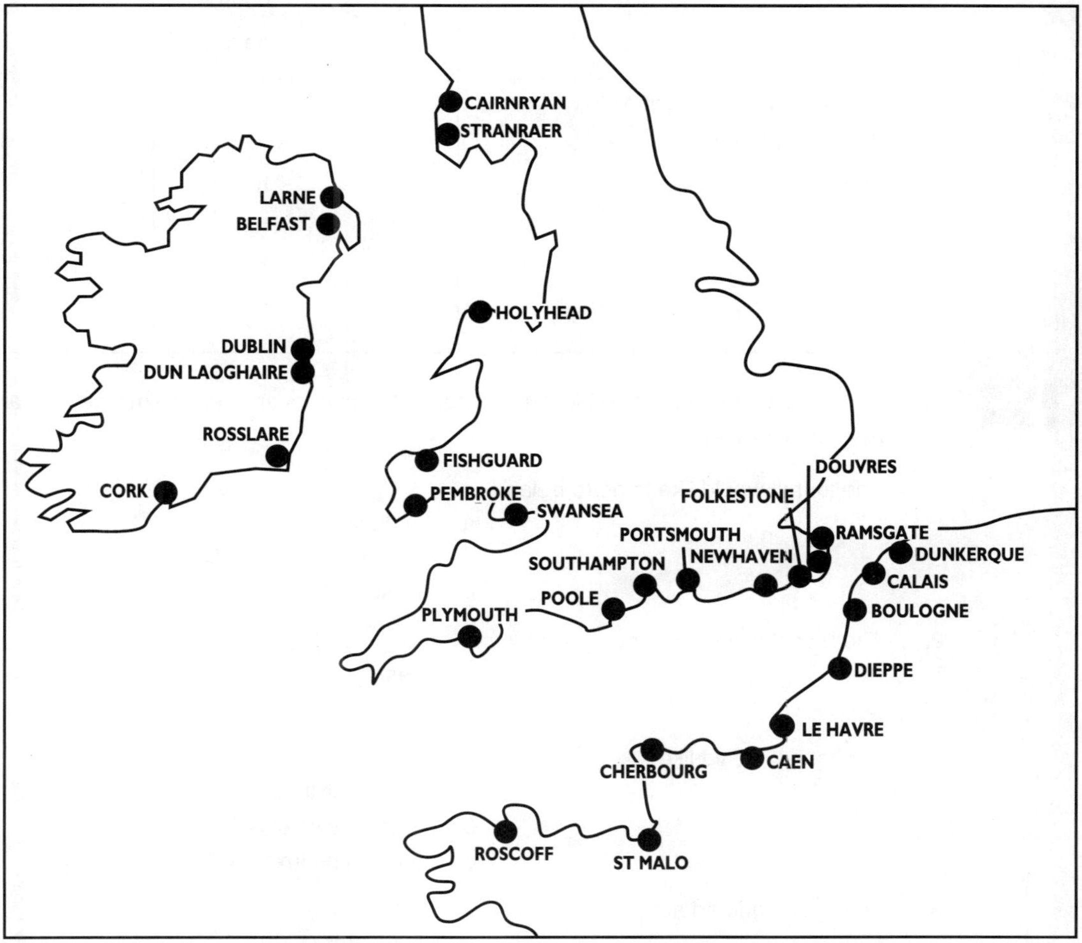

TRAVEL INFORMATION

 (b) Listen to the tape again to take down further details.
Mark on the table below the various crossings mentioned, their durations and prices. (See example 1)

Trajets Routes			Durée de la traversée Duration of crossing	Prix Price
Direct/direct				
1. de: Le Havre		à: Rosslare	21 heures	4700 F
2. de:		à:	heures	F
3. de:		à:	heures	F
4. de:		à:	heures	F
Par la Grande Bretagne Via Great Britain				
1. de:		à:	h	F
2. de:		à:	h	F
3. de:		à:	h	F
4. de:		à:	h	F

 (c) Listen once more to the dialogue and choose the correct answers below (several answers may be possible):

1. The tourist would like to go to Ireland
   a. in June
   b. in July
   c. in August

2. The tourist would prefer to travel by train
   a. yes
   b. no

3. The tourist would like:
   a. a cabin with shower for 2
   b. a cabin with shower for 4
   c. a cabin de luxe for 2

4. The prices quoted are:
   a. single fares
   b. return fares
   c. APEX
   d. standard

TRAVEL INFORMATION

Listening 2:

(a) Listen to the travel information assistant replying to three customers and indicate in which order the dialogues are heard by numbering the maps below.

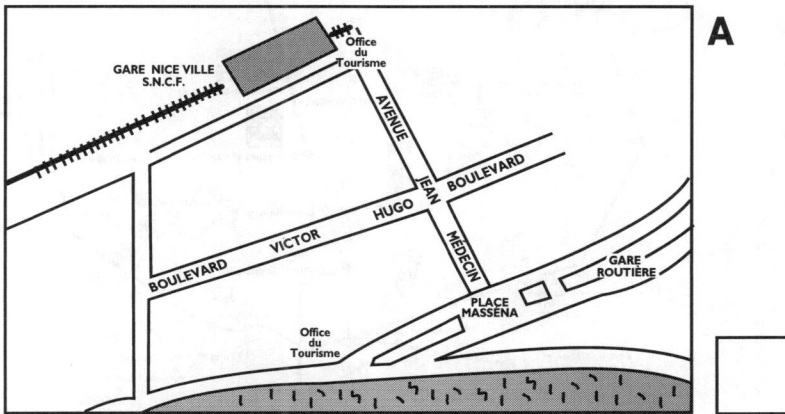

Gare routière et gare SNCF à Nice

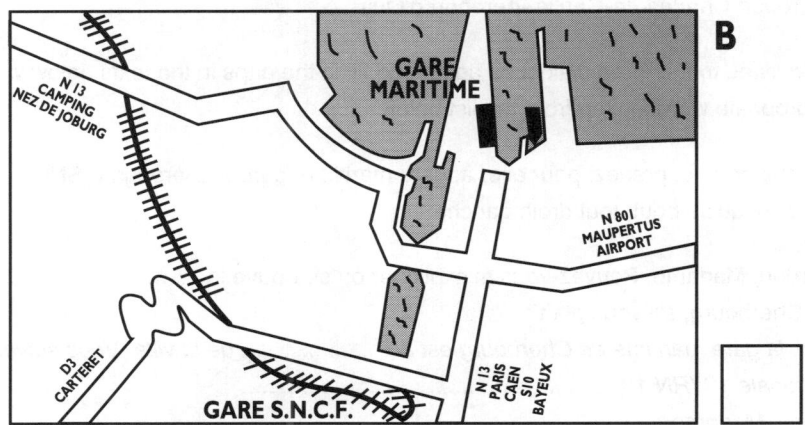

Gare maritime de Cherbourg

TRAVEL INFORMATION

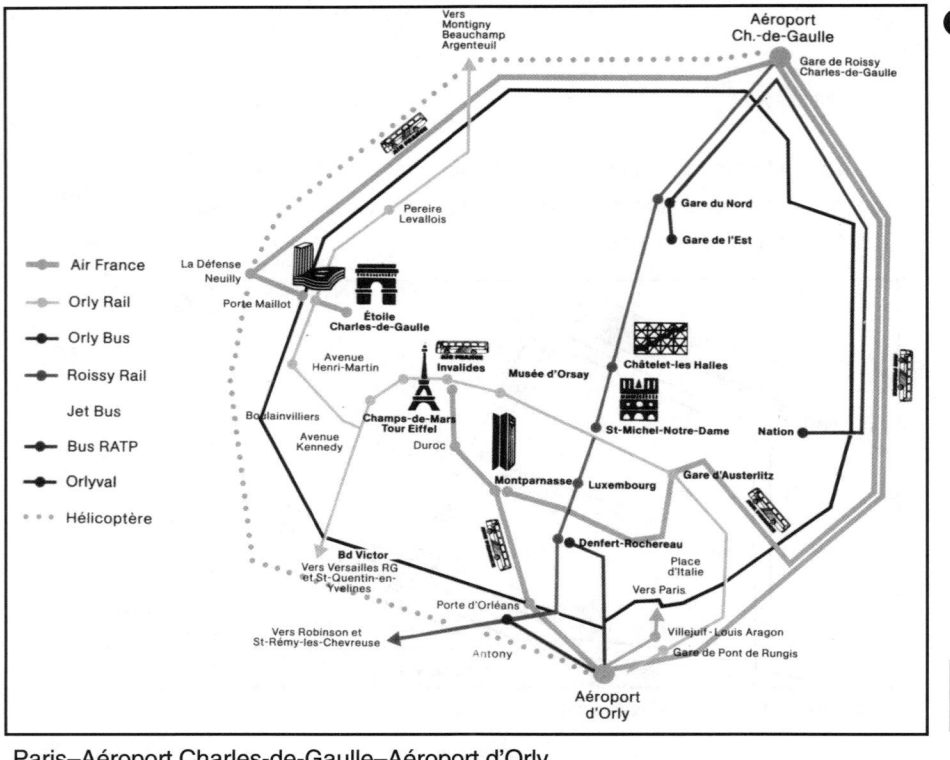

Paris–Aéroport Charles-de-Gaulle–Aéroport d'Orly

 (b) Now listen to the three dialogues again and fill in the gaps in the texts below with the appropriate words taken from the list below:

je vous en prie; prenez; pour aller à; gare maritime; gare routière; gare SNCF; aéroport; nord; jusqu'au bout; tout droit; gauche

1. Pardon, Madame. Pouvez-vous m'expliquer où se trouve la .... de Cherbourg, s'il vous plaît?
Oui, la gare maritime de Cherbourg est au .... de la ville. Vous suivez la route nationale 13 (RN 13) ....
Merci, Madame,
....

2. Pardon, Madame, où se trouve la ....de Nice?
La gare routière se trouve dans le centre, juste à côté de la place Masséna.
D'accord. Et la ....?
La gare SNCF est dans un autre quartier. Toujours à partir de la place Masséna, vous .... l'avenue Jean Médecin, vers le nord, et continuez .... jusqu'à la gare. Celle-ci est sur le côté .... de l'avenue.
Merci bien.
Je vous en prie.

TRAVEL INFORMATION

3. Pardon, le plus simple pour aller à l'aéroport Charles-de-Gaulle à partir du centre de Paris, s'il vous plaît?

   Le plus simple .... l'aéroport Roissy–Charles-de-Gaulle est de prendre le RER ligne B. Ça s'appelle ROISSY–RAIL. Ça prend seulement 35 minutes. En arrivant à la station de RER de l' .... vous prenez une navette qui vous conduit à l'aérogare 1 ou 2.

How to say it

Combien de temps	dure le voyage?		How long	does the journey last?	
Combien d'heures			For how many hours		
Le voyage	dure	dix heures	The journey	lasts	ten hours
La traversée	prend	deux jours	The crossing	takes	two days
Vous pouvez	faire la traversée directe		You can	cross directly	
	passer par l'Angleterre			go through England	
Cela	fait	... francs	That costs ... francs		
	coûte				
Où se trouve	la gare maritime?		Where is	the ferry terminal?	
	l'aéroport?			the airport?	
D'accord			Agreed		
			OK		
La gare SNCF	se trouve	dans le centre ville	The SNCF station	is	in the city centre
La gare routière		au nord de la ville	The bus station		to the north of the city

Giving information about departure and arrival times
Issuing travel documents

Listening 3:

Listen to the travel agent telling tourists how to get from Paris to various European cities and fill in the grid below.

At The Travel Agency
À L'Agence de Voyages

De Paris à:	en car/by coach durée/duration	en train/by train durée/duration	en avion/by plane durée/duration
1. Rome			
2. Londres			
3. Amsterdam			

83

TRAVEL INFORMATION

Listening 4:

(a) Now listen to the end of the same conversation between the travel agent and the tourists and circle in the following documents the departure and arrival times of the train, plane or coach they are going to take.

1.

SNCF	PARIS–ROME		
Paris–Gare-de-Lyon	18.47	20.56	22.22
Chambéry	23.51	02.18	
Torino	02.51	05.46	07.13
Genoa	04.40	07.51	09.48
Roma–Termini	09.35	13.40	14.44

SNCF	ROME–PARIS	
Roma–Termini	16.15	19.10
Genoa	21.59	00.13
Torino	00.10	02.05
Chambéry	03.12	04.56
Paris–Gare-de-Lyon	08.52	10.07

2.

LONDRES	AIR FRANCE
Heathrow	Départ PARIS–Charles-de-Gaulle
	Départ ⟶ Arrivée (heure locale)
	07.30 07.40
	07.40 07.50
	08.20 08.30
	09.00 09.10
	09.30 09.45
	Destination PARIS–Charles-de-Gaulle
	Départ ⟶ Arrivée (heure locale)
	17.30 19.35
	18.45 20.50
	19.10 21.15
	20.00 22.05

3.

EUROCARS		ITINERAIRES ET HORAIRES		
07.00	22.30	Paris–Charenton	15.30	07.00
07.30	23.00	Paris–Villette	15.00	06.30
13.30	05.00	Breda	09.00	00.30
14.15	05.45	Rotterdam	08.15	23.45
14.45	06.15	La Haye	07.45	23.15
15.00	06.30	Utrecht	07.30	23.00
15.30	07.00	Amsterdam	07.00	22.30

TRAVEL INFORMATION

 (b) Listen again to the end of the conversation between the travel agent and the tourists and complete the following tickets with the missing details.

1.

SNCF		Billet		Classe: 2
ALLER	Heures	RETOUR		Heures
Départ: PARIS–Gare-de-Lyon	....	Départ:		....
Arrivée:	14h44	Arrivée: PARIS–Gare-de-Lyon		10h07
Date:		Date:		
Réservation couchettes:		Aller: No. 22		PRIX
		Retour: No. 56		........F

2.

AIR FRANCE				
Nom:				
Prénom:				
		Dates	Heures	
			Départ	Arrivée
De:	PARIS	....	08h20	....
À:	....			
À:	PARIS	30/05	....	20h50
TARIF:	.... F			

3.

EUROCARS			
Nom:			
Prénom:			
		Aller	Retour
		Heures	
De:	....	22h30	07h00
À:	....	07h00	22h30
		Dates	
		....	
Prix:	.... F		

TRAVEL INFORMATION

How to say it

Le train	part	à	... heures	The train	leaves	at	... o'clock
	arrive		midi		arrives		midday
Le car	part	le	mardi	The coach	leaves	on	Tuesday
	arrive		samedi		arrives		Saturday
Le bateau	part de		Cherbourg	The boat	leaves from		Cherbourg
	arrive à		Rosslare		arrives at		Rosslare

Selling and booking travel and tours

Listening 5:

Listen to a tourist enquiring about holidays in Tunisia and choose the correct answers below (several answers may be possible).

1. The tourist wants to go to Tunisia:
    a. from April 10 to April 17
    b. from April 17 to April 24
    c. from April 24 to April 30

2. The only way to go to Tunisia is by charter flight:

    True ☐   False ☐

3. Which of the following meals are included if you go *en pension complète* (full board)?
    a. le petit déjeuner (breakfast)
    b. le déjeuner (lunch)
    c. le dîner (dinner)

4. Which meal is not included if you go *demi-pension* (half-board)?

5. Do the prices of 1640F and 1410F for a stay in the Hôtel-Club Hammamet include the flight fare?

    Yes ☐   No ☐

6. The *Découverte de la Tunisie* tour costs:
    a. 2840F
    b. 2140F
    c. 2410F

TRAVEL INFORMATION

7. The *Circuit Sud Tunisien* tour is cheaper than the *Découverte de la Tunisie* tour.

   True ☐   False ☐

8. Hiring a car costs:
   a. 2000F a day
   b. 200F a week
   c. 2000F a week

Listening 6:

Listen to the end of the conversation between the same travel agent and tourist and complete the registration form below.

NOUVELLES FRONTIÈRES
FICHE D'INSCRIPTION

Voyage
Destination: TUNISIE
Ville de départ: PARIS
Date de départ: ....   **Date de retour:** ....

Circuit: DECOUVERTE DE LA TUNISIE

Participants

Nom	Prénom	Date de Naissance	Nationalité	Profession

Adresse: ....
Téléphone domicile: ....
Téléphone travail: ....
Montant à payer: .... F

☐ par chèque   ☐ par carte de crédit   ☐ en espèces

TRAVEL INFORMATION

Language Practice

Exercise 1:

(a) Replace the drawings below by the corresponding French word.

1. *Vous pouvez aller en Norvège en* .... *ou en* ....

    Et en .... , *c'est aussi possible?*

    Oui, c'est possible. Et même en .... *si vous préférez.*

2. *Vous préférez visiter la vallée de la Loire en* .... , *ou en* .... *de location?*

    Non, je préfère visiter à .... , *à* .... *ou à* ....

    Alors, bon voyage!

(b) Now fill in the following sentences with 'en' or 'à'.

1. Vous allez en Espagne .... avion?
    Non, ... train.

2. Vous visitez la région .... voiture?
    Non, ... autocar.

3. Vous préférez voyager .... voiture?
    Non, ... bicyclette, ou .... pied.

4. Vous allez en Afrique .... bateau?
    Non, ... avion.

TRAVEL INFORMATION

Exercise 2:

(a) Fill in the following sentences with 'en', 'au' or 'aux'.

Example: **la** Belgique   aller **en** Belgique
           le Canada   aller **au** Canada
           les Pays-Bas   aller **aux** Pays-Bas

1. la Suisse   aller .... Suisse
2. la Russie   aller .... Russie
3. le Portugal   aller .... Portugal
4. le Cameroun   aller .... Cameroun
5. la Chine   aller .... Chine

(b) Now, fill in the following sentences with 'à' and 'en' or 'au' (you can check whether a word is masculine or feminine in the glossary).

Example: Vous allez **à** Bruxelles, **en** Belgique?
           Vous allez **à** Lisbonne, **au** Portugal?

1. Vous allez .... Genève, ... Suisse?
2. Vous allez .... Copenhague, ... Danemark?
3. Vous allez .... Athènes, ... Grèce?
4. Vous allez .... Varsovie, ... Pologne?
5. Vous allez .... Florence, ... Italie?
6. Vous allez .... Yaoundé, ... Cameroun?

Exercise 3:

You are working at the information desk of a major tourist office. Give the following information to tourists enquiring about transport. Then check your answers on the tape.

1.
SNCF	
TGV No. 28	
Paris–Gare-de-Lyon	09h35
Lyon–Perrache	11h40

TRAVEL INFORMATION

2.

CARS AVIGNON–APT
(tous les jours sauf les 25 décembre et 1er mai)

Départ Avignon	06h35	16h17	Départ Apt	08h30	18h00
Arrivée Apt	07h45	17h30	Arrivée Avignon	09h40	19h15

3.

AIR FRANCE
Départ PARIS (Aéroport Charles-de-Gaulle)

	Départ Paris ⟶ Arrivée Dakar	
DAKAR	10h30	15h35
(Sénégal)	*11h00	16h40
	13h30	18h45
	+16h45	22h30
* Tous les jours sauf dimanche		+ dimanche seulement

Exercise 4:

The travel agency Nouvelles Frontières has just published its new brochure. Before you can advise tourists, check if you understand the description of the following holiday options in France by answering the questions below.

1. HÔTEL LES CLARINES

SEJOUR GOLF

HOTEL LES CLARINES, VERCORS FRA SE 05

Stage de golf. A proximité immédiate du golf 18 trous de Corrençon. Un hôtel calme et confortable avec piscine.
Options stages de golf

HOTEL LES CLARINES, DANS LE VERCORS FRA SE 15

SEJOUR GOLF		
PRIX PAR PERSONNE PAR SEMAINE ET EN DEMI-PENSION	CHAMBRE DOUBLE bain/télévision	CHAMBRE DOUBLE douche
SAISON		
12 juin/3 juillet, 4 septembre/9 octobre	2 100 F	1 640 F
HAUTE SAISON		
3 juillet/4 septembre	2 400 F	1 930 F

- enfant accompagné de 2 adultes : réduction 50% de 2 à 6 ans et 30% de 6 à 12 ans
- OPTION GOLF : stages du lundi au samedi chaque semaine du 15 juin au 12 septembre. initiation : 1 990 F ; perfectionnement : 2 450 F ; classement : 2 800 F. Réduction de 10% les 3 premières semaines et les 2 dernières. Stage Junior School - 7/13 ans : dont les parents font un stage 900 F, pour les autres 1 300 F. Consultez la fiche technique détaillée. Forfait 6 Green Fees (licence exigée) haute saison : 1 000 F ; autres : 800 F

TRAVEL INFORMATION

(a) What sport is available to tourists? ....

(b) Are rates given for one week or for two weeks? ....

(c) Are rates given for full-board, half-board or bed and breakfast? ....

(d) Would a 14-year-old pay the same rates as an adult? ....

(e) What does the rate 2400F relate to? ....

2. SEPT JOURS EN LIBERTÉ EN CORSE

7 JOURS EN LIBERTE FCO FC 03

CIRCUITS VOITURE + HOTELS			PRIX PAR PERSONNE EN DEMI-PENSION
7 jours	BASE 2 PERSONNES	BASE 3 PERSONNES	BASE 4 PERSONNES
3 avril/26 juin	2 930 F	2 680 F	2 560 F
26 juin/17 juillet	3 270 F	3 020 F	2 900 F
21 août/11 septembre	3 270 F	3 020 F	2 900 F
11 septembre/31 octobre	2 930 F	2 680 F	2 560 F

- base véhicule de catégorie A ; supplément par véhicule et par semaine : Cat. B, + 270 F ; Cat. C, + 520 F
- enfant : de 0 à 2 ans, gratuit ; de 2 à 12 ans, partageant la chambre de 2 adultes, réduction de 20%
- départ aéroport Ajaccio, Bastia, Calvi, Figari selon vols
- retour possible à une autre agence (aéroport ou ville) que celle du départ (prévenir en prenant le véhicule)
- hôtels 3 étoiles supplément 35 F/nuit payable sur place ▪ chambre individuelle : environ 115 F
- cette formule n'existe pas du 15 juillet au 21 août

(a) How does a tourist travel in Corsica? ....

(b) Is there more than one airport where one can land? ....

(c) Are hotel nights included in the cost? ....

(d) What does the cost of 3270F relate to? ....

....

TRAVEL INFORMATION

3. RÉSIDENCE HOTEL LES PINS

RESIDENCE HOTEL LES PINS FRA FC 02

NOUVEAU

A quelques minutes de Montpellier, dans une pinède protégée, la Résidence Hôtelière Les Pins vous offre 80 chambres spacieuses et confortables, conçues comme un espace à vivre (bureau, terrasse, 9 chaînes de télévision, toilettes séparées), où vous pourrez goûter aux joies des plages et de l'arrière pays. Egalement sur place, piscine, fitness, jacuzzi, tennis.

RESIDENCE HOTEL LES PINS FRA FC 02

A LA CARTE	CHAMBRE DOUBLE		CHAMBRE INDIVIDUELLE	
PRIX PAR PERSONNE EN NUITS ET PETITS DEJEUNERS	par jour	par semaine	par jour	par semaine
1er avril/30 juin	260 F	1 710 F	420 F	2 780 F
1er juillet/31 août	240 F	1 590 F	390 F	2 590 F
1er septembre/31 octobre	260 F	1 710 F	420 F	2 780 F

■ située à quelques minutes de Montpellier dans une pinède protégée. A l'hôtel, piscine, fitness, jacuzzi, tennis ■ repas : 110 F

(a) How many bedrooms are there in this hotel? ....

(b) What is the nearest town? ....

(c) List three sports that are available at the Hôtel les Pins. ....

....

(d) What meals are included in the rates? ....

(e) What does the amount of 110F refer to? ....

Exercise 5:

You are working at the information desk of a travel agency in England when a French client arrives. Listen to the client and answer the questions as prompted below. You play the part of the assistant.

At The Travel Agency

À L'Agence de Voyages

Visitor	Bonjour.
Assistant	*Greet the client and offer help.*

TRAVEL INFORMATION

Visitor   Je voudrais aller à Paris le 18 décembre, s'il vous plaît.
Assistant   *Ask the client if she wants to travel by train, by plane or by coach.*
Visitor   Je ne sais pas. Quels sont les prix d'un aller-retour en train, en avion et en car, s'il vous plaît?
Assistant   *Give the client the information (see information sheet).*
Visitor   Combien de temps dure le voyage en train, en avion, en car?
Assistant   *Give the client the information (see information sheet).*
Visitor   Est-ce qu'il y a un vol le 18 décembre?
Assistant   *Tell the client that there are flights every day.*
Visitor   Quelle est l'heure de départ et l'heure d'arrivée?
Assistant   *Give the client the information (see information sheet).*
Visitor   Où se trouve l'aéroport?
Assistant   *Give the client the information (see information sheet).*
Visitor   Je voudrais réserver un aller-retour en avion pour le 18 décembre.
Assistant   *Ask her name and make the plane booking.*
Visitor   Isabelle LECLERC, L - E - C - L - E - R - C.

	FICHE D'INFORMATION			
	Durée	Tarif aller-retour	Départ	Arrivée
1. TRAIN	19h00	£132.00	15h35	10h48
2. AVION	01h30	£215.00	13h14 (tous les jours)	14h42
3. CAR	23h00	£106.00	14h22 (tous les jours)	13h36

1. Gare située au centre ville.
2. Aéroport à 5 km au nord de la ville (accès par le car spécial aéroport qui part de la gare routière: prix £5.35).
3. Gare routière située en face de l'église Sainte Marie.

TRAVEL INFORMATION

 ## TRAVELLING BY TRAIN

When the spirit of adventure takes hold and you decide to break out of Paris and explore the rest of France, you will be preparing yourself to encounter the SNCF or *Société Nationale des Chemins de Fer Français,* the French railway company of course!

When you have decided on your destination, you must then find the *gare* (railway station) from which you should leave.

The main railway stations in Paris are:

Gare du Nord for the north of France and Belgium
Gare de Lyon for the south-east of France and for Italy
Gare Montparnasse for the west of France
Gare St Lazare for the north-west including the port of Le Havre
Gare d'Austerlitz for the south-west of France
Gare de l'Est for the east of France and for Germany

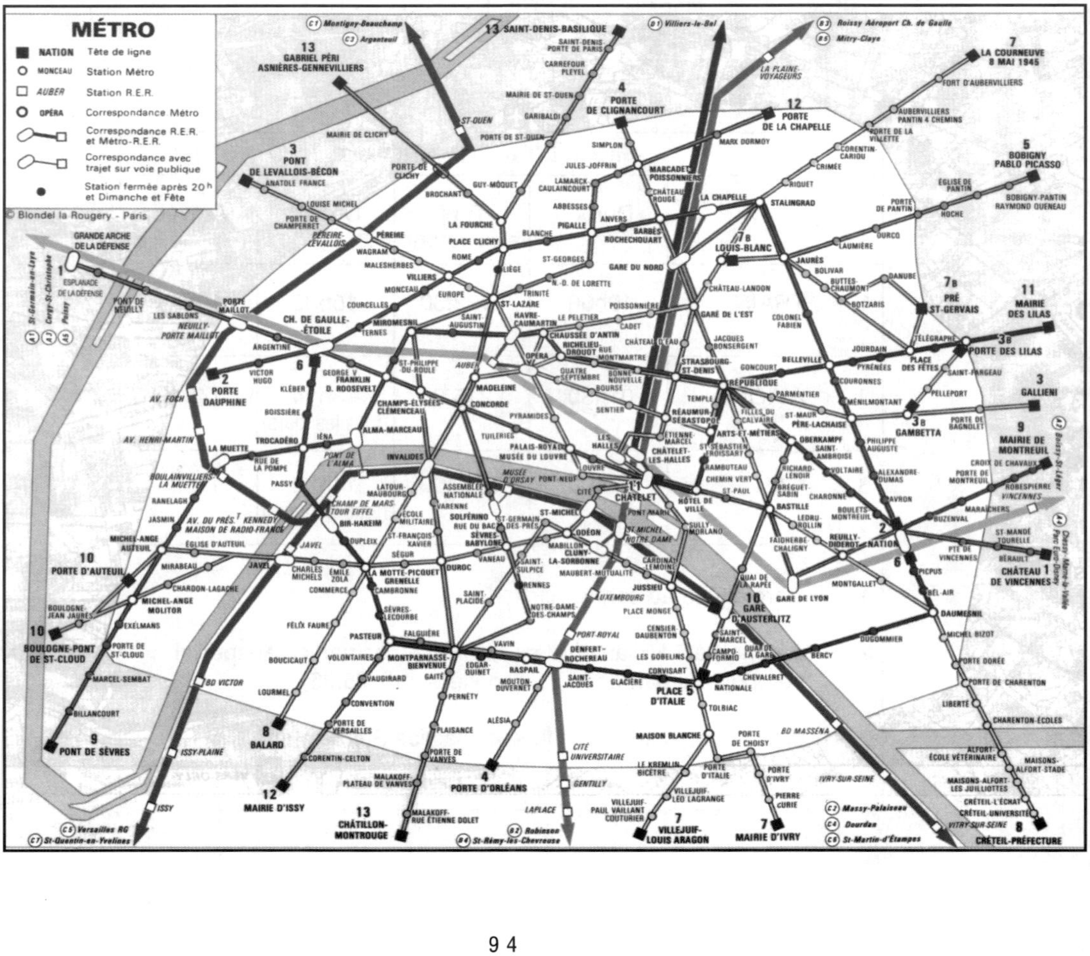

TRAVEL INFORMATION

Remember

Many trains have first and second-class carriages but some are all first-class and others all second-class. Passengers with second-class tickets will have to pay a supplement if found to be travelling in a first-class carriage.

It is also worth noting that in France, trains do leave at the stated time if not one or two minutes before it. By the time you board the train you should have already *composté* (punched) your ticket in the machine at the entrance to the *quais* (platforms) or *voies* (tracks). It looks like a litter bin, orange in colour with a flashing green arrow. Your ticket is not valid unless you do this and the alternative is an encounter with the *contrôleur* (ticket inspector) who will not hesitate to fine you on the spot!

Reservations are usually not required on standard trains, although when choosing your seat it is advisable to check whether it has been reserved and for what part of the journey. This could save a lot of bother.

On the high speed train or TGV *(train à grande vitesse)* you must reserve your seat. There is an additional charge for this which may vary according to the time of day and the route you travel. No standing is allowed as the TGV can reach speeds of around two hundred miles per hour. Any additional charge is compensated for by the great comfort and, most of all, the reduction in travel time. For example, a standard train journey from Paris to Lyon would take around 6 hours, the TGV will have you there in 2 hours 15 minutes. Since its introduction on the Paris–Lyon line the TGV has spread in all directions.

TRAVEL INFORMATION

Les réductions

There are considerable reductions available for everyone as rail travel really is part of French life. Be sure to investigate what is on offer. It could save you up to 50% of the fare!

The *Calendrier Voyages,* a free leaflet which shows you the off-peak travelling times, is available at all train stations in France.

There are certain times when reductions are greatest. At especially busy times, no reductions are available. This information is clearly colour-coded on the free calendar.

Reductions for special categories

There are special reductions available for people over 60, under 26, under 15, travelling as a couple, and so on. And of course there are run-about tickets which can be great value if you are doing a lot of travel on three, five or ten days within a one-month period.

Information on reductions is also available outside France from international railway travel offices.

TRAVEL INFORMATION

The Extras

Finally, for the special needs of travellers, SNCF provide additional services. Many main line trains have an excellent *wagon-restaurant* (restaurant car). With the *trains-couchettes* you can reserve a bed for the night; if you would really like to do it in style and wake up to a served breakfast, you can avail of the *Wagon-Lits* service (sleeping cars). When you want to bring your car along too, the *Train Auto-Couchettes* option will allow you to do this. If you wanted to bring the kitchen sink too it probably would be possible!

SPORTS AND LEISURE

UNIT 7

Objectives

At the end of this unit you will be able to:

- Greet and welcome visitors

- Give information on activities and facilities

- Give information on regulations and safety rules

- Ask someone what he or she would like to do

- Suggest doing something

- Ask about medical conditions and symptoms

- Respond to requests for assistance

SPORTS AND LEISURE

Giving information on activities, facilities and regulations

Listening 1:

 (a) Listen to the leisure assistant greeting and welcoming a group of tourists which has just arrived at the holiday village of Waterville. Tick the activities available in the village on the vocabulary list below.

	Piscine couverte/Indoor swimming pool	☐
	Piscine découverte/Outdoor swimming pool	☐
	Voile/Sailing	☐
	Tennis/Tennis	☐
	Ski nautique/Water skiing	☐
	Plongée libre/Snorkelling	☐
	Plongée avec bouteille/Scuba diving	☐
	Parcours de golf/Golf course	☐

SPORTS AND LEISURE

- Randonnée à pied/Walking ☐
- Randonnée à vélo/Cycling ☐
- Randonnée à cheval/Pony trekking ☐
- Tir à l'arc/Archery ☐
- Musculation/Weight training ☐
- Mise en forme/Keep fit ☐
- Planche à voile/Wind surfing ☐
- Vélo Tout Terrain (VTT)/Mountain biking ☐
- Equitation/Horse riding ☐
- Arts appliqués/Craft workshop ☐
- Pêche/Fishing ☐

SPORTS AND LEISURE

 (b) Listen again and tick the statements below in the appropriate columns.

	True	False
1. There are two restaurants.		
2. Children are not catered for in this village.		
3. You can go dancing.		
4. There are two 18-hole golf courses.		
5. You can play bridge.		
6. All activities are fee paying.		

Listening 2:

 Listen to the receptionist at the desk of this hotel leisure centre and try to list all the rules and regulations he is indicating to the visitor by completing the sentences below *en français* (in French).

The following words will help you to do so:
le sauna, le jacuzzi, le bonnet de bain, réserver, fumer, les enfants

1. .... est obligatoire.

2. .... de moins de 15 ans ne sont pas admis.

3. .... sont interdits aux enfants.

4. Il faut ....

5. Il est interdit de ....

GIVING INFORMATION ON ACTIVITIES AND REGULATIONS AND SUGGESTING ACTIVITIES

Listening 3:

 (a) Listen to the leisure assistant suggesting possible activities to a group of visitors and fill in their programme for the day's activities.

Eilí Bay Adventure Centre Samedi 26 Juin	
Matin:	....
13h00 — 14h30:	déjeuner
Après-midi:	....
19h30:	dîner
22h30:	....

SPORTS AND LEISURE

 (b) Now listen again and list all seven activities mentioned in the conversation.

1. ....   2. ....
3. ....   4. ....
5. ....   6. ....
7. ....

How to say it

| Que voulez-vous faire? | What would you like to do? |
| Qu'est-ce que vous préférez? | What would you prefer? |

| N'oubliez pas | vos gilets de sauvetage | Don't forget | your life jackets |
| | votre raquette | | your racquet |

Listening 4:

 (a) Listen to the receptionist giving information to a newly-arrived visitor about some activities and the required equipment for each. Match the sport with the required equipment.

SPORT   EQUIPMENT

1. Faire du tennis   a. Des chaussures spéciales

2. Faire du VTT   b. Un gilet de sauvetage

3. Faire de l'escalade   c. Un casque

SPORTS AND LEISURE

4. Faire du cheval

d. Des chaussures de tennis

5. Faire de la planche à voile

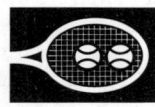
e. Une raquette et des balles

6. Faire du rafting

f. Une bombe et des bottes

7. Faire du canoë-kayak

8. Faire du ski nautique

 (b) Listen again and indicate whether you can hire the items listed below.

Emprunter/Louer
To borrow/Hire

		Yes	No
1.	Des chaussures spéciales	☐	☐
2.	Un gilet de sauvetage	☐	☐
3.	Un casque	☐	☐
4.	Des chaussures de tennis	☐	☐
5.	Une raquette	☐	☐
6.	Une bombe	☐	☐
7.	Des bottes	☐	☐

SPORTS AND LEISURE

ILLNESSES AND INJURIES

Listening 5:

A tour guide is discussing health-related issues with a group of tourists who are planning a holiday on the French island of Martinique. Listen to the conversation and select the correct answers from the list below.

HELP!

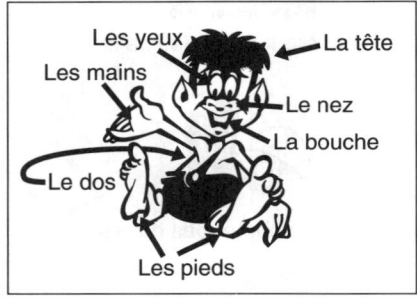

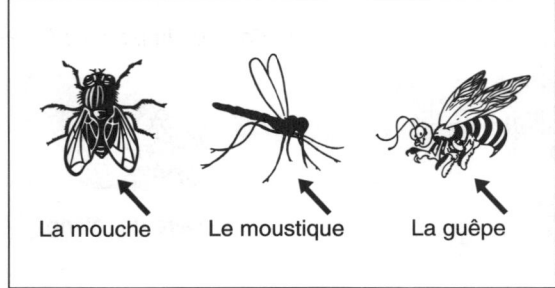

1. The group is going on a
   a. hill walking holiday
   b. pony trekking holiday
   c. cycling holiday

2. One of the participants suffers from
   a. malaria
   b. diphtheria
   c. diabetes

3. Another participant is allergic to
   a. horses
   b. pollen
   c. mosquitoes

4. In Martinique, there are lots of
   a. flies
   b. mosquitoes
   c. wasps

5. Another participant has problems with his
   a. feet
   b. back
   c. eyes

SPORTS AND LEISURE

6. The recommended vaccinations are
   a. anti-tetanus
   b. anti-malaria
   c. anti-polio

Listening 6:

(a) The participants are now in Martinique and they have stopped at a campsite for the first night of their trek. Listen to the dialogues where the participants complain about a variety of ailments and indicate the dialogue number beside each illustration as in the example.

A   (Cut finger)   3   (Example)

B   (Broken ankle)   ☐

C   (Headache)   ☐

D   (Upset stomach)   ☐

E   (Mosquito bites)   ☐

F   (Toothache)   ☐

(b) Listen to the same passages again and choose the answer on the right which matches the statement or question on the left.

1. J'ai mal à l'estomac.   a. Vous voulez de l'aspirine?
2. J'ai très mal à la tête.   b. J'appelle une ambulance.
3. Je me suis coupé le doigt.   c. Vous voulez que j'appelle un dentiste?
4. J'ai très mal aux dents.   d. Tenez, c'est une pommade . . .
5. Je me suis cassé la cheville.   e. Prenez ces cachets . . .
6. Vous avez quelque chose contre les moustiques? f. Il faut désinfecter . . .

SPORTS AND LEISURE

How to say it

Etes-vous en bonne santé?	Are you in good health?
Avez-vous des problèmes de santé?	Have you got health problems?
Vous avez mal où?	Where does it hurt?

Prenez   ces cachets
              cette pommade
	Take these pills
	           this cream

J'appelle   un médecin
              une ambulance
	I'll call a doctor
	           an ambulance

Ne vous inquiétez pas	Do not worry

J'ai mal   à la tête
            à l'estomac
            aux dents
	I have a headache
	           a stomach ache
	           a toothache

Language Practice

Exercise 1:

Look at the Club Med advertisements for holidays in Guadeloupe and Martinique and write the names of the sports in French opposite the symbols.

Au sud de la Guadeloupe
LA CARAVELLE
CONFORT / SITE

Le bonheur à La Caravelle c'est:
- Le lieu idéal pour les baignades dans une mer chaude et claire, le bronzage sur une plage sublime.
- le lieu idéal pour faire du sport à volonté: kayak, tennis, planche à voile et fitness
- le lieu idéal pour faire des excursions: du shopping à St Barth, la forêt tropicale et le survol d'îles aux noms poétiques: les Saintes, Marie-Galante et la Désirade.

....
....
....
....
....
....
....
....

Au sud de la Martinique
LES BOUCANIERS
CONFORT / SITE

Le bonheur aux Boucaniers c'est:
- une ambiance tonique dans ce village sans enfants
- tous les symboles des tropiques: cocotiers, hibiscus, flamboyants, … et une mer à 28°
- un festival de sports nautiques: plongée, ski nautique, voile et planche à voile
- des sorties en mer au clair de lune

....
....
....
....
....
....

SPORTS AND LEISURE

Exercise 2:

Listen to the cues on the tape and build up sentences based on the models below.

    Faire de la voile   **Vous pouvez faire de la voile**
    Jouer au volley-ball   **Vous pouvez jouer au volley-ball**

1. Faire du ski nautique   ....
2. Faire de la plongée libre   ....
3. Faire du vélo tout terrain   ....
4. Faire de l'escalade   ....
5. Faire de la planche à voile   ....
6. Faire du canoë-kayak   ....
7. Jouer au tennis   ....
8. Jouer au golf   ....
9. Jouer au squash   ....
10. Jouer au football   ....

SPORTS AND LEISURE

Exercise 3:

Look at the extract from the list of activity holidays offered by Bord Fáilte and answer the questions *en anglais* (in English).

Organisme	Période	Durée du Séjour	Lieu	Prix	Hébergement	Age	Activités
Club des 4 Vents	Juillet/Août	3 semaines	Co. Meath	8 200 F	Centre	14-17	1 sem. vélo, 1 sem. équitation. 1 sem. activités sociales et culturelles
Association Regards	Été	3 semaines	Westport	6 450 F	En famille, camping, cottage	13-17	Stage sportif à la carte : golf, tennis, canoë, vélo, roulotte, pêche, équitation, aquarelle.
	Juillet-Août	2 semaines	Drumshambo	4 900 F	Cottage	11+	Groupes de 15 personnes. Stage organisé et encadré par l'École Française de Pêche. Autres dates sur demande.
Marmottes Chamois Interlingua M.C.I	Juillet/Août	10 jours	Dublin	6 925 F (10 jours)	en famille	15-17	Circuit sportif et culturel à pied/vélo.
Nouvelles Frontières	Toute l'année	13 jours / 1 semaine	Kerry Connemara Toute l'Irlande	6 100 F 6 660 F 1 210 F	Guesthouses / Guesthouse/ Chez l'habitant		Randonnée pédestre. Demi-pension. Circuit "La route des pubs" à vélo. Option mountain bike (VTT) possible.
U.C.P.A.	Été	15 jours	Connemara	6 800 F	En centre	16-17	Séjours multi-sports. En vélo, à pied, kayak de mer, surf.

1. Name the organisation which offers a three-week stay with a different activity every week.
   ....
2. What are the three activities?
   ....
3. You want to go on a camping/activity-based holiday. Where can you go?
   ....
4. Name five of the activities you would be able to practise there.
   ....
5. You want to visit Kerry with Nouvelles Frontières. What type of accommodation is offered to you?
   ....
6. Is pony trekking part of the package?
   ....
7. Can you go to Connemara with UCPA (Union des Centres de Plein Air) all year round?
   ....
8. Name two sports you can do with UCPA.
   ....

SPORTS AND LEISURE

Exercise 4:

Look at the leaflet below and imagine you are working as a leisure assistant in Delphi. A group of French holiday-makers has just arrived at the centre and you give them information about the activities available.

Note: Check the answers on the tape but remember that they are model answers only.

Activities

LAND BASED:
 Abseiling.
 Pony-Trekking.
 Mountaineering, (including Low/High-level, Navigation, Rescue, etc.)
 Rock-Climbing.
 Archery.
 Ropes/Assault Course.
 Orienteering.
 'It's a Knock-Out'.
 Mountain-Biking.
 Cycling.
 Expeditions.
 The Delphi Decathlon— the ultimate outdoor challenge.

WATER BASED:
 Surfing.
 Sailing.
 White-Water Rafting.
 Canoeing (including Sea Kayaking, White-Water Canoeing and Canoe-Surfing).
 Water-Skiing.
 Wind-Surfing.
 Aquasausage (a five-man aquatic Roller-Coaster, towed behind a speed-boat, see photograph on right).
 Surf-Skiing.
 Sub-Aqua.

 Also available locally: Golf, Paint-ball games, Clay-Pigeon Shooting etc.

Family Holidays: Phone for separate brochure.

Courses/Holidays

- Tailor-Made Courses.
- Multi-Activity Taster Holidays.
- Mountaineering Courses, including Navigation, Rescue, etc.
- Watersports Holidays, including specialist Sailing/Windsurfing, Canoeing, Surfing and Sub-Aqua courses.
- Pony-Trekking Holidays.
- Adventure Safari - touring the West Coast of Ireland by Land-Rover, experiencing exciting Adventure Sports en-route.
- Winter Courses (even Christmas), including Hill-Walking, Pony-Trekking, etc.

SPORTS AND LEISURE

Exercise 5:

You are a leisure assistant in a holiday village. A French visitor is asking you about the various activities on offer in the village. Answer the questions as prompted below.

Note: Check the answers on the tape but remember that they are model answers only.

Visitor	Bonjour.
Assistant	*Return the greeting and offer your help.*
Visitor	Quelles sont les activités auxquelles je peux participer ce matin?
Assistant	*Say that he can use the indoor swimming pool, do aerobics or windsurfing.*
Visitor	Le bonnet de bain est obligatoire dans la piscine?
Assistant	*Say that it is, but that he can hire one at the pool.*
Visitor	Et cet après-midi, qu'est-ce que vous me conseillez?
Assistant	*Tell him that for the afternoon, there is a mountain bike outing organised, or he can do horse riding or archery.*
Visitor	Il faut réserver pour la randonnée VTT?
Assistant	*Tell him that, yes, he should book for the mountain bike outing.*
Visitor	Et ce soir, quel est le programme?
Assistant	*Tell him that there is a* son et lumière *organised for 10.00 p.m. but that he should book the tickets before 4.00 p.m.*
Visitor	Les billets coûtent combien pour le spectacle?
Assistant	*Tell him that the tickets are £8 each.*
Visitor	D'accord. Au fait, ma femme a très mal à la tête. Est-ce que vous avez quelque chose?
Assistant	*Say yes and offer him aspirin tablets.*
Visitor	Merci beaucoup.
Assistant	*Say goodbye and wish him a nice day.*

SPORTS AND LEISURE

TIME ON YOUR HANDS

If it's sport and leisure activities you're looking for, France is definitely the place to go. There is a great variety of things to do and the French seem to keep inventing new ones every year! Leisure time is seen as something to be used actively, whether for physical or mental exercise. Most towns in France have a *Maison de la Culture* (cultural centre) which offers activities to suit young and old from pottery-making, cinema or theatre workshops, to folk-dancing. There really is no excuse for boredom!

Le Sport

Most people associate France, perhaps, with rugby, cycling and rally driving. But there are many other sports which are practised by French people. The best known are probably *le foot* (soccer), *le basket-ball* (or simply *le basket*), *le volley, le hand, le squash, le tennis, la natation* (swimming) and of course *le ski* and *la luge* (tobogganing).

In winter, skiing is a very popular sport in France and it attracts many people from abroad to enjoy it at French resorts. In summer the ski resorts are also open; this allows the active holiday-maker to practise some of the other interesting activities organised in the mountains for the off-peak season or even in good winters when there is little snow.

Guide de haute montagne

Here are some sports you may like to try:

Le ski green or *le ski gold sur herbe* — yes, you can ski on the grass! Special skis are used for this.

SPORTS AND LEISURE

l'alpinisme	mountaineering
l'escalade	rock climbing
la spéléologie	pot-holing
l'équitation	horse riding
le VTT — vélo tout terrain	mountain biking
le canoë-kayak	canoeing
le parapente	parachute gliding
l'aquarelle	watercolour painting — for those who want to relax
l'escrime	fencing

You can also avail of theatre, music and dance workshops — and all this half way up a mountain!

Seaside resorts in France have become more developed too; they offer many activities apart from the well-known *ski nautique* (water skiing). For example, *la planche à voile* (wind-surfing) or *l'hydrospeed* (jet skiing).

EXCURSIONS AND TOURS

UNIT 8

Objectives

At the end of this unit you will be able to:

- Greet and welcome

- Provide information about excursions and tours

- Describe attractions, sites and scenery

- Make suggestions on places of interest, local crafts, and events

- Ask someone what he or she would like to do

- Suggest doing something

- Invite someone to do something

- Give information and respond to enquiries about weather conditions

Place de la Grande Boucherie, Strasbourg

EXCURSIONS AND TOURS

PROVIDING INFORMATION ABOUT EXCURSIONS AND TOURS
DESCRIBING ATTRACTIONS, SITES AND SCENERY

Listening 1:

The local tourist information officer in Cahors is answering questions about possible tours in the area.

 (a) Listen to the first part of the dialogue so as to complete the following chart. Circle the correct information as you hear it.

1. The Cahors–Figeac tour takes
   a. one day
   b. two days
   c. three days

2. How long is the Cahors–Figeac tour?
   a. 40 km
   b. 50 km
   c. 60 km

3. What distance is Rocamadour from Figeac?
   a. 25 km
   b. 30 km
   c. 40 km

4. How long is the Rocamadour tour?
   a. 45 km
   b. 55 km
   c. 65 km

5. How long does the visit of the Padirac caves *(grottes de Padirac)* take?
   a. 1 hour
   b. 2 hours
   c. 3 hours

EXCURSIONS AND TOURS

 (b) Listen again to the itineraries described by the local tourist information officer, and fill in the gaps with the appropriate word from the following list:

visite, bateau, voiture, circuit, carte, environs, châteaux

Bonjour, Madame, pouvez-vous nous dire quelles sont les visites intéressantes dans les environs, s'il vous plaît?
Oui, bien sûr. Vous êtes en . . . . ?
Oui, et nous sommes dans la région pour trois jours.
D'accord. Et, avez-vous une . . . . de la région?
Oui, la voici.
Bon, alors il y a beaucoup de choses à voir dans les . . . . Vous voyez, vous avez plusieurs circuits possibles. Vous pouvez par exemple faire un . . . . entre Cahors et Figeac, c'est un circuit très agréable d'une journée. Il fait environ 50 (cinquante) kilomètres. Vous pouvez aussi aller à Rocamadour, c'est à seulement 30 (trente) kilomètres au nord de Cahors. En deux jours, vous pouvez faire un circuit très varié avec des . . . ., des villages pittoresques et bien sûr, vous avez la . . . . des grottes à ne pas manquer. Ce circuit au départ de Rocamadour fait environ 65 (soixante-cinq) kilomètres.
Ces grottes sont importantes?
Oui, ce sont les grottes de Padirac. Elles sont immenses; la visite se fait en . . . . et dure deux heures.
Ça a l'air intéressant. Vous pouvez nous décrire les différents circuits, s'il vous plaît?

Listening 2:

 (a) Listen to the second part of the dialogue, where the tourist information officer gives more details about the attractions in the Cahors region.

Listen to the itineraries described and tick the attractions mentioned in the list below as often as you hear them:

Château (Example)	✓	✓	✓	✓	✓	
Village						
Église						
Grottes						
Gorges						
Panorama						
Station thermale						
Marché (spécialités gastronomiques)						
Baignade						
Pêche						

EXCURSIONS AND TOURS

 (b) First, identify the meanings of the symbols below. Then, listen to the itineraries again. While looking at the map below, identify which attractions correspond to each place on the route, and cross off the symbols that have been placed on the map by mistake.

Légende
Key

- Panorama / View point
- Église / Church
- Station thermale / Spa
- Château / Castle
- Gorges / Canyons
- Baignade / Swimming
- Village ancien / Old village
- Grottes / Caves
- Pêche / Fishing
- Marché (spécialités gastronomiques) / Market (good food specialities)

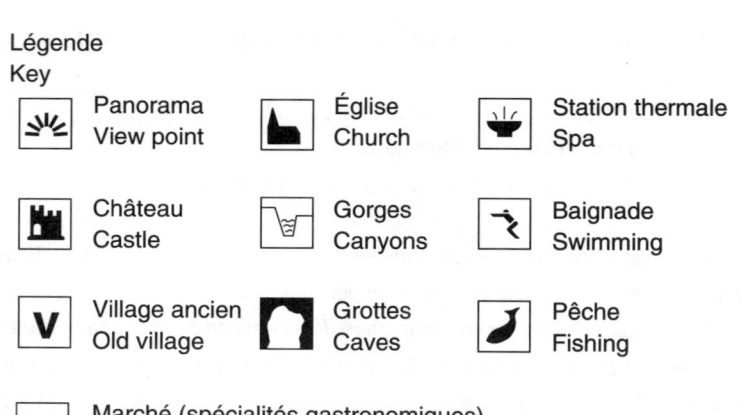

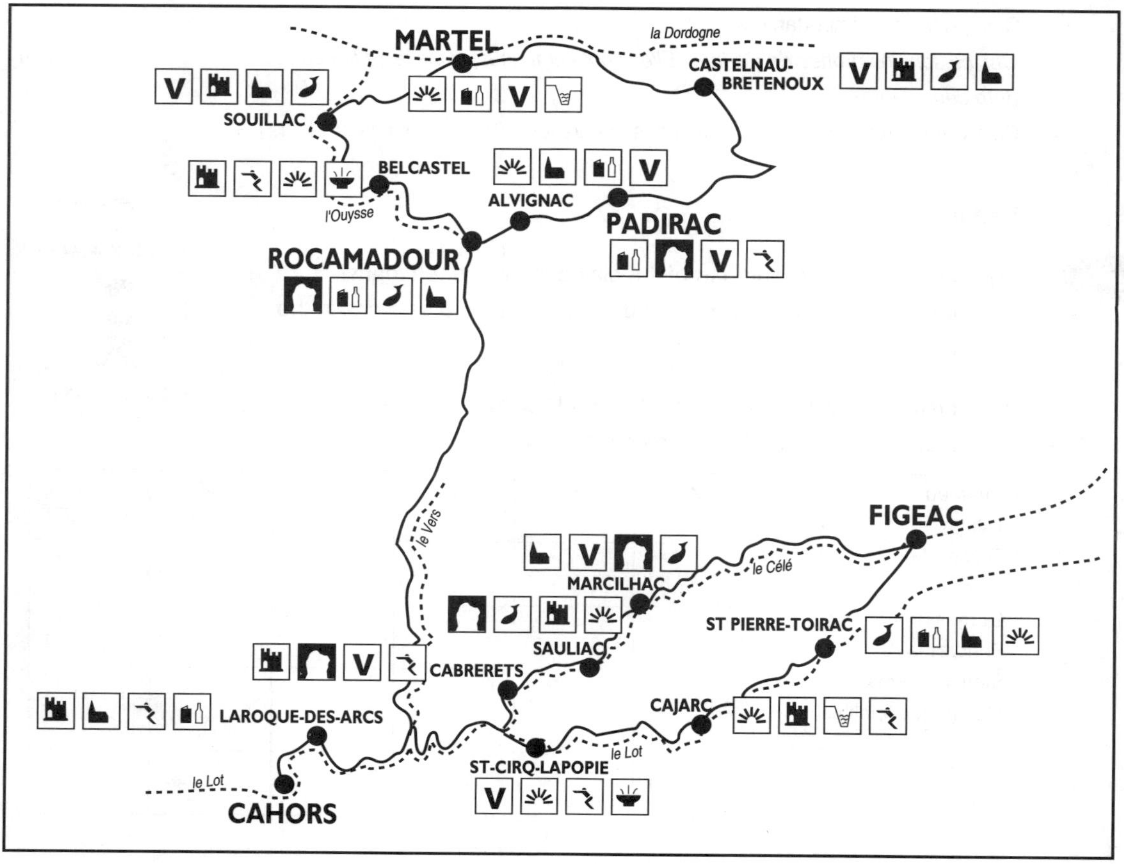

EXCURSIONS AND TOURS

 (c) Listen again to the itineraries described by the local information officer and fill in the gaps with the following verbs or expressions, which may be used several times in the dialogue (replay the tape if you find it helpful):

il y a; intéressant(s) à voir, à faire, à visiter; vous avez; vous suivez; vous passez; vous allez; vous pouvez; vous trouvez.

Avec plaisir. Alors, pour le premier, la balade entre Cahors et Figeac, vous .... d'abord la vallée du Lot, puis la vallée du Célé au retour. C'est très agréable. .... plusieurs châteaux .... notamment à Cajarc, Sauliac et Cabrerets. Vous .... aussi plusieurs petits villages avec de vieilles maisons typiques de la région, par exemple à St Cirq-Lapopie et Marcilhac.

À St Cirq-Lapopie, ... un très beau panorama sur la vallée du Lot; et à Cajarc, ... aussi un panorama magnifique et des gorges impressionnantes. Si cela vous intéresse, ... également des églises anciennes dans plusieurs villages, notamment à St Pierre-Toirac et Marcilhac. Vous .... aussi visiter de petites grottes sur ce circuit, à Marcilhac et Cabrerets. Finalement, si cela vous tente, ... aussi des possibilités de baignade dans la rivière à Cajarc et Laroque-des-Arcs. Vous voyez, c'est un circuit très varié.

Oui, ce doit être très joli. Et qu'est-ce qu'il y a d'intéressant .... du côté de Rocamadour?

Eh bien, ... aussi beaucoup de sites intéressants .... à partir de Rocamadour. Vous .... l'embarras du choix. D'abord .... plusieurs grands châteaux et de jolies églises très bien préservées. Au nord-est de Rocamadour vous .... le château de Belcastel avec un panorama magnifique sur la vallée de la Dordogne. À Souillac, vous .... un village très animé avec un château et une église du douzième (12e) siècle. Ensuite, vous .... au village médiéval de Martel, lui aussi très bien préservé. À Martel, vous .... un marché avec des spécialités gastronomiques de la région. Vous .... la vallée de la Dordogne jusqu'à Castelnau-Bretenoux où .... un village pittoresque et un très grand château du onzième (11e) siècle. Au retour vous .... par la station thermale d'Alvignac.

EXCURSIONS AND TOURS

How to say it

Quel est le circuit le plus intéressant?		Which is the most interesting tour?
Quels sont les villages les plus pittoresques?		Which are the most picturesque villages?

Il y a | un château / une église | **à** | voir / visiter

There is | a castle / church | to | see / visit

C'est | un circuit / une visite | **d'** un jour / une semaine **de** deux jours / quatre jours

It is | a | one day / one week / two day / four day | tour / visit

Où est-ce qu'on peut | aller à la pêche? / faire des achats?

Where | can we | go fishing? / do some shopping?

Qu'est-ce qui vous intéresse? What are you interested in?

Avec plaisir It's my pleasure / You're welcome

Listening 3:

(a) Listen to a travel agent giving information about a two-week package tour in Quebec.

Indicate, on the map below, the itinerary of the tour called 'La balade du St Laurent'.

AT THE TRAVEL AGENCY
À L'AGENCE DE VOYAGES

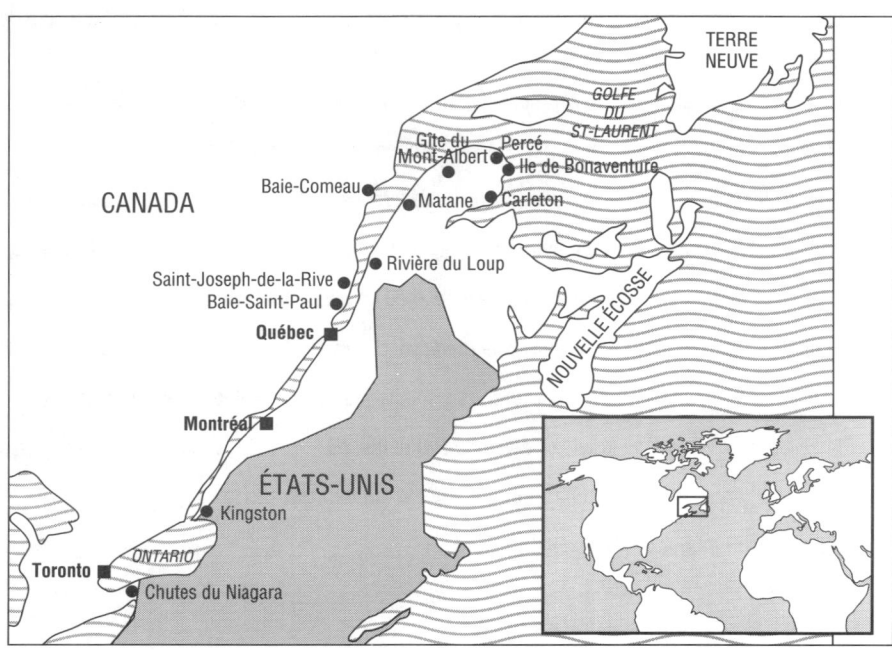

EXCURSIONS AND TOURS

(b) Listen again to the travel agent and tick the right answer.

1. On the first day you fly from Paris to:
   - a. Quebec
   - b. Montreal
   - c. Toronto

2. On the second day, you go to the Niagara Falls by:
   - a. coach
   - b. train
   - c. car

3. On the third day, you go on:
   - a. a city/town tour
   - b. a visit to the museum
   - c. a cruise

4. On the fourth day, in Montreal, you visit:
   - a. the opera house
   - b. the Olympic stadium
   - c. the castle

5. On the fifth day, you stay overnight in:
   - a. Montreal
   - b. Charlevoix
   - c. Baie St Paul

6. On the sixth day, you visit:
   - a. a bakery
   - b. a paper mill
   - c. an island

7. On the seventh day, you cross the St Laurent river in:
   - a. 1 hour 30 mins
   - b. 2 hours
   - c. 2 hours 30 mins

8. You spend the eighth day in:
   - a. a castle
   - b. a gîte
   - c. a hotel

EXCURSIONS AND TOURS

9. On the ninth day, you taste local specialities of:
   a. vegetables
   b. fish
   c. wine

10. You spend the tenth night in:
    a. Bonaventure
    b. Percé
    c. Carleton

11. On the eleventh day, you travel by:
    a. car
    b. train
    c. coach

12. On the twelfth day, you visit:
    a. towns
    b. villages
    c. mountains

13. On the thirteenth day, you visit:
    a. the cathedral
    b. the Acadian museum
    c. the Frontenac castle

14. On the fourteenth day, you do:
    a. a guided tour of Montreal
    b. a guided tour of Quebec
    c. shopping in Montreal

15. On the fifteenth day, you arrive in Paris:
    a. in the morning
    b. in the afternoon
    c. at night

EXCURSIONS AND TOURS

MAKING SUGGESTIONS ON PLACES OF INTEREST, LOCAL CRAFTS AND EVENTS

TOURIST INFORMATION

INFORMATIONS

Listening 4:

(a) Listen to the guides answering questions about night entertainment in Périgueux, and tick the options which the two tourists express interest in:

1. un cabaret ☐
2. un concert de musique classique ☐
3. une boîte de nuit ☐
4. un grand restaurant renommé ☐
5. un petit restaurant pas cher ☐
6. un spectacle folklorique ☐
7. un spectacle son et lumière ☐
8. une promenade tranquille ☐

(b) Listen again to the dialogues and complete the table below with the corresponding entertainment:

A. en face des Arènes Romaines (example)   (4) un grand restaurant renommé

B. au Musée du Périgord   ( )

C. dans les Arènes Romaines   ( )

D. à la Cathédrale   ( )

E. à proximité de la Cathédrale   ( )

(c) Listen once more and indicate at what time the following events start:

1. le spectacle folklorique   ....
2. le spectacle son et lumière   ....
3. le concert de musique classique   ....

EXCURSIONS AND TOURS

Listening 5:

 (a) Listen to the guide advising tourists on local crafts and specialities in Alsace and circle the items that you hear mentioned in the first dialogue (box 1).

(b) Listen to the four dialogues now and match the comments on the right-hand side below with the appropriate items on the left-hand side.

1.

l'artisanat	
la parfumerie	
la poterie	
la peinture sur verres	C'est très original
la sculpture sur pierre	
les articles en bois	

2.

la tarte aux fruits	
la tarte aux pommes	
la tarte flambée	
la tarte au kirch	C'est délicieux
la tarte tatin	
la tarte au fromage	

3.

les paniers en osier	
les articles en cristal	
les produits d'artisanat	
les poteries miniatures	C'est joli, pas cher et original
les bouquets de fleurs séchées	
les tableaux	

4.

les moules à gâteau	
les jouets en bois	C'est vraiment typique
les costumes folkloriques	C'est un beau souvenir
les poupées folkloriques	C'est plus cher
les petits meubles en bois	C'est très apprécié
les articles de sport	

122

EXCURSIONS AND TOURS

 (c) Listen to the four dialogues again and identify where the items can be found by circling the appropriate numbers:

	Dialogues			
à proximité de la cathédrale	1	2	3	4
le marché sur la place	1	2	3	4
le quartier de l'Europe	1	2	3	4
à côté du Musée d'Alsace	1	2	3	4
tout près de l'hôtel	1	2	3	4
la vieille ville	1	2	3	4
un peu partout	1	2	3	4

GIVING INFORMATION AND REPLYING TO QUERIES ABOUT WEATHER CONDITIONS

HOW TO SAY IT

Quel temps fait-il?			What is the weather like?		
Il	fait	beau	It	is	fine
	va faire	chaud	The weather	is going to be	hot
Il	y a	du brouillard	There	is	some fog
	va y avoir	de la pluie		is going to be	some rain
Il	pleut		It	is raining	
	va pleuvoir			is going to rain	

EXCURSIONS AND TOURS

Listening 6:

(a) Look at the map below and listen to the weatherwoman giving the weather forecast in France for this morning; then, insert the appropriate symbols and complete the sentences below the map:

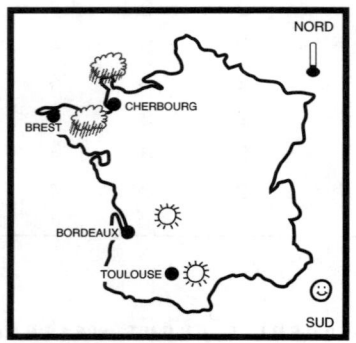

- BEAU
- FROID
- SOLEIL
- PLUIE

matin

Ce matin, il fait ☐ ....   Ce matin, il y a ☐ du ....

☐ ....   ☐ de la ....

(b) Look at the second map below and do the same thing with the weather forecast given for this evening:

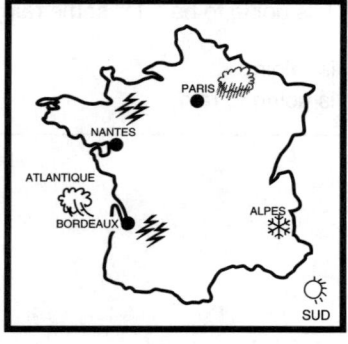

- FRAIS
- VENT(S)
- ORAGE(S)
- NEIGE

soir

Ce soir, il va faire ☐ ....   Ce soir, il va y avoir ☐ du ....

☐ de la ....

☐ de la ....

☐ des ....

124

EXCURSIONS AND TOURS

(c) Look at the third map below and do the same thing with the weather forecast for tomorrow:

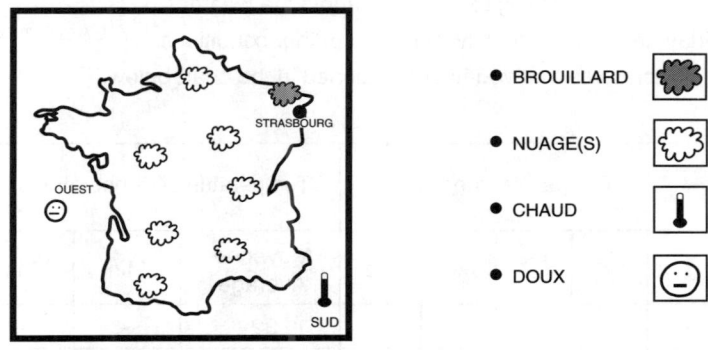

demain

Demain, il va faire ☐ ....   Demain, il va y avoir ☐ des ....
☐ ....   ☐ du ....

(d) Now, listen to the end of the weather forecast which covers the rest of Europe, and place the appropriate symbols in the spaces provided:

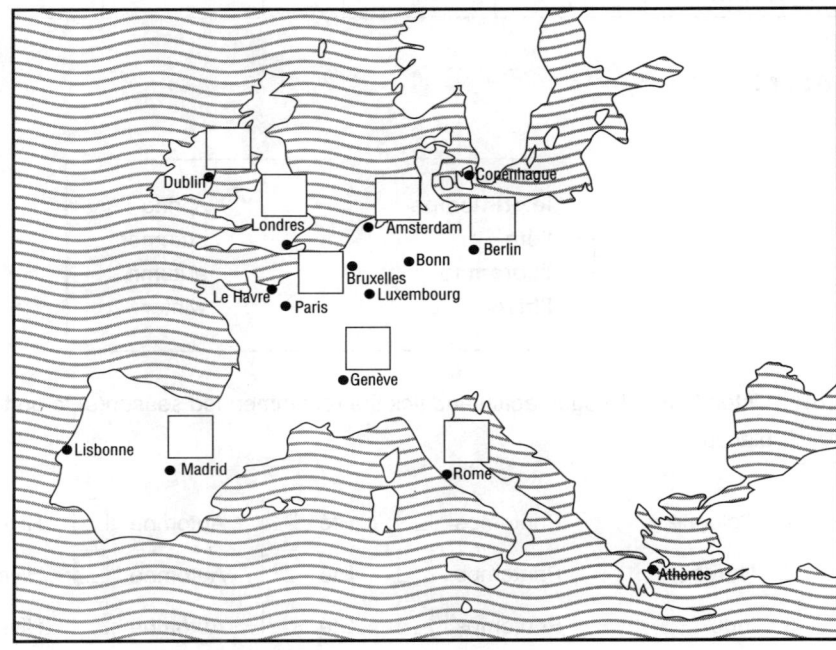

EXCURSIONS AND TOURS

AT THE TRAVEL AGENCY
À L'AGENCE DE VOYAGES

Listening 7:

(a) Listen to the travel agent replying to enquiries about the weather in various holiday destinations in July; tick the weather conditions and fill in the temperatures that you hear mentioned in the chart below.

Destination / Destination	Temps/Weather					Températures/Temperatures		
	🌡 (hot)	🌡 (cold)	☀	☁	⚡	Moyenne / Average	Min	Max
1. Pologne (e.g.)	✓				✓	32	–	–
2. Norvège							–	–
3. Inde							–	–
4. Cuba						–		
5. Mexique						–		
6. Australie							–	–
7. Tahiti							–	–
8. Turquie							–	–

HELP!

le printemps	spring
l'été	summer
l'automne	autumn
l'hiver	winter

(b) Listen to the dialogue again and tick the recommended season(s) to go to the following places:

1. Pologne   Printemps ☐ Été ☐ Automne ☐ Hiver ☐
2. Norvège   Printemps ☐ Été ☐ Automne ☐ Hiver ☐
3. Inde   Printemps ☐ Été ☐ Automne ☐ Hiver ☐
4. Mexique   Printemps ☐ Été ☐ Automne ☐ Hiver ☐

EXCURSIONS AND TOURS

LANGUAGE PRACTICE

Exercise 1:

Listen again to the itineraries around Cahors and Rocamadour in Listening 1 and 2, and match the attractions mentioned with the corresponding adjectives.

Attractions: les visites, un circuit, des villages, châteaux, villages, maisons, un panorama, des gorges, un circuit, châteaux, églises, un village, des spécialités.

Descriptions (adjectives):

1. .... très animé		2. .... médiéval	
3. .... intéressant**es**		4. .... typiques	
5. .... très varié		6. .... très agréable	
7. .... impressionnantes		8. .... intéressant**s**	
9. .... gastronomiques		10. grands	
11. .... pittoresques		12. petits	
13. .... magnifique		14. jolies	

Exercise 2:

(a) With the help of the key below, describe the following tour starting from St Germain-en-Laye (au départ de St Germain-en-Laye), west of Paris.

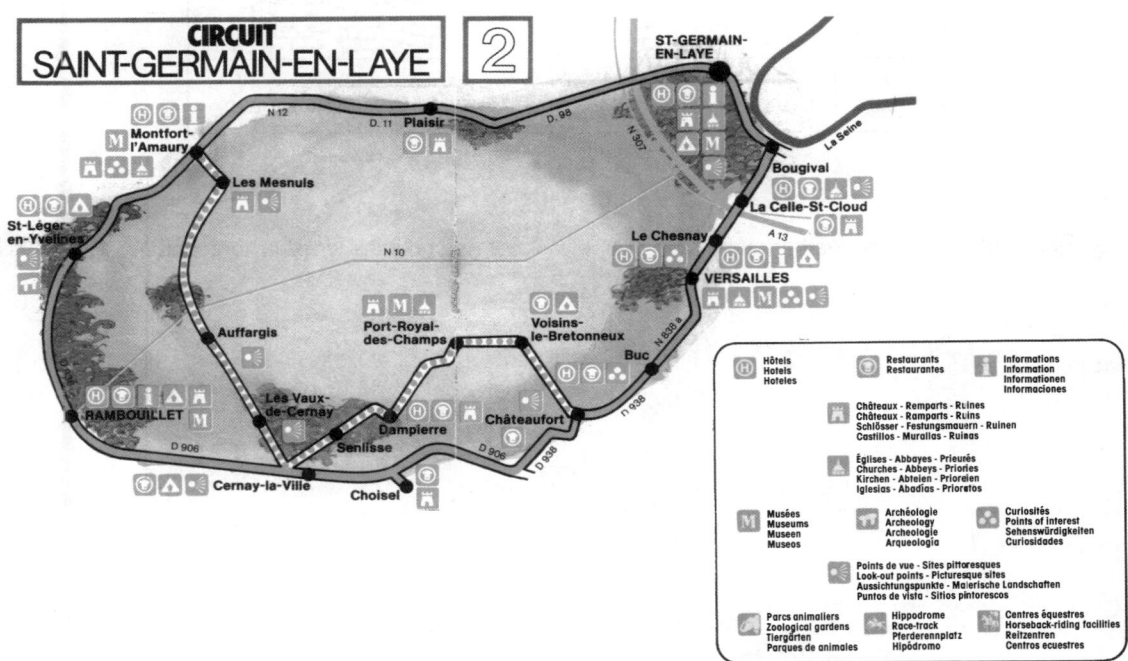

EXCURSIONS AND TOURS

 (b) Now, use a map of your local area and outline possible tours or visits

Exercise 3:

 (a) Describe the weather on the weather map below:
La météo en Europe.

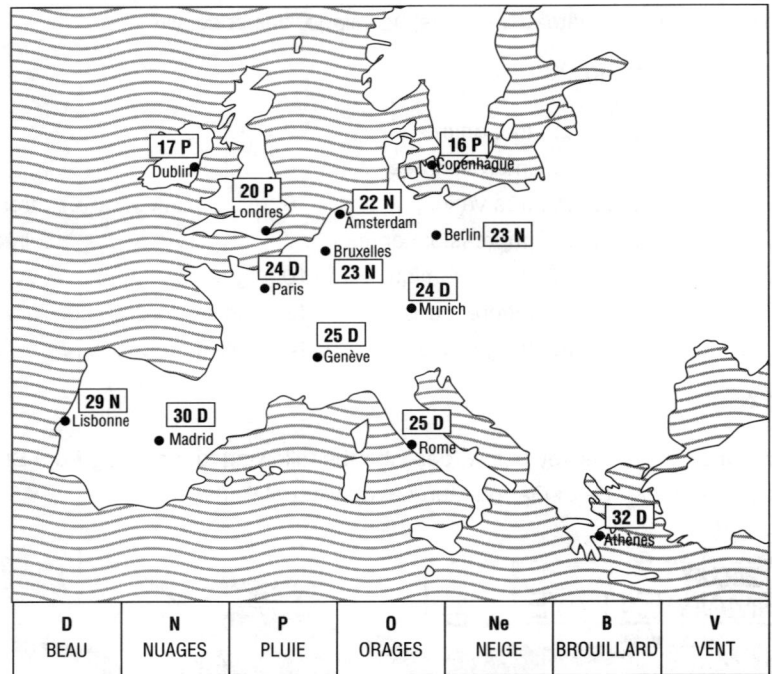

 (b) Use the weather map in today's newspaper and give the weather forecast.

EXCURSIONS AND TOURS

Exercise 4:

 The document below presents a package holiday in Ireland. Look at it and answer the questions below:

LA VIE DE CHATEAU

BATEAU + VOTRE VOITURE + CHATEAUX-HOTELS

Dromoland Castle

Pour ce circuit, nous avons choisi des châteaux-hôtels, réputés aussi bien pour leur site que pour leur charme et leur grand confort, tous classés en catégorie A ou A*.

Deux nuits sont prévues aux principales étapes afin de vous permettre de découvrir l'Irlande sans précipitation.

DEPART DE FRANCE DU
1er AVRIL AU 7 SEPTEMBRE

Jours pairs en avril/mai/août, jours impairs en juin/juillet/septembre (sauf jeudi du 25 juin au 27 août).

1er jour : Le Havre ou Cherbourg
Embarquement et départ pour l'Irlande à bord du Saint-Killian, en cabine de luxe.

2e jour : Rosslare - Killiney (Dublin) 155 km
Arrivée vers 14 h. Débarquement. Départ pour Dublin par Wexford et le Comté de Wicklow, jardin de l'Irlande. Installation au Fitzpatrick Castle à Killiney.

3e jour : Killiney
Notre suggestion : visite de Dublin (15 km), et excursion à Glendalough (ruines d'un centre monastique dans un cadre naturel magnifique). Nuit à Killiney.

4e jour : Killiney - Cong (280 km)
Par Athlone, sur le Lough Ree l'un des plus beaux lacs du Shannon, et par Galway capitale de l'Irlande de l'Ouest. Installation à l'Ashford Castle à Cong, au cœur du Connemara.

5e jour : Cong
Notre suggestion : découverte du Connemara et du Comté de Mayo, région sauvage par excellence. Nuit à Cong.

6e jour : Cong - Newmarket on Fergus (130 km)
Le long de la baie de Galway par Ballyvaughan, et en suivant la côte, par les falaises de Moher (à pic de 200 mètres). Installation à l'hôtel Dromoland Castle à Newmarket.

7e jour : Newmarket - Kenmare (170 km)
Par Limerick, le pittoresque village d'Adare, Killarney et ses lacs. Installation au Park Hôtel à Kenmare.

8e jour : Kenmare
Notre suggestion : excursion de l'anneau de Kerry ou des Péninsules de Dingle et Beara qui offrent de remarquables paysages de mer et de montagne. Nuit à Kenmare.

9e jour : Kenmare - Cashel (180 km)
Par Glengariff, le col de Keimaneigh et le parc forestier de Gougane Barra, Macroom, la vallée de la Lee, Mallow, Cahir et son château et Tipperary.

10e jour : Cashel - Rosslare (180 km)
Par Clonmel, la vallée de la Suir, Waterford et ses cristalleries et Wexford. Embarquement à Rosslare à 16 h. Départ à 17 h., en cabine luxe.

11e jour : Le Havre ou Cherbourg
Arrivée en France. Débarquement.

EXCURSIONS AND TOURS

1. What is the name of this tour? . . . .
2. What does the package include?
   . . . .
3. Can you take this holiday in October? . . . .
4. Do people spend each night in a different place?. . . . .
5. In the list below tick the attractions that are mentioned in the brochure?

   a. visit to a monastic site

   b. visit to a cathedral

   c. visit to a forest park

   d. visit to a crystal factory

Exercise 5:

You are working as a guide. Some visitors are enquiring about evening entertainment and shopping in Dublin.

Listen to the visitors and answer the questions as prompted below.
You play the part of the guide.

TOURIST INFORMATION

INFORMATIONS

Visitor 1	Qu'est-ce qu'on peut faire à Dublin le soir?
Guide	*Say there are many things to do. Ask the visitor what he is interested in.*
Visitor 1	J'aimerais trouver un petit restaurant pas cher et ensuite écouter de la musique irlandaise.
Guide	*Say that there are many good restaurants near Grafton Street and that there are many pubs with Irish music near the hotel.*
Visitor 1	Merci. Et à quelle heure ferment les pubs?
Guide	*Say that pubs close at 11.30 p.m.*
Visitor 1	D'accord. Merci.
Guide	*Tell the visitor he is welcome and wish him a pleasant evening.*
Visitor 2	Je voudrais faire des achats demain. Que me conseillez-vous?
Guide	*Tell the visitor that there are five shops near the hotel; that you recommend pottery, Aran jumpers (les pulls d'Aran) and Waterford crystal (le cristal de Waterford).*
Visitor 2	J'aimerais trouver quelque chose d'original et pas cher.
Guide	*Suggest he buy a tape of Irish music.*
Visitor 2	C'est une excellente idée. Merci.
Guide	*Tell the visitor he is welcome.*

EXCURSIONS AND TOURS

 ## A TRIP AROUND THE PARKS

For the tourist wishing to take a day tour or excursion there are lots of interesting and exciting things to see and do in the various parks around France.

Les Parcs Naturels et Régionaux

For the visitor who wishes to get to know the real France, its culture and traditions, its history and folklore, there is no better way than to explore some of the natural regional parks where you can see how the Marshes of Poitou were reclaimed and farmed, or how the Old Mill at Nieul (near La Rochelle) worked. These places of interest usually present an audio-visual show of the history of the region.

Lovers of wildlife will find many parks in which protected species of animals may be spotted. These parks are designed to preserve the natural beauty and special character of their region and because France is a country of variety you can be sure of an interesting visit each time. How about the *Parc des Volcans* (Volcano Park) in the Auvergne region, for an exciting view of France?

EXCURSIONS AND TOURS

Les Écomusées

A type of interpretive centre or folk museum, the *Écomusée*, allows visitors to witness the traditional way of life of a region. These are usually 'inhabited' by people who are carrying on the traditional work of the area — sugar-making with a windmill, distillation of kirsch or operation of a traditional farm. It can be a little like stepping into another world for a day.

Les Parcs d'Attractions

The best known French fun parks are *Asterix, Mirapolis, Big Bang, Schtroumpfs, Zygofolies* and *Futuroscope*. Much like the latest arrival in Paris, *Eurodisney*, these parks are based around a theme or comic strip characters. For an entry fee, visitors may avail of unlimited entertainment within the complex. Some of these parks have not been as successful with French people as with visiting tourists.

Mirapolis

EXCURSIONS AND TOURS

Les Parcs Nautiques
For an all-in price you can have unlimited fun on the water slides and rapids in *Aquacity* (near Toulon) or in any of the other water parks, (*Aqualand, Nautipark, Aquasplash,* etc.). Be sure to practise your crash-landing beforehand!
With all of these options for day trips throughout France, everybody should find something of interest.

CONFERENCES AND FAIRS   UNIT 9

Objectives

At the end of this unit you will be able to:

- Greet and welcome

- Register delegates

- Give information on programme of events and other services

- Direct delegates and visitors inside and outside the centre or fair

- Give information literature

- Give information on starting and finishing times of events

Place Charles-de-Gaulle, popularly called Place-de-l'Étoile

CONFERENCES AND FAIRS

DIRECTING DELEGATES OUTSIDE AND INSIDE THE CONFERENCE CENTRE
GIVING INFORMATION ON SERVICES

Listening 1:

Listen to one of the organisers at the reception desk of the conference answering queries from French delegates, either on the phone or directly at the desk.

Look at the map (page 137) for help and then tick the correct answer(s):

A. 1. To get from the airport to the university, one can take:

    a. a bus ☐
    b. a train ☐
    c. a taxi ☐

    2. Which bus can you take from the airport to the university?

    a. 40A ☐
    b. 41 ☐
    c. 41A ☐

B. 1. The taxi fare from the airport to the hotel is:

    a. £10 ☐
    b. £12 ☐
    c. £10–12 ☐

    2. How far is the last bus stop from the hotel?

    a. five minutes' walk ☐
    b. fifteen minutes' walk ☐
    c. twenty minutes' walk ☐

C. 1. Which of these buses can you **not** take from the university to the city centre?

    a. 11 ☐
    b. 11A ☐
    c. 13 ☐
    d. 13A ☐
    e. 19 ☐
    f. 19A ☐

135

CONFERENCES AND FAIRS

2. How much is the bus fare from the university to the city centre?
   a. 85 pence ☐
   b. 90 pence ☐
   c. 95 pence ☐
   d. £1.05 ☐

3. At what time is the last bus?
   a. 11.00 p.m. ☐
   b. 11.15 p.m. ☐
   c. 11.30 p.m. ☐
   d. 11.45 p.m. ☐

D. 1. What are the telephone numbers of VIP Radio Taxis?
   a. 468 3333 ☐
   b. 478 3333 ☐
   c. 488 3782 ☐
   d. 478 3782 ☐

E. 1. Where does the shuttle-bus to the airport leave from?
   a. Westmoreland Street ☐
   b. Busáras ☐
   c. North Wall Quay ☐

2. When does the shuttle-bus leave?
   a. On the hour ☐
   b. Every half hour ☐
   c. Every fifteen minutes ☐

F. 1. Telephoning from Ireland, what is the international access code?
   a. 16 ☐
   b. 00 ☐
   c. 19 ☐

CONFERENCES AND FAIRS

2. Telephoning to France, what is the international country code for France?

   a. 03 ☐
   b. 30 ☐
   c. 353 ☐
   d. 33 ☐

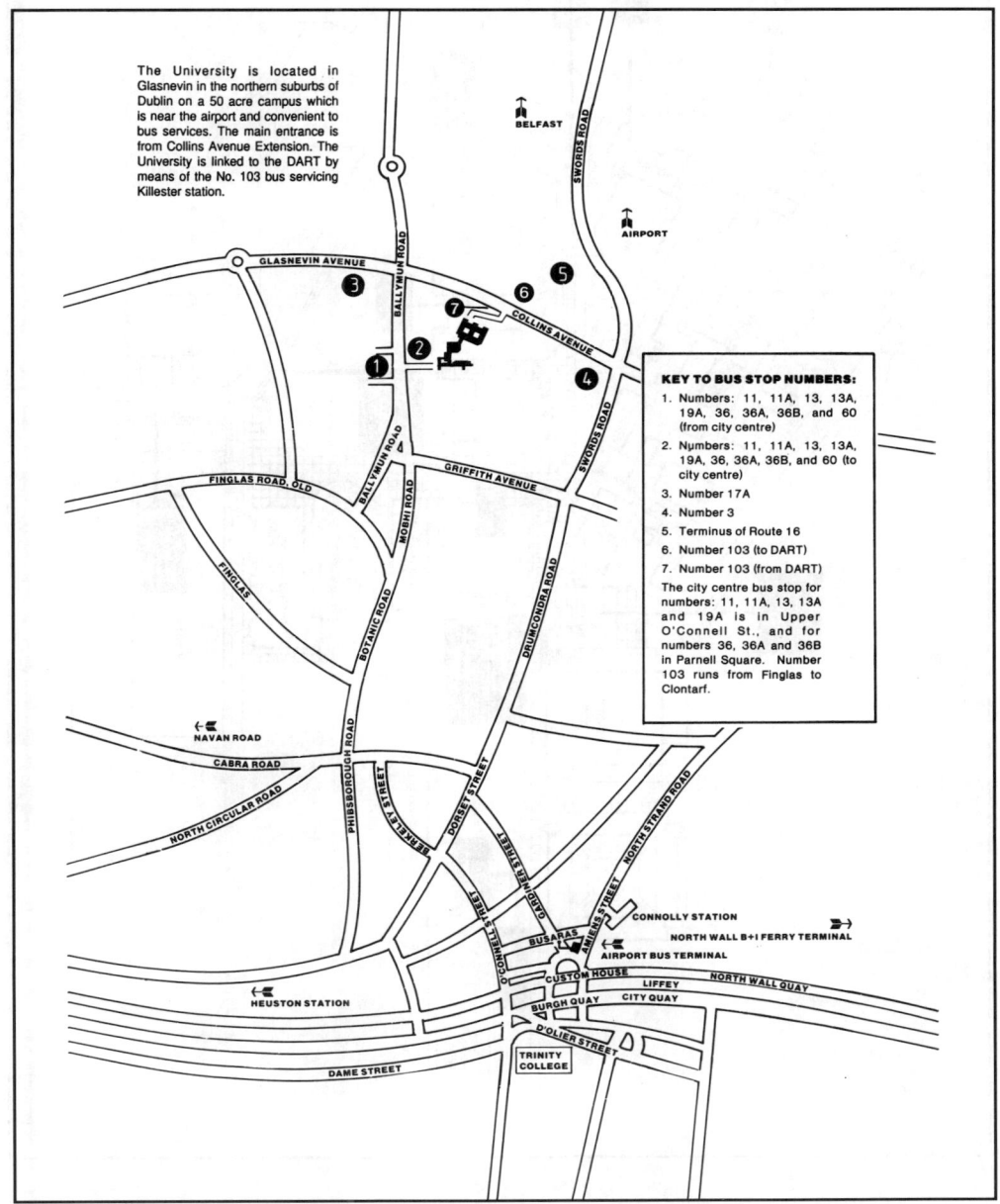

AT THE CONFERENCE CENTRE

AU CENTRE DE CONFÉRENCES

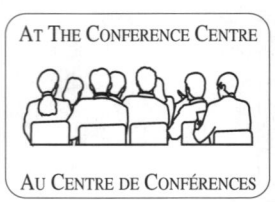

Listening 2:

(a) Listen to one of the organisers at the reception desk of the conference answering queries from French delegates. Then number on the map below the order in which the various places are mentioned.

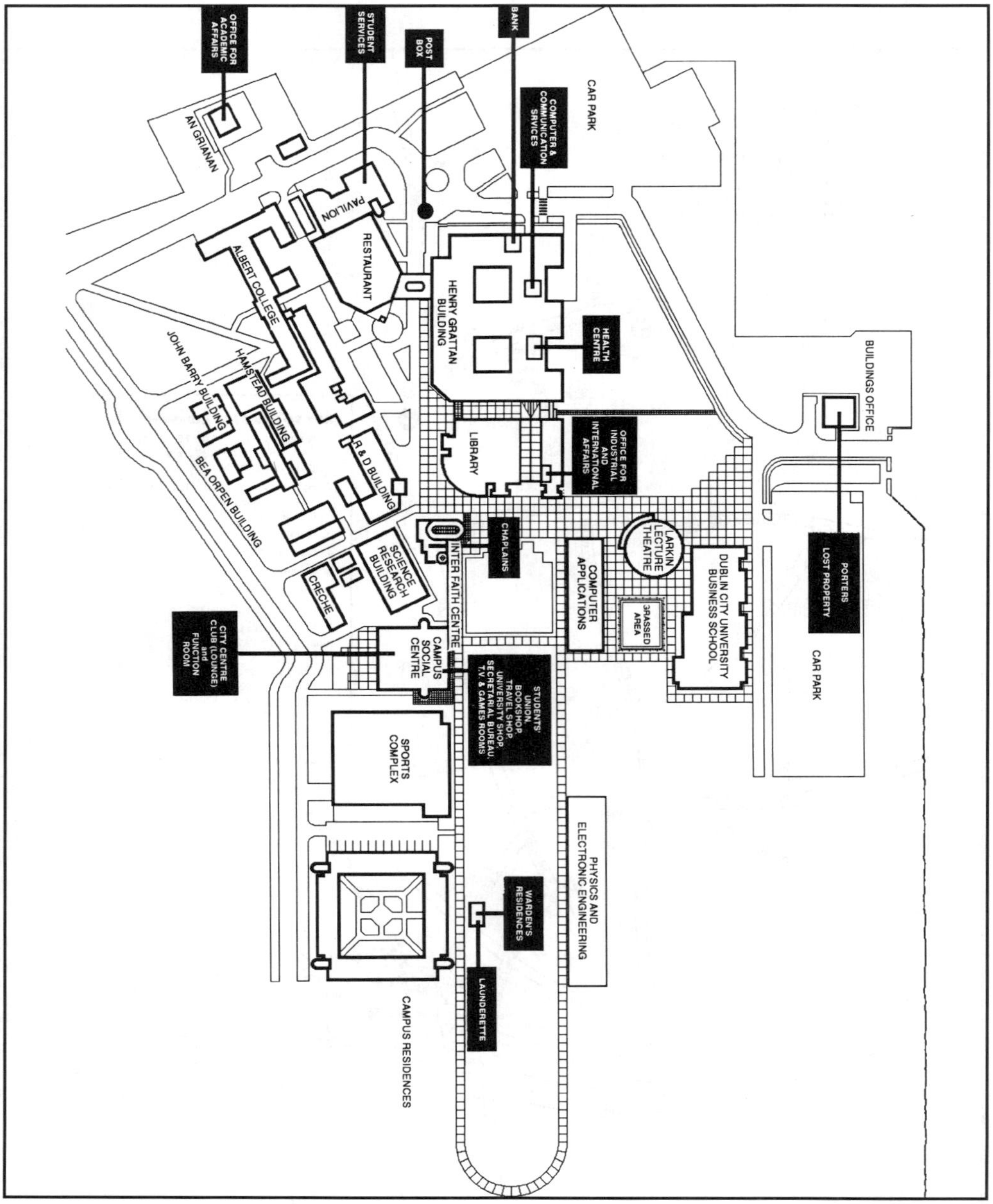

CONFERENCES AND FAIRS

(b) Listen again to the same dialogue. Then fill in the missing details below:

Sports Complex

Opening hours: ....

Fee for each visit: ....

Bar

Opening hours: ....

Closed: ....

Students' Shop

Opening hours: ....

Closed: ....
....

Bank

Opening hours: ....
....

Closed: ....
....

Location: ....
....
....

Library

Opening hours: ....
....
....
....

Closed: ....
....

Location: ....
....
....

Residence Office

Opening hours: ....

Telephone number: ....

Fax number: ....

Restaurant

Breakfast served from: ....

139

CONFERENCES AND FAIRS

REGISTERING DELEGATES AND GIVING INFORMATION
ON PROGRAMME OF EVENTS

AT THE CONFERENCE CENTRE

AU CENTRE DE CONFÉRENCES

Listening 3:

Listen to one of the organisers registering the French participants at the International Conference for Tourism Studies. Check whether the information in the grid below is correct or complete; if it is not, amend or complete the document accordingly. Then fill in the last column.

International Conference for Tourism Studies June 24–25–26, 1994						
Name	Temple Bar Hotel	Student Residences	Extra Nights	Accompanying Persons	Amount Paid £	Amount Due £
BRAULT Alice		✓	0	1	370	
.... Martine	✓		0	0	236	
.... André		✓	0	2	185	
.... Marcel	✓		0	0	185	
SEBILLE Christine	✓		2	0	308	
TISSOT Gabriel		✓	0	0	185	

Registration and Accommodation Fees	
Student Residences:	(3 nights: 24–25–26 June) £185
	Additional night £19.50 per night per person
Temple Bar Hotel:	(3 nights: 24–25–26 June) £236
	Additional night £36 per night per person

HOW TO SAY IT

Pour aller	du centre ville de l'aéroport	à	l'université l'hôtel	To go from	the city centre the airport	to	the university the hotel
J'aimerais savoir	combien coûte un billet comment on va au centre ville			I would like to know	how much a ticket costs how one gets to the city centre		
Vous avez	réservé une chambre double payé £185			You have	booked a double room paid £185		
Comment payez-vous? Vous payez comment?				How are you going to pay?			

140

CONFERENCES AND FAIRS

Listening 4:

Listen to one of the organisers announcing changes for the first day of the Conference and amend the programme of events below accordingly.

International Conference For Tourism Studies

June 24–25–26, 1994

Programme/Programme of Events

Date et heures Date and time	Activités/Activity	Emplacement/Location
Jeudi 24 juin **Thursday 24 June**		
09.00–09.30	Inscriptions/Registration	Réception/Reception
09.30–11.00	Séance plénière/Plenary session Accueil et ouverture/Welcome and opening	Amphithéâtre Larkin/ Larkin Lecture Theatre
11.00–11.30	Pause-café/Coffee	S255
11.30–13.00	Ateliers A à D/Workshops A to D	A: S217 B: S219 C: S220 D: S218
13.00–14.30	Déjeuner/Lunch	Restaurant
14.30–15.30	Ateliers E à H/Workshops E to H	E: S217 F: S219 G: S218 H: S220
15.30–16.00	Pause-café/Coffee	S255
16.00–17.30.	Ateliers I à L/Workshops I to L	I: S122 J: S122 K: S121 L: S123
18.00	Bus pour le centre ville/ Buses to city centre	Parking/ Car park
18.30	Réception organisée par le Maire Reception hosted by Lord Mayor	Mansion House

CONFERENCES AND FAIRS

G IVING INFORMATION ON TRADE FAIR
D IRECTING VISITORS INSIDE TRADE FAIR

Listening 5:

Listen to one of the organisers of the 20th World Tourism and Travel Fair giving information about the fair and fill in the fact sheet below:

20e Salon Mondial du Tourisme et des Voyages
20th World Tourism and Travel Fair

Lieu/Location:

Dates/Dates:

Journées réservées aux professionnels/Trade only days:

Heures d'ouverture/Opening hours:

Journées grand public/Open to the public:

Heures d'ouverture/Opening hours:

Exposants/Exhibitors:

Étrangers/Foreign:

Français/French:

Surfaces louées/Total floor area let: m²

Visiteurs attendus/Expected number of visitors:

Renseignements/Information:

Numéro de téléphone/Telephone number:

Numéro de Fax/Fax number:

CONFERENCES AND FAIRS

Listening 6:

Listen to the hostess at the reception desk of the 20th World Tourism and Travel Fair telling visitors where various stands and facilities are. Then fill in the missing information in the floor plans below:

20ᵉ SALON MONDIAL DU TOURISME ET DES VOYAGES

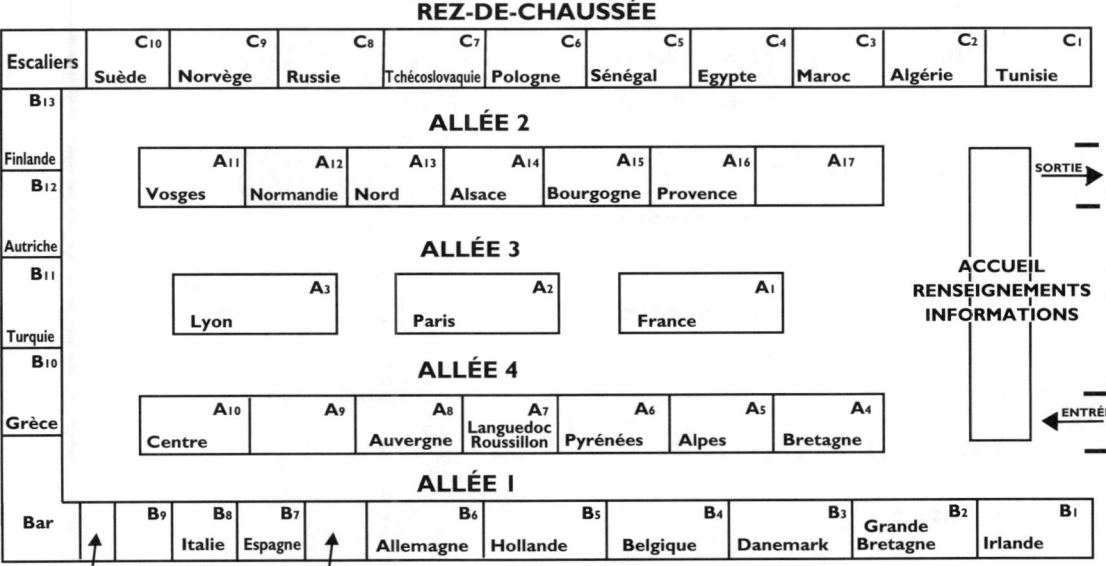

CONFERENCES AND FAIRS

Listening 7:

Listen to the same hostess giving the programme of presentations to be held in 'Salle de l'Europe' and complete the document below:

AT THE TRADE FAIR

AU SALON

Salle de l'Europe		
Thursday 16 June		
16.00:	Presentation on	....
............:	Presentation on	....
Friday 17 June		
............:	Presentation on	....
............:	Presentation on	....
............:	Presentation on	....
............:	Presentation on	....

LANGUAGE PRACTICE

Exercise 1:

Complete the following sentences:
Example:
        Le stand 12 est le stand **de la** Tunisie
        Le stand 14 est le stand **du** Portugal
        Le stand 17 est le stand **des** États-Unis
        Le stand 18 est le stand **de** l'Italie

1. Le stand 1 est le stand .... Belgique (la)
2. Le stand 2 est le stand .... Danemark (le)
3. Le stand 3 est le stand .... Espagne (l')
4. Le stand 4 est le stand .... Amérique du Sud (l')
5. Le stand 5 est le stand .... Népal (le)
6. Le stand 6 est le stand .... Maroc (le)
7. Le stand 7 est le stand .... Normandie (la)
8. Le stand 8 est le stand .... Nord (le)

CONFERENCES AND FAIRS

9. Le stand 9 est le stand .... Alpes (les)
10. Le stand 10 est le stand .... Pyrénées (les)
11. Le stand 11 est le stand .... Auvergne (l')
12. Le stand 12 est le stand .... Antilles (les)

Exercise 2:

You are working at the reception desk of the 20th World Tourism and Travel Fair. Listen to the tourists asking you where various stands and facilities are. Use the floor plan (page 143) to answer the queries.

AT THE TRADE FAIR

AU SALON

Check your answers in the answer keys section.

Exercise 3:

Listen to the information given on the tape and with the help of the document on page 141, complete the programme of events below *en anglais* (in English).

International Conference for Tourism Studies
June 24–25–26, 1994

Date: Vendredi 25 juin/Friday 25 June

Heures/Time	Activités/Activity	Emplacement/Location
09.30–11.00	Séance plénière/Plenary session	Amphithéâtre Larkin Larkin Lecture Theatre
11.00–11.30	....	....
11.30–13.00	....	N: ....
		O: ....
		P: ....
		Q: ....
13.00–14.30	....	....
14.30–16.00	....	R: ....
		S: ....
		T: ....
16.00–16.30	....	....
16.30–17.30	....	....
18.00	Bus pour la réception au château Buses to the Castle for reception	....

CONFERENCES AND FAIRS

Exercise 4:

You are working at the reception desk of a conference centre. A French participant arrives. Listen to the participant and answer the questions as prompted below.

You play the part of the assistant.

Participant	Bonjour.
Assistant	*Greet the participant and ask her if she is attending the Conference on Tourism.*
Participant	Oui, Monsieur.
Assistant	*Ask her name and the name of her company.*
Participant	Je m'appelle Valérie Petit et je travaille pour Eurovoyages. Quels sont les sujets des conférences, à quelle heure est-ce que cela commence et dans quelle salle?
Assistant	*Give her the following information:* *Monday (today) at 10.00 a.m. — lecture on travel agencies* *Tuesday at 9.30 a.m. — lecture on agri-tourism (le tourisme vert)* *Wednesday at 11.00 a.m. — lecture on business tourism (le tourisme des affaires)* *Thursday at 10.30 a.m. — lecture on leisure centres.* *All the lectures finish at 4.30 p.m and they are held in the Conference Room on the ground floor, at the end of the corridor on the left.*
Participant	Est-ce qu'il y a un restaurant sur place?
Assistant	*Tell her that there is no restaurant in the Conference Centre but that there is one fifty metres away opposite the railway station.*
Participant	Est-ce que vous pouvez me dire où se trouvent les toilettes et le vestiaire?
Assistant	*Tell her that the ladies' toilets are to the right next to the lift and that the cloakroom is next to the reception desk.*
Participant	Je vous remercie.
Assistant	*Wish her a good day.*

CONFERENCES AND FAIRS

FRANCE FOR BUSINESS

In the last ten years, France has become particularly well equipped for business tourism and today the business person travelling to and through France can benefit from a great range of services designed to ensure that as little precious time as possible is lost in travel.

Les Palais des Congrès

Many cities in France have purpose-built conference centres, *Palais des Congrès*; one of the largest of these is in Paris at the Porte Maillot, convenient to travellers from the airports. Most cities, too, have many excellent hotels for business people and good transport facilities.

Un Voyage d'Affaires (A Business Trip)

If you decided to attend the famous food fair in Lyon, to the south-east of Paris, you could start your journey with a business class seat on an Air France flight to Paris. This will allow you to use meeting room facilities at the airport on arrival if you need. Once in Paris you can take a TGV to Lyon and avail of the services of a business carriage on the train. This will be equipped with microphones, overhead projectors, video systems and sound proofing. There will even be enough room for group table meetings which can be carried on as normal with only the gentle rocking of the train (despite its high speed) to remind you that you are not in the office.

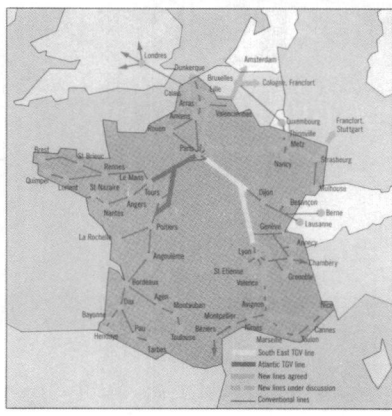

CONFERENCES AND FAIRS

Incentives: Stimulation — Challenges

Developments in business tourism within France include the *voyage de stimulation* (incentive business trip) and the in-company or inter-company survival test or challenge.

The *voyage de stimulation* is intended to encourage greater participation in conferences by organising them in totally new surroundings such as the Victoria Falls in Zimbabwe or the exotic French West Indies. With a new environment and the chance, for example, to go on safari or take in a morning's skiing, executives are more likely to attend and, in the more relaxed environment, communications and relations between staff, as well as the flow of new business ideas improves greatly.

Another exciting development in business tourism in France, *les Challenges*, is the best way for a company to test the endurance and drive of its staff. Thrown into the heart of somewhere like the Scottish Highlands with a map and a compass and 72 hours to reach a certain point, or dropped at the top of a mountain river armed with only a wet suit and told to reach the bottom on foot, the employee really gets a chance to see what he or she is made of!

Companies see this as a great way to forge links between staff members of various levels, many of whom would never normally address each other as anything other than *Monsieur* or *Madame*. For the organisers it represents a chance to invent more and more new ideas which can be tried out on unsuspecting victims!

It is good for tourism too: some challenges cost up to 150,000 francs per company and with up to 100 companies taking part at a time the rewards speak for themselves.

TEST YOUR COMPETENCE 2

Note:
Exercises 1 to 6 are for grammar revision. The remaining exercises are based on Units 5 to 9 and in each case the first is a written comprehension exercise and the second a production exercise.

Exercise 1:

Fill in the blanks in the second column as shown in the example (and see Grammar Summary 3):

(a) Example: **un** musée intéressant   **une** cathédrale intéressan**te**

1. un souvenir original   une visite ....
2. un château ancien   une maison ....
3. un village pittoresque   une rue ....
4. un panorama magnifique   une église ....
5. un passeport allemand   une voiture ....

(b) Example: **un** musée intéressant   **des** musée**s** intéressant**s**

1. une visite agréable   des visites ....
2. une grotte immense   des grottes ....
3. un bateau irlandais   des bateaux ....
4. une spécialité française   des spécialités ....
5. un circuit varié   des circuits ....

Exercise 2:

Rewrite the following sentences as shown in the examples (and see Grammar Summary 8):

(a) Examples: **Le** voyage dure deux heures/**il** dure deux heures
                La traversée dure cinq heures/**elle** dure cinq heures

1. Le musée est fermé le mardi.   ....
2. Monsieur Sanchez est espagnol.   ....
3. L'avion part à 18h15.   ....
4. La rivière est magnifique.   ....
5. L'église est à gauche.   ....
6. Madame Martin est belge.   ....

TEST YOUR COMPETENCE 2

(b) Examples: **Les musées** sont fermés le mardi/**Ils** sont fermés le mardi.
Les boutiques sont ouvertes le dimanche/**Elles** sont ouvertes le dimanche.

Note: You may check in the glossary if in doubt whether noun is masculine or feminine.

1. Les grottes sont impressionnantes. ....

2. Monsieur Leblanc et Monsieur Joubert sont à l'Hôtel Concorde.

   ....

3. Les hôtels ont une piscine. ....

4. Madame Seibert et Madame Calmy sont en réunion.

   ....

5. Les toilettes sont au fond du couloir.

   ....

6. Les ascenseurs sont à votre gauche.

   ....

Exercise 3:

Transform the following sentences as shown in the examples (and see Grammar Summary 8):

(a) Example: **Prenez** le bus No 41/Vous devez **prendre** le bus No 41.

1. Allez à la gare. ....
2. Tournez à gauche. ....
3. Prenez une douche. ....
4. Payez à la caisse. ....
5. Passez par Paris. ....
6. Faites attention. ....

TEST YOUR COMPETENCE 2

(b) Example: Vous devez **aller** tout droit/**Allez** tout droit.

1. Vous devez téléphoner à Madame Richet. ....
2. Vous devez acheter une carte postale. ....
3. Vous devez visiter la Tour Eiffel. ....
4. Vous devez choisir un restaurant. ....
5. Vous devez sortir par la porte B. ....
6. Vous devez partir le samedi. ....

Exercise 4:

Transform the following sentences as shown in the example (and see Grammar Summary 8 [e]):

Example: Le bateau **part** à 8h15/Le bateau **va partir** à 8h15.

1. Ce matin, Marc fait du tennis.

   ....

2. L'avion arrive dans vingt minutes.

   ....

3. Elle visite les Antilles. ....
4. Il pleut. ....
5. Il fait beau. ....
6. Il y a du vent. ....

Exercise 5:

Change the following sentences as shown in the examples (and see Grammar Summary 10):

(a) Example: La famille visite le Québec/La famille **ne** visite **pas** le Québec.

1. Le musée est ouvert le lundi.
   ....

2. Le restaurant est fermé en décembre.
   ....

3. Le gîte est situé à St Jean.
   ....

4. La visite est gratuite.
   ....

5. L'avion arrive à 18 heures.
   ....

6. Paul fait de la plongée sous-marine.
   ....

(b) Example: Il y a **une** piscine dans l'hôtel/Il **n'**y a **pas de** piscine dans l'hôtel.
   Il y a **des** rivières dans la région/Il **n'**y a **pas de** rivières dans la région.

1. Il y a une poste sur la place.
   ....

2. Il y a un bus pour Avignon.
   ....

3. Il y a des chambres libres.
   ....

4. Il y a des cinémas en ville.
   ....

5. Il y a un concert ce soir.
   ....

6. Il y a une boutique de souvenirs.
   ....

TEST YOUR COMPETENCE 2

Exercise 6:

Transform the following sentences as shown in the examples (and see Grammar Summary 9):

Examples: **Vous avez** l'heure?   **Avez-vous** l'heure?
                                                                       Est-ce que vous avez l'heure?

1. Vous voulez un dépliant?

   ....
   ....

2. Vous allez en Irlande en bateau?

   ....
   ....

3. Vous désirez le menu?

   ....
   ....

4. Vous prenez le train ou l'avion?

   ....
   ....

5. Vous acceptez les cartes de crédit?

   ....
   ....

6. Vous passez par la Suisse ou par l'Italie?

   ....
   ....

Exercise 7:

Read the document on Loubressac (on page 155) and tick the correct answer:
1. This document is:

    a. an advertisement for a flower shop   ☐

    b. a holiday brochure   ☐

    c. a local tourist information fact sheet   ☐

TEST YOUR COMPETENCE 2

2. Among the attractions listed below, which ones do **not** appear in the list below the photograph?

   a. fortified village ☐
   b. good restaurants ☐
   c. riverside walks ☐
   d. beautiful view ☐
   e. old church ☐

3. Is there a good hotel in the village?

   Yes ☐   No ☐

4. The local celebrations take place in:

   a. June ☐
   b. July ☐
   c. August ☐
   d. September ☐

5. Which of the following sports are mentioned in the document?

   a. golf ☐
   b. swimming ☐
   c. hill-walking ☐
   d. tennis ☐

6. Is there a campsite in the village?

   Yes ☐   No ☐

TEST YOUR COMPETENCE 2

DÉCOUVREZ...

LES PLUS BEAUX VILLAGES DE FRANCE

Loubressac

— Son vieux village fortifié du XVe siècle dans un site remarquable.
— Son panorama magnifique.
— Ses grands espaces, ses randonnées.
— Ses maisons fleuries.
— Ses restaurants réputés.

UN VILLAGE VIVANT EST HEUREUX DE VOUS ACCUEILLIR

HEBERGEMENT
— Gîte d'étape. Tél. 65.38.25.52.
— Gîtes ruraux.
— Locations en meublés.
— Salle municipale à votre disposition pour réunions familiales, clubs, congrès, repas, banquets, méchouis...
— Camping " La Garrigue " Tél. 65.38.34.88

ANIMATION
— Tennis.
— Randonnées pédestres accompagnées.
— Fête locale annuelle le deuxième dimanche de Juillet.
— Concours Photos Amateurs en Juillet-Août.
— Concours Poésie.

RESTAURANTS
— LOU CANTOU .... Tél. 65.38.20.58
— CHEZ ALICE .... Tél. 65.38.19.15
— LA CREPERIE, à Py .... Tél. 65.38.52.09
— CHEZ SUZIE, au Trouillé .... Tél. 65.38.49.42

EXPOSITIONS
— A côté du Panorama Est : GALERIE DU CLOS
  Suzanne MEROT-MAURY, Artiste Peintre.
— A côté du Panorama Ouest :
  Jeremy ANNETT, Artiste Peintre.
— Sur la place : L'ARTISANE.

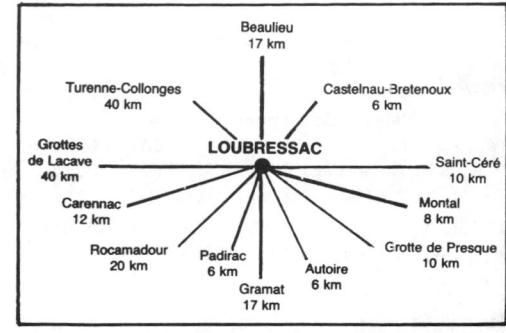

S.I. Mairie de LOUBRESSAC —— 46130 BRETENOUX
Tél. 65.38.18.30

Imp. Y. MARMOL - St-Céré

TEST YOUR COMPETENCE 2

Exercise 8:

You are working as a tourist information officer in Dublin. French-speaking tourists come in looking for information on James Joyce's tower and George Bernard Shaw's house. Based on the documents below, you give them as much information as possible on these two sites (access, opening hours, admission rates, facilities).

JAMES JOYCE TOWER
SANDYCOVE

Tel. (01) 2809265/2808571 Fax (01) 2802641
(8 miles from Dublin – Bus No. 8 & Dart Rail Service)

1993
OPENING HOURS
April and October
Monday - Friday   10.00 - 17.00 hours
May to September inclusive
Monday - Saturday   10.00 - 17.00 hours
Sundays & Public Holidays   14.00 - 18.00 hours
Closed for lunch 13.00 - 14.00 weekdays

ADMISSION	INDIVIDUAL	GROUPS
Adults (18 yrs. & over)	£1.75	£1.25
Senior Citizens & Students (12 - 17 yrs.)	£1.40	£1.10
Children (3 - 11 yrs.)	£0.90p	£0.70p

Family Ticket: £5.00 (2 Adults & 3/4 children)

Facilities: Bookshop

Combined Dublin Writers Museum/James Joyce Tower or George Bernard Shaw House tickets available

James Joyce

GEORGE BERNARD SHAW HOUSE
33 Synge Street, Dublin 2.
Telephone:(01) 722077 Fax:(01) 722231

1993
OPENING HOURS:
May - September Inclusive:
Monday - Saturday   10.00 - 17.00 hours
Sundays & Public Holidays   14.00 - 18.00 hours

ADMISSION	INDIVIDUAL	GROUPS
Adults (18 yrs. & over)	£1.75	£1.25
Senior Citizens & Students (12 - 17 yrs.)	£1.40	£1.10
Children (3 - 11 yrs.)	£0.90p	£0.70p

Family Ticket: £5.00p (2 Adults & 3/4 children)

Facilities: Bookshop

Combined Dublin Writers Museum/James Joyce Tower or George Bernard Shaw House tickets available

TOURS AVAILABLE IN FOREIGN LANGUAGES.

Designed & Printed
by C.R.C. Workshops

TEST YOUR COMPETENCE 2

Exercise 9:

Read the document on 'L'Irlande en autocar' and answer the following questions:

1. How will you be travelling in Ireland?
   a) by train ☐
   b) by car ☐
   c) by coach ☐

2. Which of the following regions will you be visiting?
   a) Dublin ☐
   b) Kerry ☐
   c) Donegal ☐
   d) Connemara ☐
   e) Belfast ☐

3. Where will you spend your first night?
   a) in a hotel ☐
   b) on a coach ☐
   c) on a ferry-boat ☐
   d) on a train ☐

4. Which of the following attractions are mentioned in the document?
   a) a museum ☐
   b) a cathedral ☐
   c) cliffs ☐
   d) an interpretive centre ☐
   e) an abbey ☐
   f) a distillery ☐

5. Will you be staying in . . . . ?
   a) two-star hotels ☐
   b) three-star hotels ☐
   c) four-star hotels ☐

6. Are lunches included in the price?
   Yes ☐   No ☐

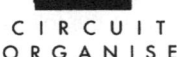

CIRCUIT ORGANISE

L'IRLANDE EN AUTOCAR
IRL CO 05

10 JOURS

Circuit en autocar à partir de Paris. L'Irlande traditionnelle : le Connemara, l'Anneau de Kerry, Killarney, Dublin. Le folklore unique d'un pays si proche et si éloigné pourtant de nos traditions.
Hébergement en hôtels

ITINERAIRE :
1er JOUR : départ de Paris vers midi pour Cherbourg ou Le Havre. Embarquement. Nuit à bord en couchettes.
2e JOUR : arrivée en début d'après-midi à Rosslare, transfert à Cork et nuit.
3e JOUR : départ de Cork vers Killarney par la belle route traversant Lee-Valley et Macroom (petite ville charmante) Tour d'orientation et visite de Muckross House (demeure du 19e siècle, parc et musée). Nuit à Killarney.
4e JOUR : Killarney (en passant par Adare, très joli village)-Limerick, par les falaises de Moher-Galway. Visite libre de la ville. Nuit à Galway.
5e JOUR : Galway. Journée libre. Soirée pubs. Nuit à Galway. (Possibilité d'excursion aux îles d'Aran).
6e JOUR : excursion de la journée dans le Connemara avec visite de l'abbaye de Kylemore. Nuit à Galway.
7e JOUR : Galway-Athlone, visite du site historique Clonmacnoise. Nuit à Dublin.
8e JOUR : demi-journée visite avec St-Patrick's cathédrale et Trinity College. Après-midi libre. Nuit à Dublin.
9e JOUR : Dublin-Glendalough-Rosslare. Embarquement et nuit à bord.
10e JOUR : arrivée au Havre ou à Cherbourg. Retour sur Paris.
(20 à 40 personnes).

▼

LE PRIX COMPREND :
- le transport en autocar
- la traversée France-Irlande en bateau (couchettes de 4 personnes), lignes Irish Ferries
- l'hébergement en Irlande en hôtels*** (chambres doubles)
- les petits déjeuners irlandais et les dîners
- l'assurance
- un accompagnateur Nouvelles Frontières de Paris à Paris

NE COMPREND PAS :
- les déjeuners (prévoir 100 F par jour)
- les repas sur le bateau
- les visites et entrées non prévues au programme

TEST YOUR COMPETENCE 2

Exercise 10:

You are working as a tourist information officer in Galway. French-speaking tourists come in looking for information on the Aran Islands. Based on the information below, you give them as much information as possible on how to get to the Aran Islands.

TOURIST INFORMATION

INFORMATIONS

Aran Islands, County Galway

The three Aran Islands — Inishmore, Inishmaan and Inishere — lie about 48 km from Galway across the mouth of the Bay, 16 km from Connemara and 10 km from Doolin in County Clare.

Inishmore
Location: The most northerly and largest island is located 48 km from Galway and 16 km from Ros a'Mhil (Rossaveal) in Connemara.
Access: By Ferry: From Galway 3 sailings daily returning 5.00 p.m. Aran Ferries. Tel: (091) 68903 office hours; (091) 92447 after hours.
From Ros a'Mhil (Rossaveal) 38 km west of Galway. There are 3 or 4 sailings daily. Aran Ferries.
By Air: From Galway Airport (8 km east of Galway at Carnmore). Several flights daily. Contact Aer Arann. Tel: (091) 55437.

Inishmaan
Location: Inishmaan — the middle island — lies to the south-east of Inishmore across Gregory's Sound.
Access: By Ferry: From Spiddal — 18 km west of Galway — which operates 3 crossings daily from June to 9 September.
Connecting bus operates from Galway station. For further details: Tel: (091) 62131.
By air: From Galway Airport and from Inishmore and Inishere. Several flights daily. Contact Aer Arann.

Inishere
Location: The smallest of the Aran Islands lies 8 km north-west of Doolin in County Clare.
Access: By Ferry: From Doolin — 12 or more return sailings daily — leaving Doolin on the hour and returning from Inishere on the half hours. Crossing takes 25/30 minutes.
Contact: Doolin Ferries. Tel: (065) 74189.
From Spiddal — 18 km west of Galway. Three crossings daily from June to 9 September. Connecting bus operates from Galway station.
For further details. Tel: (091) 62131.
By Air: From Galway Airport and from Inishmore and Inishmaan. There are several flights daily. Contact Aer Arann.

TEST YOUR COMPETENCE 2

Exercise 11:

Read the document on the town of Antibes and where appropriate tick the correct answers:

1. Where is Antibes?
    ....

2. If you choose this holiday, you will be staying in:

    a) a campsite ☐
    b) an hotel ☐
    c) a private villa ☐
    d) an apartment house ☐

3. Which of the following facilities is situated on the spot:

    a) a beach ☐
    b) a golf course ☐
    c) a swimming pool ☐
    d) a tennis court ☐

4. Which sports are offered in the vicinity of the Résidence:

    a) skiing ☐
    b) horseriding ☐
    c) snorkelling ☐
    d) sailing ☐
    e) cycling ☐
    f) golf ☐
    g) waterskiing ☐
    h) tennis ☐
    i) fishing ☐
    j) archery ☐
    k) weightlifting ☐
    l) windsurfing ☐

5. Which sports are specially available for children?
    ....

6. Can you guess one of the animals you can watch in the 'Marineland Show'?
....

ANTIBES

COTE D'AZUR

Antibes, sa vieille ville,
ses célèbres rues,
ses musées, son port,
ses remparts,
ses fleurs...
Et les bistrots,
les boutiques,
la vie nocturne,
le célèbre festival de
jazz de Juan-Les-Pins !

La Résidence

Votre Résidence est située à l'orée du Cap d'Antibes, à mi-chemin de l'animation d'Antibes et des plages de Juan-les-Pins, dans le complexe résidentiel du Tanit.

LES LOISIRS DE VOTRE RESIDENCE

Vous vous dorez au soleil autour de la piscine (possibilité de location de matériel de plage). Le décor est somptueux.

LES LOISIRS ALENTOUR

Ecole de voile du port d'Antibes (500 m) avec location de matériel et stages de planche à voile, dériveur, catamaran. Ski nautique (2 km). Plongée sous-marine à Juan-les-Pins. Tennis-clubs (1 à 2 km), cours collectifs et stages. 3 golfs 18 trous à Biot (8 km), à Cannes-Mougins (10 km) et à Valbonne (12 km). Centre hippique de Vaugrenier (8 km). ULM, tir à l'arc, mini-golf, location de vélos...

Spécial forme
Le centre "Thalazur" à Antibes (8 km) et deux grands centres de thalassothérapie à Marina-Baie des Anges (8 km), qui utilisent les techniques les plus modernes de soins, remise en forme et revitalisation.

Pour vous, les enfants !
Des stages d'optimist à l'école de voile du port d'Antibes, pour vous les 7-12 ans. Et si vous avez moins de 16 ans, des stages de tennis au club de la Roseraie. Surtout, ne manquez pas le grand show d'orques, de dauphins et d'otaries du Marineland (7 km).

Vos escapades
La vieille ville, le château Grimaldi qui abrite le musée Picasso. Le musée naval et napoléonien, le musée d'archéologie, le musée d'histoire locale et le musée Peynet, le marché sur le cours Masséna. Le Cap d'Antibes. Et toute cette belle région aimée des peintres et des artistes : Vallauris, Biot, Vence, Saint-Paul-de-Vence, Grasse, Nice. Et fêtes, spectacles, concerts, expositions, night-clubs et casinos.

BIEN-ÊTRE ET CONFORT

Votre appartement (p. 9)
Studio-cabine 4/5 pers.,
2 pièces 4/5 pers. et
2 pièces-cabine 6/7 pers.

Les services et commerces
Réception, ascenseurs. Laverie. Local planches à voile et vélos. Parking couvert payant. A proximité immédiate, supérette (indépendante des services Pierre & Vacances), et à 500 m, tous les services et commerces.

Tarifs en fin de catalogue.

TEST YOUR COMPETENCE 2

Exercise 12:

Read the brochure below and on the next page, on the Adventure Centre and Hostel at Eilí Bay, Belmullet, County Mayo and give as much information as possible to a French-speaking tourist who would like to spend a weekend break in the Centre. Advise him or her on its location, cost and available activities.

Canoeing
Our instructors can introduce novices to this skillful sport, while experienced paddlers can sample the spectacular surf of the nearby Atlantic.

Nature Studies
The vast tracts of blanket bog, rich in plant and animal life and the towering cliffs and uninhabited islands which act as a refuge to many species of birds, make the area alive with Birdlife, Flora and Fauna.

Windsurfing
Elly Bay is a mecca for windsurfers of all abilities. Sample Ireland's fastest growing and thrilling sport with a beginner course at 10° West.

Cycling.
Our location offers the visitor a multitude of scenic cycling routes. So why not take a bike from 10° west and explore secluded coves, towering cliffs or majestic mountains. The abundance of local folklore and heritage sites allow plenty of opportunities for a refreshing stop with an interesting story.

Sailing
Discover the wonderful sport of dinghy sailing in the sheltered waters of Elly Bay. For the beginner there's no better introduction to this exciting sport than a course at 10°West.

Swimming
One couldn't pick a more ideal location to learn to swim than the crystal clear water of the blue flag beach at Elly Bay. Swimming tuition by experienced I.A.S.A. instructors is uniquely offered at 10° West.

Hillwalking
The combination of the spectacular cliff walks of Erris with the renowned Bangor trail through the Nephin Beg Mountains make our location a hillwalkers paradise.

Golf
The addition of probably the most challenging 18 hole championship links golf course in Ireland compliments the variety of activities available in Erris.

10° West

Our adventure centre is located in the remote barony of Erris, Co. Mayo. This area is characterised by its spectacular scenery and unspoiled natural amenities.

Erris is unequalled for its scenic variety. Colourful moors and bogs, mystical mountains, appealing lakes and streams, sand dunes and golden beaches are all part of the Erris experience. It is a district of natural beauty with mystic islands bordering its coast.

Our ideal location, excellent facilities and qualified instructors make 10° West perfect for an adventure holiday.

TEST YOUR COMPETENCE 2

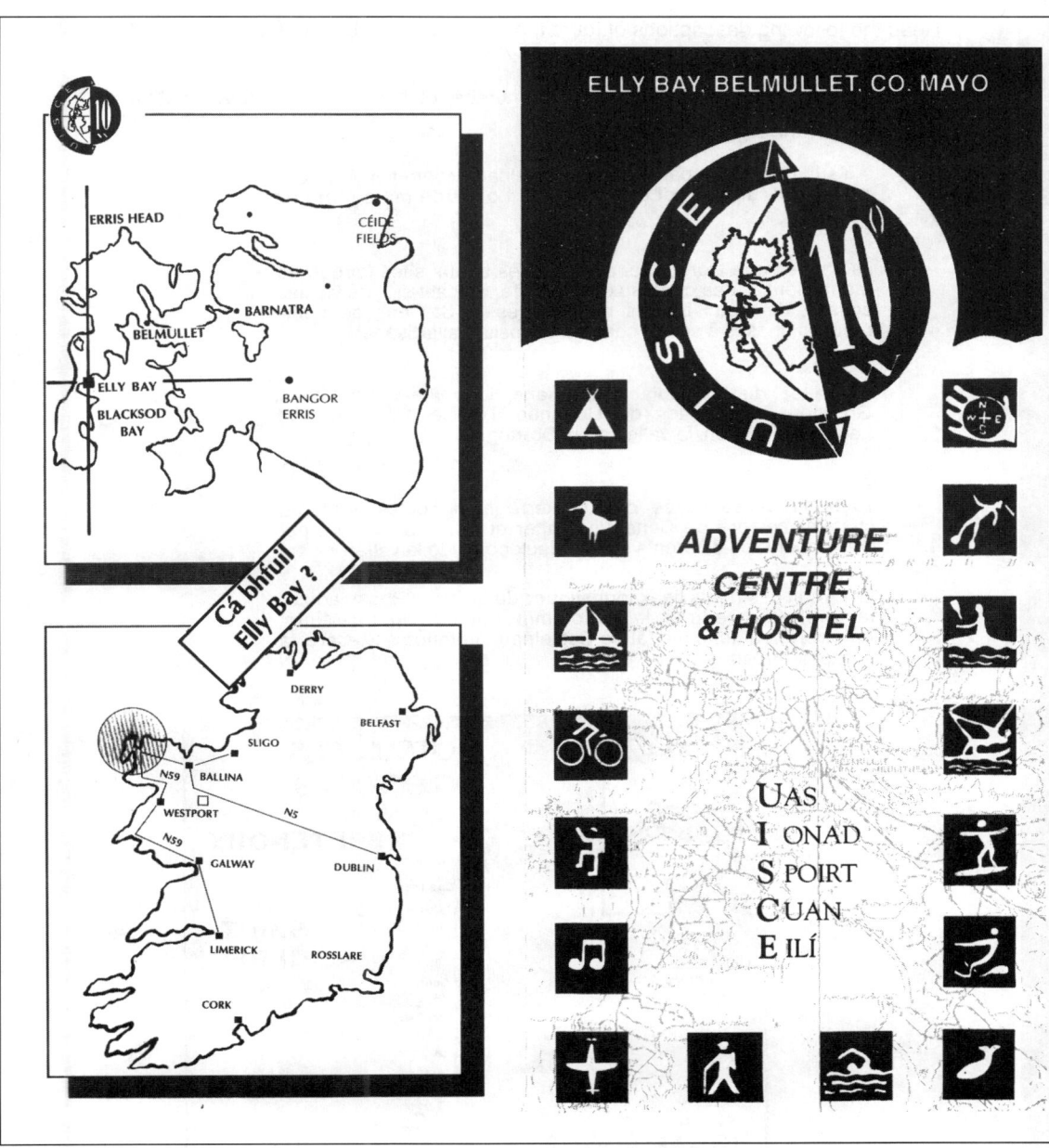

TEST YOUR COMPETENCE 2

Exercise 13:

Read the following descriptions of tours that are offered in the Quercy region (South-West of France):

Give each map on the following pages the number of its corresponding description.

Then number the signposts on page 167.

1. Au sud de Cahors par Cieurac, Castelnau-Montratier, Montcuq et Sauzet, un aspect attachant du Lot, rude mais plein de chaleur.

2. La vallée de la Dordogne, avec de très beaux sites (cirque de Montvalent...), des châteaux (La Treyne, Belcastel...), de vieilles églises, de vieux bourgs pittoresques. A St-Céré, de nombreuses choses à voir (y compris expositions, artisanat...).

3. La vallée du Lot, puis la Bouriane, le château de Linars, Gourdon, les Grottes de Cougnac, l'église XIIe siècle de Lamothe-Fénelon, la vallée de la Dordogne.

4. Toute la basse vallée du Lot, terre à vignobles, jusqu'au château célèbre de Bonaguil. L'aller et le retour se font par deux itinéraires différents sur les deux côtés de la vallée.

5. Le circuit des hauts lieux touristiques du Quercy: Rocamadour, le gouffre de Padirac, la station minérale d'Alvignac-Miers, Autoire, le château féodal de Castelnau-Bretenoux, St-Céré, la grotte de Presque.

(a)

[Map: circuit des merveilles, 75 KILOMETRES — showing Bretenoux, Castelnau, Loubressac, Saint Céré, Autoire, Grottes de Presque, La Cave, Miers, Gouffre de Padirac, Le Boutel, Alvignac, Thégra, Calès, Lavergne, Rocamadour, Gramat]

(b)

(c)

(d)

(e)

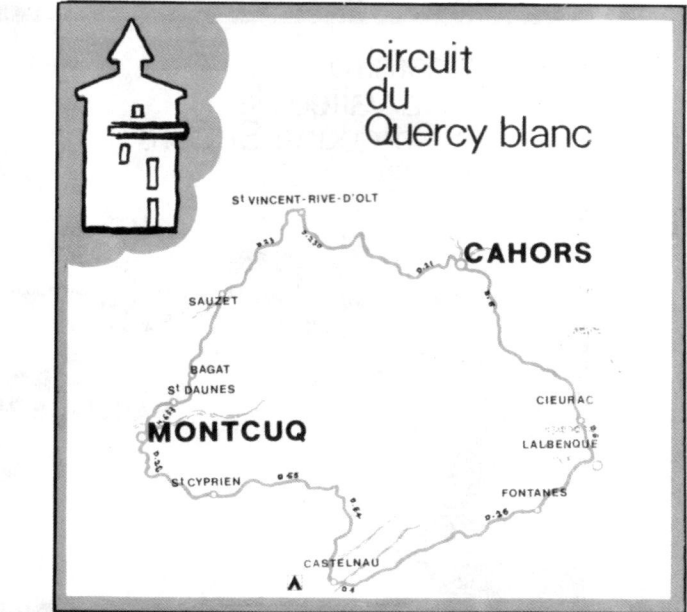

TEST YOUR COMPETENCE 2

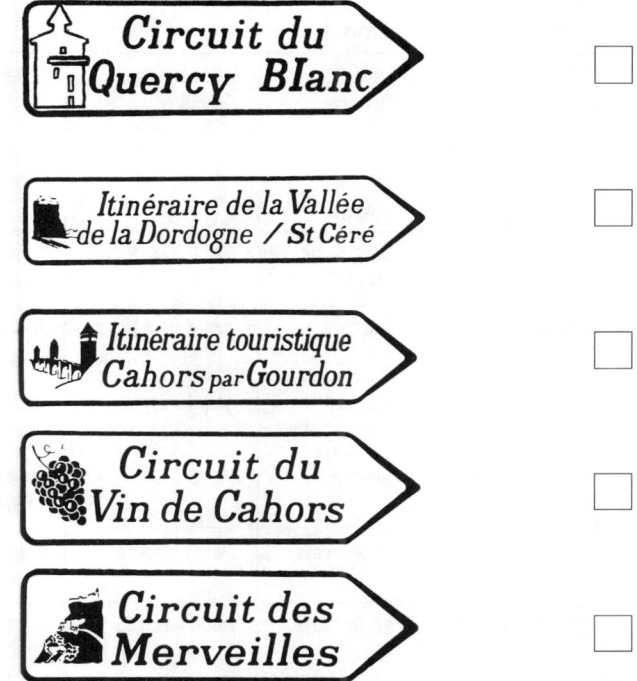

Exercise 14:

You are working at the information desk of Bus Éireann. French-speaking tourists come looking for information on day-tours from Dublin.

Based on the document below, give them as much information as possible on day-tours available on Sundays and then on Fridays.

TEST YOUR COMPETENCE 2

Day Tour Programme

	Tour	Depart	Return	Days of Operation	Dates of Operation	Fares
CD1	Dublin City Sightseeing	11.15	15.00	Mon-Sat excl. public holidays	May 4-Sept 26	Adult £9 Child £4.50
CD2	Glendalough and Wicklow Panorama	10.30	17.45	Daily except Friday	March 30-Sept 26	Adult £12 Child £6
CD3	Avondale, Glendalough and Wicklow Hills	09.30	16.30	Fridays	June 5-Sept 18	Adult £12 Child £6
CD5	Boyne Valley (including visit to Newgrange)	10.00	17.45	Sun, Tues, Thurs	May 12-Sept 27	Adult £12 Child £6
CD6	Powerscourt Gardens and Pine Forest	14.15	18.00	Sundays	May 3-Sept 13	Adult £10 Child £5
CD7	Kilkenny (including visit to Kilkenny Castle)	09.30	18.30	Wednesdays	May 20-Sept 16	Adult £13 Child £6.50
CD9	Russborough House and Blessington Lakes	13.30	18.00	Wednesdays	June 24-Aug 26	Adult £10 Child £5
CD11	Waterford, New Ross (including lunch and cruise)	09.00	21.00	Mondays and Thursdays	July 13-Aug 24 May 21-Sept 24	Adult £23 Child £12
CD14	Glen of Aherlow	09.00	21.00	Saturdays	July 11, 25 Aug 8, 22 Sept 5	Adult £16 Child £8
CD15	Coach tour and Shannon cruise (including visit to Lockes Distillery)	09.30	19.00	Tuesdays	June 16-Sept 15	Adult £16 Child £8
CD16	Lough Erne scenic Drive (including visit to Marble Arch Caves)	09.00	21.00	Saturdays	July 4, 18 Aug 1, 15, 29	Adult £17 Child £8.50

Exercise 15:

Read the two documents on the 'Parc International d'Expositions Paris-Nord' (pages 170-171) and answer the following questions:

1. What is the 'Parc International d'Expositions de Paris-Nord'?

    a) a public park ☐   b) an amusement park ☐   c) a trade exhibition centre ☐

2. Name four modes of transport one can take to get to it:

    ....; ....; ....; ....

TEST YOUR COMPETENCE 2

3. Where is the taxi rank situated?

   ....

4. Are **all** the car parks always open?   Yes ☐   No ☐

5. Are the car parks free?   Yes ☐   No ☐

6. Is there a specific mode of transport
   to get from the car parks to the esplanade?   Yes ☐   No ☐

7. Explain what RER stands for.

   ....

8. How often are there métros to and from Paris?

   a) every hour ☐   b) every half-hour ☐   c) every fifteen minutes ☐

9. Match the following signs with the appropriate sentence:

   (a) [sign]   (b) [sign]   (c) [sign]   (d) [sign]   (e) [sign]   (f) [sign]

   (g) [sign]   (h) [sign]   (i) [sign]   (j) [sign]   (k) [sign]   (l) [sign]

   1. On peut acheter des fleurs.   ....
   2. On peut retirer de l'argent à un distributeur.   ....
   3. On peut rencontrer des amis.   ....
   4. On peut changer des dollars.   ....
   5. On peut poster une lettre.   ....
   6. On peut acheter un journal.   ....
   7. On peut boire une bière ou un café.   ....
   8. On peut déjeuner à la carte.   ....
   9. On peut voir un docteur.   ....
   10. On peut réserver un billet d'avion.   ....
   11. On peut obtenir des renseignements.   ....
   12. On peut donner des photos à développer.   ....

L'arrivée des visiteurs

Si le visiteur arrive en voiture

Un accès spécial lui est réservé à partir de la bretelle de l'autoroute A 104 signalé : « PARC DES EXPOSITIONS - VISITEURS ».

Selon l'importance des manifestations un ou plusieurs parkings sont ouverts (P1 - P2 - P3 - P4 - P6) avec tarif horaire ou journalier.

Depuis son parking le visiteur emprunte, soit un chemin piétonnier, soit l'une des cabines sur rail du nouveau SK qui roule sans fin sur le mail central jusqu'à l'esplanade.

Si le visiteur arrive en taxi ou en car

Il est déposé ou repris en charge au TERMINAL TAXIS situé sous l'esplanade centrale, ou au TERMINAL AUTOCARS à proximité de la gare du RER en bordure de l'esplanade.

Si le visiteur arrive en train

Le RER, Métro Express Régional, s'arrête à la station « PARC DES EXPOSITIONS », tous les quarts d'heure dans les deux sens.

De la gare, le visiteur emprunte un passage couvert de 150 m qui le mène directement à l'esplanade centrale.

Prenez la cabine en marche

La Société SOULE a mis au point un système de transport sur courtes distances totalement automatique, le SK.
14 petites cabines sur rail, tractées par un câble sans fin, circulent sur une voie double à une vitesse de 20 km/h, soit 5 fois plus vite qu'un trottoir roulant. Elles ralentissent pour la montée et la descente.
Sa mise en service sur le Parc a constitué une première mondiale pour ce type de transport.

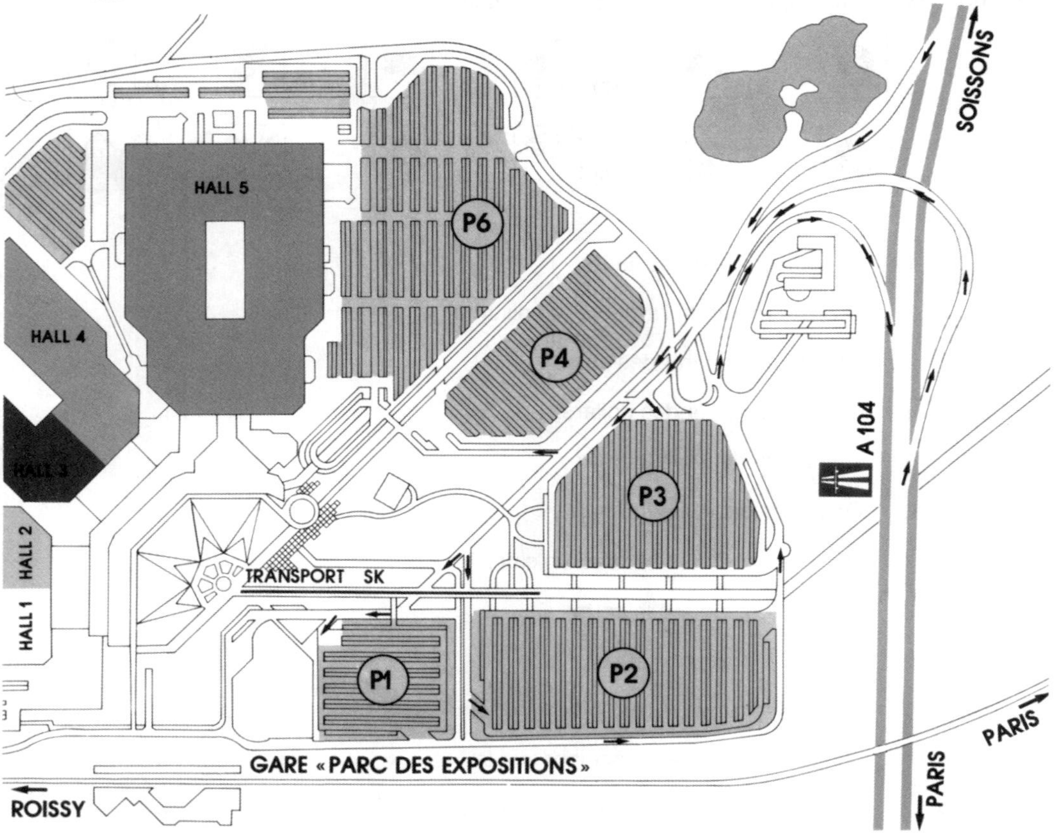

TEST YOUR COMPETENCE 2

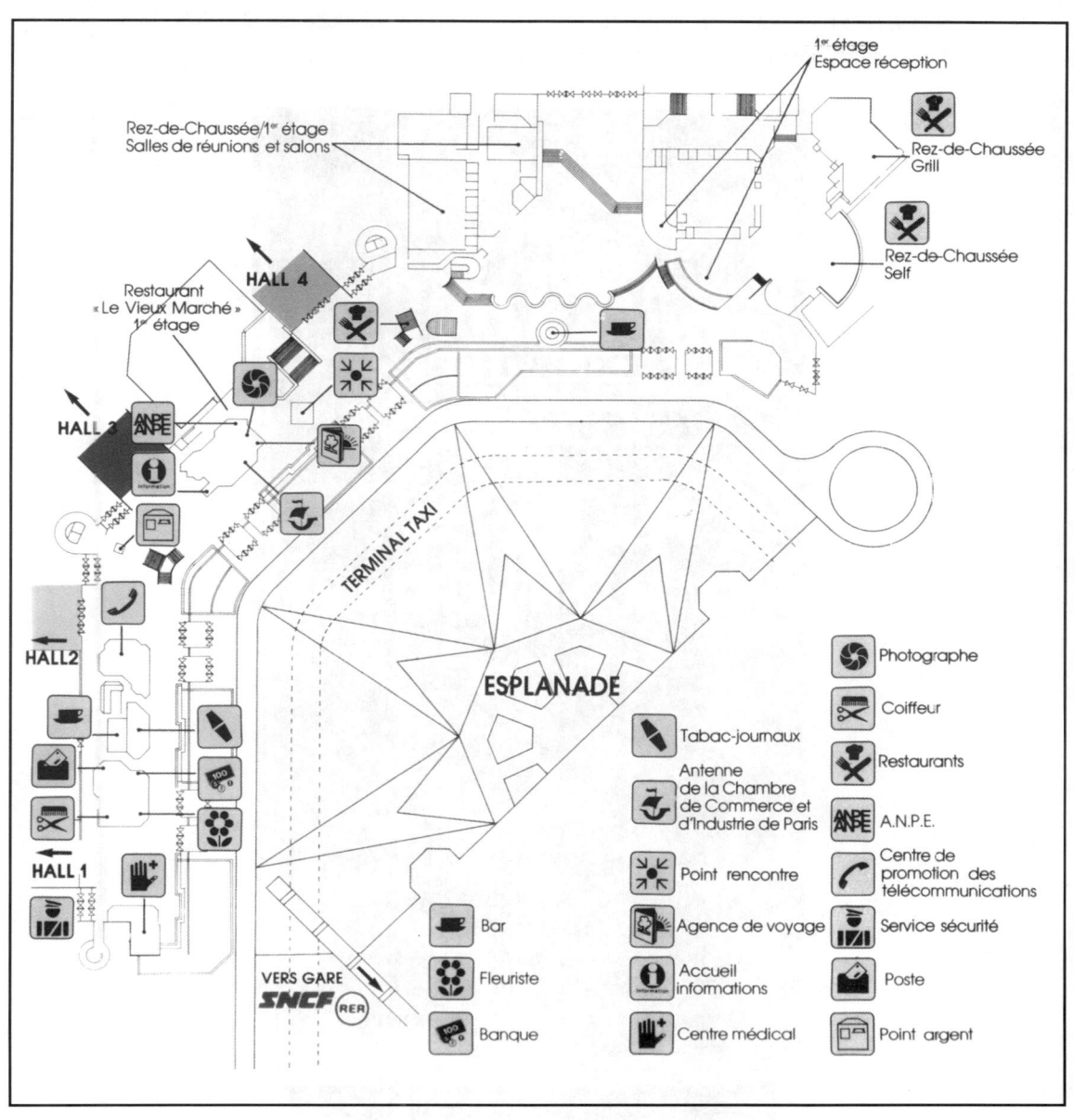

TEST YOUR COMPETENCE 2

Exercise 16:

You are working for the organising committee of the National Catering Exhibition. French-speaking exhibitors ring up looking for information on this trade fair. Based on the document below, give them as much information as possible on the fair (location of R.D.S., how to get there, dates, opening hours, admittance, etc).

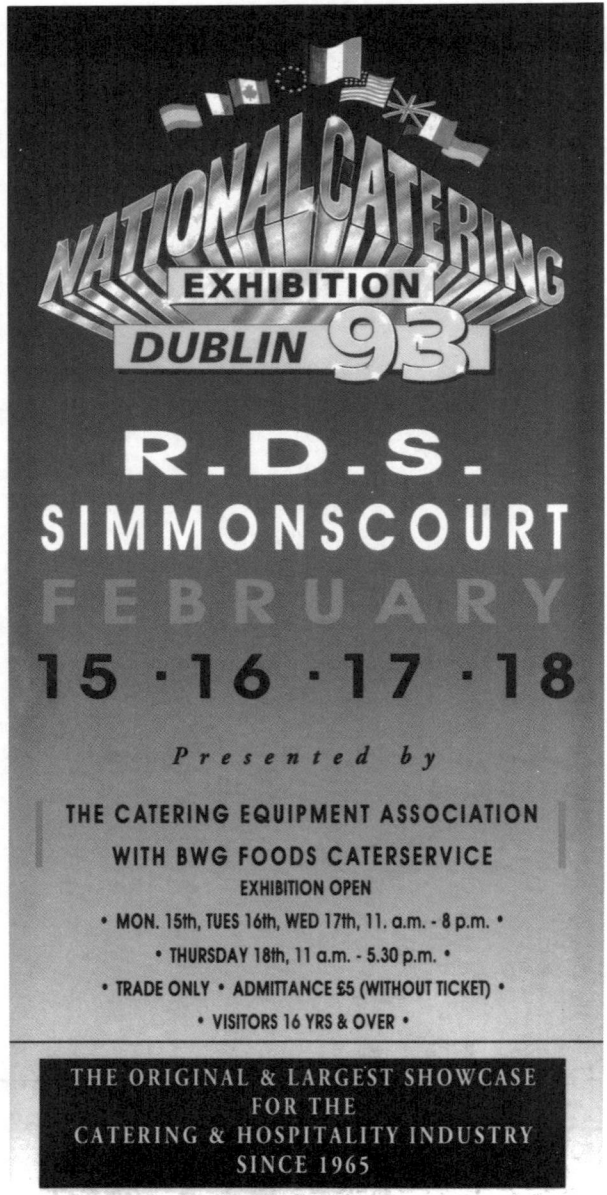

GRAMMAR SUMMARY

French grammar has been kept to a minimum in the nine units, but for those who would like to know a bit more about how the French language functions, this chapter provides a summary of the main points.

Grammatical terms are essential tools in understanding the way any language works; these are the basic terms used in this section:

- **Nouns:**
  A noun is a word used for naming — people, places, objects, animals or concepts,
  e.g. **Ann; France; car; horse; tourism.**

- **Articles:**
  An article is a word meaning **the** or **a**. It is used before a noun or its accompanying adjective.
  The is called the *definite* article.
  A and **an** are called *indefinite* articles.

- **Adjectives:**
  An adjective is a word which describes a noun and gives more information about it,
  e.g. an **old** castle, a **good** idea.

- **Demonstrative adjectives:**
  In English, demonstrative adjectives include, **this, that, these** and **those** and they are used to point out which person or object you are talking about.

- **Possessive adjectives:**
  In English, possessive adjectives include **my, your, his, her,** and so on. They refer to the possessor and their form never varies, so, for example, *singular* and *plural* are the same.

- **Adverbs:**
  An adverb is a word used to give extra information about, or modify, verbs, adjectives or other adverbs, e.g. he speaks **quickly**, this is **very** interesting, they eat **too quickly**.

- **Comparatives:**
  This term refers to the way an adjective or adverb changes when two or more things are being compared, e.g. big changing to big**ger** or fast changing to fast**er**.

- **Verbs:**
  A verb is a word which expresses an action or a fact, e.g. **to turn, to be, to want.**
  a) A *regular* verb will follow the same pattern or rule as a number of other verbs in its tenses.
  There are, of course, exceptions to the rules. These are called *irregular* verbs.

GRAMMAR SUMMARY

b) **Present tense:** the present tense is used to describe:
   1. An action occurring in the present: e.g. I **make** a phone call.
   2. A fact in the present: e.g. the line **is** engaged.
   3. What normally happens: e.g. the train **arrives** at 8 o'clock.

   There are two forms of the present tense in English but only one in French.
   I play tennis; I am playing tennis.

c) **Imperative:**
   The imperative is used to make a request, give advice, a direction or an order,
   e.g. **go** to the station, **visit** the old town, **wait** a minute.

d) **Infinitive:**
   The infinitive is a form of the verb which does not change for *tenses* or *persons*
   (**I, you, she,** etc.); it usually consists of **to** followed by the verb.
   It is the part of the verb you find in the dictionary, e.g. **to turn, to be.**

e) **Immediate future:**
   In English, this is the form **I am going** to . . . or **it is going** to . . .

f) **Conditional forms:**
   This is usually translated by *would* in English and is so called because there is often
   a condition involved: I **would** do something, **if** I could.
   It is also used for other purposes, e.g. being polite: I **would** like . . .

Note:

It is helpful to know that three basic principles apply to French grammar: **gender, number** and **agreement.**

   Gender: French *nouns* are either *masculine* or *feminine*.
   Number: The number of a *noun* refers to whether it is *singular* or *plural*.
   Agreement: In French, the agreement system is far more widespread than in English.
   So for example:

   (a) *articles* agree with *nouns:*
       la banque, **les** banques

   (b) *adjectives* agree with *nouns* in *gender* and *number:*
       le grand hôtel, **la** grand**e** poste
       les grand**s** hôtels, **les** grand**es** postes

   (c) *verbs* agree with *subjects:*
       vous arriv**ez** à quelle heure?
       elle arrive à neuf heures?

(d) *pronouns* agree with the *noun* they represent: e.g.
Je vous **le** passe (le = **le** poste)
Je vous **la** passe (la = **la** chambre)

1. Nouns

In French all nouns are either *masculine* or *feminine*. The *gender* is indicated by the *article:*
masculine: **le** (the) or **un** (a/an)
feminine: **la** (the) or **une** (a/an)
e.g. **la** France; **une** voiture; **un** cheval; **le** tourisme.

So remember to learn the *article* every time you learn a new noun.

If the noun ends with an **e** in the *masculine* form it remains the same in the *feminine* form,
e.g. **le** secrétaire/**la** secrétaire.
If the noun does not end in **e** the *feminine* form is obtained by adding an **e** to the *masculine* form:
un client/**une** client**e**
un Irlandais/**une** Irlandais**e**

In the *plural* form, as a general rule, *feminine* and *masculine* nouns take an **s** which is not pronounced:
un train/des train**s**
une voiture/des voiture**s**

There are however exceptions to the rule:

- nouns ending in **s** or **x** do not change:
 un congrès/des congrès
 un prix/des prix
- some nouns add an **x** instead of an **s**:
 un château/des château**x**
- others change their endings:
 un cheval/des chev**aux**

2. Articles

In French, unlike English, all *nouns* are preceded by an article and the articles must agree in *number* and *gender* with the *noun* they go with.

GRAMMAR SUMMARY

(a) **Definite** article

	masculine	feminine
singular	le	la
plural	les	

- **le** and **la**, followed by a word beginning with a vowel or a non-pronounced 'h', change to **l'**:
  une université/**l'**université
  un hôtel/**l'**hôtel
- **le** and **les** preceded by **à** or **de** combine with them to give:
  à + le = **au**
      les = **aux**

  de + le = **du**
      les = **des**

  aller **au** centre ville (to go into town)
  aller **aux** États-Unis (to go to the United States)
  la durée **du** voyage (the duration of the journey)
  la durée **des** circuits (the duration of the tours)

  However, **la** and **l'** do *not* combine with **à** and **de**:
  à côté **de la** boulangerie
  près **de l'**aéroport

- in some cases, French uses a definite article where English does not:
  For example with names of countries, regions:
  L'Irlande est un beau pays (Ireland is a lovely country)
  Vous aimez **la** Bretagne? (Do you like Brittany?)

- There are other cases where the French and English uses of articles differ, for example:
  fermé **le** mardi (closed on Tuesdays)

(b) **Indefinite** article

	masculine	feminine
singular	un	une
plural	des	

- After a negative, **un, une** and **des** become **de** or **d'**:

  il y a **un** château   à visiter   /   il n'y a pas   **de**   château   à visiter
        une cathédrale   **de**   cathédrale
        des musées   **de**   musées

  il y a **un** hôtel de luxe à Cherbourg/il n'y a pas **d'**hôtel de luxe à Cherbourg.

- The indefinite article is *not* used in French for giving someone's profession:
  elle est hôtesse d'accueil (she is a conference assistant)
  il est animateur (he is a leisure assistant)

3. Adjectives

In French all adjectives agree in *gender* and *number* with the *noun* they describe.

(a) In general with *feminine* nouns the adjective adds **e**:
un dépliant gratuit   **une** brochure gratuit**e**

unless it ends in **e** already:
un endroit agréable   une visite agréable

(b) Some adjectives double the final consonant in the *feminine* as well as adding **e**:
bon   bon**ne**

(c) Some adjectives change in other ways in the *feminine*:
beau   be**lle**
premier   prem**ière**

(d) In general in the *plural* **s** is added to both *masculine* and *feminine*:
des dépliants gratuit**s**   des brochures gratuite**s**

unless the adjective ends in **s** already:
un restaurant français   des restaurants français

The exceptions are similar to those for *nouns*:
un beau château   trois beau**x** château**x**

(d) Adjectives are usually placed after the *noun*:
une visite intéressante

A small number of common adjectives go before the *noun:*
un grand hôtel	un petit déjeuner
la deuxième rue à droite	bonne journée!
un bon restaurant

4. Demonstrative adjectives

Demonstrative adjectives come before the *noun* and, as *adjectives*, agree with it:

	masculine	feminine
singular	ce/cet*	cette
plural	ces	

* used with *nouns* beginning with a vowel or a non-pronounced 'h'.

ce train	**cette** conférence
cet aéroport	**ces** musées
cet hôtel

5. Possessive adjectives

In French, possessive adjectives are determined by the *number* and *gender* of the thing or things possessed.
They come before the *noun* and, as adjectives, agree with it.
mon numéro de téléphone (**my** telephone number)
ma voiture (**my** car)
mes chaussures (**my** shoes)

	masculine singular	*feminine singular*	*m and f plural*
my your (informal) his/her/its	mon ton son	ma* ta* sa*	mes tes ses
our your (formal) their	notre votre leur		nos vos leurs

* use **mon, ton, son** if the noun starts with a vowel or a non-pronounced 'h',
e.g. une adresse   **mon** adresse

The forms **ton, ta, tes** refer to a single possessor and are used when addressing someone you know well. **Votre, vos** are the polite forms; they can all be translated as *your;* when *your* refers to two or more people, you must use **votre, vos**.

6. Adverbs

These are the most common ones:

toujours (always)   bien (well)
souvent (often)   mal (badly)
quelquefois (sometimes)   beaucoup (very much)
jamais (never)   trop (too)
assez (enough)   peu (very little)

7. Comparatives

Plus in front of an adjective is equivalent to the English **more** as in **more** interesting, **bigger**, **more** expensive, etc:
c'est **plus** cher (it is more expensive or it is dearer)
c'est **plus** intéressant (it is more interesting)

Moins is equivalent to the English **less**, or **not as** . . . :
il fait **moins** chaud aujourd'hui (it is less hot today)
Dublin est **moins** grand que Paris (Dublin is not as big as Paris)

8. Verbs

A verb is usually referred to in its *infinitive* form and you have to change its ending depending on the *tense* it is in or the *person* it is used with.

> infinitive: visit**er** (to visit)
> present tense (second person): vous visit**ez** (you visit)

The subject of a verb can be a *noun* or *pronoun*.

Personal pronouns:

je (j')   I
tu   you (informal)
il/elle   he/she/it
nous   we
vous   you (formal) and/or you (plural)
ils/elles   they

Note: It and **they** can be *masculine* or *feminine* in French depending on the *gender* of the *noun* referred to:

GRAMMAR SUMMARY

la visite est intéressante — **elle** est intéressante (**it** is interesting)
le château est magnifique — **il** est magnifique (**it** is superb)
les visites sont intéressantes — **elles** sont intéressantes (**they** are interesting)
les châteaux sont magnifiques — **ils** sont magnifiques (**they** are superb)

(a) **Regular** and **irregular** verbs

Regular verbs are divided into three categories according to their endings in the *infinitive* form:

- infinitives ending in **-er**: visit**er** (to visit)
- infinitives ending in **-ir**: chois**ir** (to choose)
- infinitives ending in **-re**: attend**re** (to wait)

Irregular verbs are in a minority, but many of them are used very frequently. For example: être (to be), avoir (to have), aller (to go), faire (to do), vouloir (to want), devoir (to have to), pouvoir (to be able to).

(b) **Present tense**

In English, there are two forms of the present tense; he **speaks**, she **is speaking**. In French, there is only one present tense, which is used for both meanings.

The present tense of the three main categories of verbs is:

	Visit**er** (to visit)	Chois**ir** (to choose)	Attend**re** (to wait for)
je/j'	visit**e**	chois**is**	attend**s**
tu	visit**es**	chois**is**	attend**s**
il/elle	visit**e**	chois**it**	attend
nous	visit**ons**	chois**issons**	attend**ons**
vous	visit**ez**	chois**issez**	attend**ez**
ils/elles	visit**ent**	chois**issent**	attend**ent**

Note: The most common verbal form found in this book is the **ez** ending, that is to say the **vous** form — which is the polite or formal **you** — as opposed to **tu** — the familiar **you** — which does not appear in this book as it does not occur in professional interactions.

GRAMMAR SUMMARY

Present tense of some irregular verbs:

	Être (to be)	**Avoir** (to have)	**Aller** (to go)	**Pouvoir** (to be able to)
je/j'	suis	ai	vais	peux
tu	es	as	vas	peux
il/elle	est	a	va	peut
nous	sommes	avons	allons	pouvons
vous	êtes	avez	allez	pouvez
ils/elles	sont	ont	vont	peuvent

devoir:	vous devez	sortir	vous sortez	
faire:	vous faites	suivre	vous suivez	
mettre:	vous mettez	tenir	vous tenez	
ouvrir:	vous ouvrez	venir	vous venez	
partir:	vous partez	voir	vous voyez	
prendre:	vous prenez	vouloir	vous voulez	

(c) **Imperative**

Imperative forms are used to make a request, give advice, a direction or an order:
e.g.
allez à la gare (go to the station)
visitez la vieille ville (visit the old town)
attendez un instant (wait a minute)

(d) **Infinitive**

The infinitive is used:
1. Directly after some verbs such as:
   pouvoir: vous pouvez réserver (you can book)
   vouloir: vous voulez partir quel jour? (which day do you want to leave on?)
   devoir: vous devez réserver (you have to book)
   il faut: il faut réserver (you have to book)
   aimer: vous aimez faire du tennis? (do you like to play tennis?)
   préférer: vous préférez aller au restaurant? (do you prefer to go to a restaurant?)

2. After the preposition **à** in some expressions like: **intéressant à** visiter, **beaucoup à** voir, **des choses à** acheter . . .

GRAMMAR SUMMARY

(e) **Immediate future**

In French, the immediate future is formed with **aller** (to go) + infinitive: e.g. vous **allez** faire un circuit très intéressant (you are going to do a very interesting tour)

(f) **Conditional forms**

In this book, conditional forms are used to express polite requests. They are therefore very important in a professional context. Remember in particular the following forms:

Je **voudrais** (I would like)
J'**aimerais** (I would like)
Pourrais-je parler à . . . ? (Could I speak to . . . ?)
Pourriez-vous parler plus lentement? (Could you speak more slowly?)

9. Asking questions

There are different types of questions: questions which only require a **yes** or **no** answer, and questions which require more information and start with an interrogative word such as **where**, **when**, **what** or **which**.

(a) **Yes** or **no** questions

In French, there are three ways of asking questions with **yes** or **no** answers. Compare the three following examples:

(1) Vous allez au Québec?
(2) Est-ce que vous allez au Québec?
(3) Allez-vous au Québec?

1. The most common way of asking a **yes** or **no** question is to keep a sentence as it is, and indicate it is a question by changing the intonation, i.e. raising your voice at the end of the sentence.

   Vous allez au Québec (You go to Quebec)
   Vous allez au Québec? (Are you going to Quebec?)

2. The second common way of asking this type of question is to add **est-ce que**, or **est-ce qu'** at the beginning of a sentence.
   Est-ce que vous voulez réserver? (Do you want to book?)
   Est-ce qu'il faut un bonnet de bain? (Is a swimming cap necessary?)

GRAMMAR SUMMARY

3. The third way is far less common in everyday oral French except for polite requests. It consists in putting the subject after the verb, which is called an inversion of the subject.

| **Pouvez-vous** | signer ici? | Can you | sign here? |
| **Voulez-vous** | | Would you like to | |

(b) **Where? When? How? Why? What?** and **Who?** questions

In French there are two main ways of asking questions starting with the interrogative pronouns **where, when, how, why, what** and **who**.

1. The first is to use one of these interrogative pronouns followed by an inversion of the subject.

| Où | allez-vous? | Where | do you go to? |

Quand	allez-vous à Avignon?	When	do you go to Avignon?
Comment		How	
Pourquoi		Why	

| **Que** | recommandez-vous? | What | do you recommend? |
| **Qui** | | Who | |

Note: **À qui** voulez-vous parler? Whom do you want to speak to?

2. The second is to start the sentence with the interrogative pronoun and add the question tag **est-ce que** followed by the sentence in the normal order (subject-verb).

| Où | est-ce que vous allez? | Where | do you go to? |

Quand	est-ce que vous allez à Avignon ?	When	do you go to Avignon?
Comment		How	
Pourquoi		Why	

| **Qu'** | est-ce que vous recommandez? | What | do you recommend? |
| **Qui** | Who | | |

Note: **Que** becomes **qu'** in front of a vowel.

GRAMMAR SUMMARY

(c) **How much?** and **how many?** questions

In French **how much** and **how many** are both translated by **combien**, either on its own or with **de/d'**:

Combien		coûte le whisky? coûtent les cigarettes? est-ce que ça coûte?	**How much**	is the whiskey? are the cigarettes? does it cost?
Combien	**de** voitures **d'**enfants	avez-vous? est-ce que vous avez?	**How many** cars children	have you?

(d) **Which?** questions

Which? questions differ from the previous ones because they are not introduced by an interrogative pronoun alone but by the interrogative adjective **quel** + noun. Being an (interrogative) adjective, **quel** agrees in gender and number with the noun it refers to, becoming **quelle, quels,** or **quelles**. As for the previous question forms, the noun is then followed by either: an inversion of the subject or 'est-ce que' + sentence in normal order.

(1) **Quel** circuit | choisissez-vous?   **Which** tour | are you choosing?
    Quelle visite   visit

(2) **Quel** circuit | est-ce que vous choisissez?
    Quelle visite

Note: **À quelle** heure arrive le train? At what time does the train arrive?
No inversion of the subject.

10. Negative statements

Compare the following examples:

1. Je comprends   Je **ne** comprends **pas**.
2. Je m'appelle Julie   Je **ne** m'appelle **pas** Julie.
3. Il y a un cinéma.   Il **n'**y a **pas** de cinéma.
4. Nous avons une piscine.   Nous **n'**avons **pas** de piscine.

In French, a verb and therefore a sentence is made negative by using two words always: **ne ... pas** or **n' ... pas**, placed on both sides of the verb like the two slices of bread in a sandwich.

Note: In a negative sentence the verb **avoir** is followed by **pas de** directly followed by the noun, i.e. the article **un** or **une** is dropped, as in examples (3) and (4) above.

GRAMMAR SUMMARY

Ne . . . pas (not) is the main negative form but not the only one. Other negative forms are:

ne ... plus (not any more) (no longer)
ne ... jamais (never)
ne ... rien (nothing).

PRONUNCIATION GUIDE

This guide is intended as a brief guide to the sounds of French. However your best guide will always be to listen carefully to French speakers, try to copy them and ask them to correct your pronunciation.

You should always remember that:

- Accents can differ from one town or region to another, e.g. Paris and Marseilles or from one French-speaking country to another, e.g. France, Belgium, Switzerland, Quebec.
- Sometimes one single sound is represented by different spellings, e.g. **visite**, **visites** and **visitent** all sound exactly the same.
- A French word and an English one can look excactly the same when written down but can be pronounced quite differently, e.g. **nature**, **information**.
- Unlike English words, French words do not bear a heavy stress on one of their syllables.

Vowels

a	is similar to the **a** in cat P**a**ris b**a**teau c**a**fé
e	similar to the **e** in bed m**e**rci m**e**r
	similar to the **a** in **a**bove p**e**tit
	when French people speak fast, this sound almost disappears and you hear p'tit.
é	similar to the **é** in the English caf**é** v**é**lo caf**é** **é**glise
è/ê	similar to the **e** in best bi**è**re f**ê**te
i	similar to the **i** in police p**i**scine merc**i**

PRONUNCIATION GUIDE

o similar to the **o** in **o**dd
Gren**o**ble

at the end of a word and **ô** are slightly different; they sound more like the **o** in hell**o**.

métr**o**   all**ô**   h**ô**tel

u this sound is not found in English but it is somewhere between **u** as in **u**se and **ee** as in green. Listen carefully to French speakers and ask them to demonstrate **u** as in
d**u**   s**u**r   m**u**sée   r**u**e

eu similar to the vowel sound in s**i**r in English
h**eu**re   d**eu**x

ou similar to the **o** in English wh**o**
v**ou**s   v**ou**lez   **où**

oi like the sound of English **o**ne
tr**oi**s

au/eau as in hell**o**
chât**eau**   **au**to

Final consonants

Generally, if the last letter of a word is a consonant it is not pronounced:
peti**t**   deu**x**   fran**c**   restauran**t**   boulevar**d**

This means that in most cases the plural of nouns and adjectives sounds the same as the singular:

un **restaurant français**   des **restaurants français**

There are exceptions however:

—   neu**f** (the **f** is pronounced)
—   many words ending in **l**: origina**l**   espagno**l**
—   many words ending in **c**: Cogna**c**

PRONUNCIATION GUIDE

Other consonants

Many consonants have almost the same sound as English.
Here are the main variations and exceptions:

c	as in English except for **ci** where it remains **si** in French commer**ci**al
ç	always like the **s** in **s**it fran**ç**ais **ç**a
ch	like the English **sh** in **sh**op **ch**âteau **ch**er **ch**aud
g	before **a, o, u,** or a consonant, as in the English **g**ood **g**are
	before **e** or **i** like **s** in English lei**s**ure rou**g**e man**g**er
gn	like the sound in the middle of o**ni**on campa**gn**e monta**gn**e Avi**gn**on
h	is normally silent — when it is the initial letter of a word it is usually ignored. Thus when it is preceded by an **l'** we have l'**h**ôtel l'**h**oraire Most words starting with **h** would therefore be subject to the rule of liaison (see below) le**s** **h**ôtels le**s** **h**oraires There are some exceptions to this rule: le **h**aricot les **h**aricots (no liaison) la **H**ollande les **H**ollandais(es) (no liaison)
j	like the **s** in lei**s**ure **j**e **J**acques
qu	just as **k** in **qu**iche **qu**atre **qu**i

PRONUNCIATION GUIDE

r	one of the most difficult sounds in French for English speakers. Listen carefully to the tapes and to French speakers Pa**r**is **r**ue
s	has the same pronunciation as in English **s**ud **s**andwich égli**s**e However the **s** at the end of a word is not usually pronounced irlandai**s** musée**s** le**s** In the case of liaison (see below) the **s** at the end of a word is pronounced (like **z**)and joins the following word le**s** avenues
t	similar to the English **t** in **t**ea However in words ending in -*tion* the **t** is pronounced **s** (and not **sh**) s**t**ation
th	never like the English **th** in **th**is but like **t** in **t**ea **th**éâtre
w	this consonant is rare in French. It is usually like the **w** in **w**ater **w**hisky sand**w**ich However it is sometimes **v** as in **v**ery **w**agon

Nasals

These sounds do not have exact equivalents in English so listen carefully to their pronunciation on the cassettes.

in/im/aim	as in French tra**in**
en/an	as in French restaur**an**t, **en**trée, d**an**s, c**en**tre

PRONUNCIATION GUIDE

on   as in French
b**on**jour,   **on**ze,   b**on**

un   there is hardly any difference between this sound and the **in** sound above. However when this sound comes within a word and before a vowel, **un** is not a nasal sound and is pronounced as the vowel **u** sound
université   **u**ne

Liaisons

A liaison is when the final consonant of a word which is normally silent becomes pronounced because the next word starts with a vowel.

Liaisons are made in the following cases:

–   following the articles **les** and **des** and **aux**, the final **s** or **x** is pronounced like a **z**.
de**s** avenues   de**s** abbayes   au**x** États-Unis

–   between a pronoun subject and a verb
vou**s** allez   nou**s** avons   il**s** ont   elle**s** achètent

–   after **plus**, **moins** and **très** in front of an adjective or an adverb
plu**s** économique   moin**s** intéressant   trè**s** agréable

–   the **n** in the article **un** is fully pronounced when the next word starts with a vowel or a silent **h**

u**n** arbre   u**n** hôtel

–   numbers
deux, trois, six and dix: the final **x** and **s** are pronounced as **z** when the following noun or adjective starts with a vowel.
deu**x** avenues   troi**s** heures   si**x** enfants   soixante-di**x** ans

GLOSSARY

Key: f. = feminine
m. = masculine
sg. = singular
pl. = plural
la = feminine
le = masculine

à, in, at, to
à la ..., in the ... way
d'abord, first, at first
acadien (m.), **acadienne** (f.), Acadian
accepter, to accept
l'**accès** (m.), access
l'**accompagnateur** (see **guide accompagnateur**)
l'**accompagnatrice** (see **guide accompagnatrice**)
d'accord, all right, agreed
l'**accueil** (m.), welcome, reception
l'**achat** (m.), purchase
acheter, to buy
l'**acrylique** (m.), acrylic
l'**activité** (f.), activity, occupation
admis (m.), **admise** (f.) (see **admettre**), admitted, let in
admettre, to admit, let in
l'**adresse** (f.), address
l'**adulte** (m. or f.), adult
l'**aérogare** (f.), airport (buildings), terminal
l'**aéroport** (m.), airport
les **affaires** (f. pl.), business
l'**Afrique** (f.), Africa
l'**agence** (f.), agency, office
　　l'**agence de voyages,** travel agency
l'**agent de tourisme** (m. or f.), tourist information officer
l'**agent de voyages** (m. or f.), travel agent
agréable, pleasant, agreeable
j'ai (see **avoir**), I have
aider, to help
aimer, to like, to love
l'**alcool** (m.), alcohol
l'**allée** (f.), lane, path, avenue, aisle
l'**Allemagne** (f.), Germany
allemand (m.), **allemande** (f.), German
aller, to go
l'**aller** (m.), outward journey; single ticket
l'**aller-retour** (m.), return (ticket)

allergique, allergic
allô, hello (telephone)
alors, then, so, in that case
l'**alpinisme** (m.), mountaineering
l'**ambulance** (f.), ambulance
l'**Amérique** (f.), America
l'**amphithéâtre** (m.), amphitheatre, lecture theatre
l'**an** (m.), year
ancien (m.), **ancienne** (f.), ancient, old
l'**Angleterre** (f.), England, Britain
anglais (m.), **anglaise** (f.), English, British
l'**animal** (m.), animal, **animaux** (m.pl.), animals
l'**animateur** (m.), leisure assistant
l'**animatrice** (f.), leisure assistant
animé (m.), **animée** (f.), busy, lively
l'**année** (f.), year
l'**anniversaire** (m.), birthday, anniversary
s'annoncer, to approach, to look (weather)
l'**annuaire** (m.), telephone directory
anti-malaria, anti-malaria
anti-poliomyélitique, anti-polio
anti-tétanique, anti-tetanus
août, August
appeler, to call
　　appeler en PCV (= **Paiement Contre Vérification**), to make a reverse charge call
s'appeler, to be called
　　je m'appelle, my name is
l'**appétit** (m.), appetite
apprécier, to appreciate, like
après, after(wards)
l'**après-midi** (m.), afternoon
l'**aquarelle** (f.), watercolour painting
archéologique, archaeological
l'**architecture** (f.), architecture, structure
l'**Armistice** (m.), Armistice Day
l'**arrivée** (f.), arrival
arriver (à), to arrive (at)
l'**article** (m.), item, article
　　les **articles de sport,** sports equipment
　　les **articles en bois,** wooden crafts
　　les **articles en cristal,** crystal
l'**artisanat** (m.), arts and crafts
les **arts appliqués** (m.pl.), craft workshop
l'**ascenseur** (m.), lift
l'**Ascension** (f.), Feast of the Ascension

GLOSSARY

l'**aspirine** (f.), aspirin
assez, quite, rather
l'**Assomption** (f.), Feast of the Assumption
asthmatique, asthmatic
l'**atelier** (m.), workshop
Athènes, Athens
attendre, to wait (for); to expect
    attendez un instant, wait a minute, one moment
attention, be careful, watch out
attirer, to attract
au (m. sg.), in, at, to
l'**auberge** (f.), hostel
    l'**auberge de jeunesse**, youth hostel
aujourd'hui, today
auprès, nearby
auprès de, among
il **aura** (see **avoir**), he will have
au revoir, goodbye
aussi, also, as well
l'**Australie** (f.), Australia
l'**autobus** (m.), bus
l'**autocar** (m.), coach
l'**automne** (m.), autumn
l'**autoroute** (f.), motorway
autre, other
l'**Autriche** (f.), Austria
autrichien (m.), **autrichienne** (f.), Austrian
aux (m. or f. pl.), in, at, to
avant (**de**), before
avec, with
l'**avenue** (f.), avenue
vous **avez** (see **avoir**), you have
l'**avion** (m.), aeroplane
avoir, to have
    avoir l'air, to seem, to look like
    avoir l'embarras du choix, to have difficulty choosing/deciding
    avoir l'heure, to have the right time
    avoir lieu, to take place
    avoir mal à, to have a pain in, to hurt
    avoir quartier libre, to have a few hours off
    avoir raison, to be right
    nous **avons**, we have
avril, April

la **baignade**, bathing, swimming
le **bain**, bath
la **balade**, walk, stroll; drive
la **ballade**, ballad
la **balle**, ball
la **banque**, bank
le **bar**, bar, lounge
bas (m.), **basse** (f.), low
    la **basse ville**, lower part of the city/town
la **base de loisirs**, outdoor pursuit centre
le **basket(ball)**, basketball
le **bateau**, boat
le **bâtiment**, building
beau (m.), **belle** (f.), beautiful, fine
beaucoup, a lot, very much
beaucoup de, many
belge (m. or f.), Belgian
la **Belgique**, Belgium
la **bibliothèque**, library
bien, well, good
bien sûr, of course
(la) **bienvenue**, welcome
le **bijou**, **bijoux** (pl.), jewel(s)
le **billet**, ticket
le **billet aller-retour**, return ticket
la **bise**, a kiss on the cheek
blanc (m.), **blanche** (f.), white
la **blessure**, injury, wound
le **bois**, wood
la **boîte de nuit**, night club
la **bombe**, riding hat
bon (m.), **bonne** (f.), good
    bon appétit, enjoy your meal
    bonne journée, have a good day
    bon séjour, enjoy your stay
    bon voyage, have a good trip
bonjour, good morning/afternoon, hello
le **bonnet** (see **bonnet de bain**)
    le **bonnet de bain**, swimming cap
bonsoir, good evening
la **botte**, boot
le **Bottin**, French telephone directory
la **bouche**, mouth
la **boulangerie**, baker's (shop), bakery
le **boulevard**, boulevard
le **bouquet**, bunch, bouquet

GLOSSARY

le **bout**, end
    au bout de, at the end of
la **bouteille**, bottle
la **boutique**, shop
    la **boutique hors-taxes**, duty-free shop
le **bridge**, bridge (cards)
la **brochure**, brochure, leaflet
le **brouillard**, fog, mist
Bruxelles, Brussels
le **bureau**, office
    le **bureau de change**, bureau de change
    le **bureau d'information des foires et salons**, trade information centre
le **bus**, bus

ça, that
    ça fait, that makes
    ça veut dire, that means, that says, that is to say
le **cabaret**, cabaret
la **cabine**, cabin, changing room
le **cachet**, pill, tablet
le **cadeau**, present, gift
le **café**, coffee
    le **café au lait**, coffee made with warm milk
la **cafétéria**, cafeteria
la **caisse**, cashdesk, till
le **calendrier voyages**, travel timetable/schedule
le **calmant**, tranquilliser, sedative, painkiller
le **Cameroun**, Cameroon
le **camping**, campsite
le **campus**, campus
le **Canada**, Canada
canadien (m.), **canadienne** (f.), Canadian
le **canoë-kayak**, canoe, canoeing
le **car**, coach
le **cardigan**, cardigan
le **carnet**, book of ten metro tickets
la **carte**, card, map
    la **carte de crédit**, credit card
    la **carte orange**, weekly or monthly pass for Parisian bus and metro
    la **carte postale**, postcard
    la **carte de téléphone**, telephone card
le **casino**, casino
le **casque**, helmet

la **cathédrale**, cathedral
la **cause**, cause, reason
ce, (m.), **cette** (f.), **ces** (m. or f. pl.), this, that
la **ceinture**, belt, waist
cela, that
    cela fait, that makes
celle (f.), **celui** (m.), this one
celle-là (f.), **celui-là** (m.), that one
cent, one hundred
    cent cinquante, one hundred and fifty
le **centre**, centre
    le **centre commercial**, shopping centre
    le **centre de conférences**, conference centre
    le **centre équestre**, equestrian centre
    le **centre social**, social centre
    le **centre sportif**, sports centre
    le **centre ville**, city or town centre
certain (m.), **certaine** (f.), certain, sure
certainement, certainly
ces, these, those
c'est, it is
    c'est-à-dire, in other words
    c'est ça, that's right
    c'est combien? how much is it?
    c'est de la part de qui? who's calling, speaking?
la **chambre**, bedroom, room
    la **chambre double**, double room
    la **chambre d'hôte**, bed and breakfast
le **champagne**, champagne
le **change**, exchange, exchange rate
le **changement**, change
changer, to change
chaque, each, every
le **charter**, charter flight
le **château, châteaux** (pl.), castle(s)
chaud (m.), **chaude** (f.), hot
les **chaussures** (f.pl.), shoes
    les **chaussures de tennis**, tennis shoes
le **chèque**, cheque
cher (m.), **chère** (f.), dear, expensive
chercher, to look for
le **cheval, chevaux** (pl.), horse(s)
la **cheville**, ankle
chez l'habitant, in the owner's home (of a B & B)
chic, smart, stylish

GLOSSARY

la **Chine**, China
le **chocolat**, chocolate
choisir, to choose
le **choix**, choice
la **chose**, thing
la **chute (d'eau)**, waterfall
le **cigare**, cigar
la **cigarette**, cigarette
le **cimetière**, graveyard
le **cinéma**, cinema
cinq, five
    cinquième, fifth
cinquante, fifty
    cinquante-deux, fifty-two
    cinquante-et-un, fifty-one
le **circuit**, tour, trip
la **cité**, old town, city
la **classe**, class
le **client**, la **cliente**, customer; guest
le **climat**, climate
le **club**, club
    le **club de l'histoire**, the history club
    le **club de squash**, the squash club
le **cœur**, heart
combien? how much?
    c'est combien? how much is it?
    combien coûte . . ? how much does . . . cost?
    combien de temps? how long?
    combien d'heures? how long?
commander, to order
comme, as, like
commencer, to start, to begin
comment . . . ? how . . . ? why . . . ?
    comment ça s'écrit? how do you write this?
    comment payez-vous? how do you wish to pay?
    comment vous appelez-vous? what is your name?
le **commerce**, business, trade
la **communication**, communication
la **compagnie**, company
compétent (m.), **compétente** (f.), competent, capable
complémentaire, complementary, supplementary
le **complexe sportif**, sports complex
compliqué (m.), **compliquée** (f.), complicated

comprendre, to understand
compris (see **comprendre**), understood
le **concert**, concert
conduire, to drive
la **conférence**, conference
confortable, comfortable
conseiller, to advise
continuer, to continue
contre, against
le **contrôleur**, ticket inspector
Copenhague, Copenhagen
la **correspondance**, connection
le **correspondant**, interlocutor, person to whom one is speaking, correspondent
correspondant (m.), **correspondante** (f.), corresponding
le **costume folklorique**, folk costume, dress
le **côté**, side
    à côté de, beside
    sur le côté, on one's side
le **coton**, cotton
la **couchette**, couchette, berth, bunk
le **couloir**, corridor
se **couper**, to cut oneself
le **couple**, couple, pair
courir, to run
court (m.), **courte** (f.), short
    le **court de tennis**, tennis court
coûter, to cost
le **couvert**, place setting
le **cristal**, crystal
croire, to believe, to think
la **croisière**, cruise
le **croissant**, croissant
culturel (m.), **culturelle** (f.), cultural

la **dame**, lady
le **Danemark**, Denmark
danois (m.), **danoise** (f.), Danish
dans, in, on
la **danse**, dance, dancing
la **date**, date
    la **date de départ**, departure date
    la **date de naissance**, date of birth
    la **date de retour**, return date
le **dauphin**, dolphin

GLOSSARY

de, of, from, some
le **début**, beginning
décembre, December
décoratif (m.), **décorative** (f.), decorative, ornamental
décrire, to describe
déjà, already, before
le **déjeuner**, lunch
    déjeuner, to (have) lunch
délicieux (m.), **délicieuse** (f.), **délicieux** (pl.), delicious
demain, tomorrow
demander, to ask (for)
demi (m.), **demie** (f.), half
    une **demi-heure**, half an hour
la **dent** (f.), les **dents** (f.pl.), tooth, teeth
le **dentiste**, dentist
le **départ**, departure
au **départ de**, at the start of
le **département**, department (an administrative division in France)
dépendre (de), to depend (on)
le **dépliant**, leaflet, folder, brochure
dernier (m.), **dernière** (f.), last
se **dérouler**, to happen, to take place
des (m. or f. pl.), of, from, some
descendre, to go down, get out, disembark
désinfecter, to disinfect
désirer, to want, like, desire
désolé (m.), **désolée** (f.), sorry
la **destination**, destination
le **détail**, detail
le **deutschmark**, deutschmark
deux, two
    deux cents, two hundred
    deuxième, second
devant, in front of
devoir, to have to
diabétique, diabetic
la **différence**, difference
différent (m.), **différente** (f.), different
dimanche, Sunday
le **dîner**, dinner
    le **dîner spectacle**, dinner and show
    dîner, to have dinner, to dine
dire, to say

direct (m.), **directe** (f.), direct
le **directeur**, manager
en **direction de**, going to, heading for
la **discothèque**, disco
disons (see **dire**), let's say
à votre **disposition**, at your service, disposal
le **distributeur automatique**, cash dispenser, automatic teller machine
dites (see **dire**), tell
dix, ten
    dix-huit, eighteen
    dixième, tenth
le **doigt**, finger
je **dois** (see **devoir**), I have to, I must
il **doit** (see **devoir**), he has to, he must
le **dollar**, dollar
donc, therefore
donner, to give
le **dos**, back
double, double
la **douche**, shower
doux (m.), **douce** (f.), soft, mild
douze, twelve
    douzième, twelfth
droit (m.), **droite** (f.), straight
la **droite**, right, right-hand side
    à **droite**, on the right, to the right
du (m.), of, from, some
la **durée**, length, duration
durer, to last

l'**eau** (f.), **eaux** (pl.), water(s)
    l'**eau de toilette**, eau de toilette
l'**écomusée** (m.), interpretive centre, folk museum
écouter, to listen to
l'**écran** (m.), screen
écrire, to write
    écrit, written
l'**effet** (m.), effect
    en **effet**, in fact, indeed
également, equally, also, too, as well
l'**église** (f.), church
elle, she, it, **elles** (f.pl.), they
l'**embarras du choix** (m.), difficulty of choosing, deciding
emmener, to take (along)

GLOSSARY

l'**emplacement** (m.), place, site
emprunter (à), to borrow (from)
en, in, by; of it, of them
encadré, staffed
enchanté, pleased to meet you
encore, again, more
l'**enfant** (m. & f.), child
enfin, finally, at last
enflé (m.), **enflée** (f.), swollen
énorme, enormous, huge
enregistrer, to record
ensuite, next
entendre, to hear
entre, between
l'**entrée** (f.), entrance
    entrée interdite, no entry
l'**entreprise** (f.), company
environ, about
    les **environs** (m. pl.), surroundings, surrounding area
envoyer, to send
épeler, to spell
l'**équipe** (f.), team
l'**équipement** (m.), equipment
l'**équitation** (f.), horse-riding
l'**escalade** (f.), (rock) climbing
les **escaliers** (m. pl.), stairs
l'**escrime** (f.), fencing
l'**Espagne** (f.), Spain
espagnol (m.), **espagnole** (f.), Spanish
les **espèces** (f. pl.), cash
espérer, to hope
l'**est** (m.), east
il **est** (see **être**), he is
    est-ce qu'il y a . . . ? is there . . . ?
l'**estomac** (m.), stomach
et, and
l'**étage** (m.), floor, storey
l'**étang** (m.), pond, marsh
les **États-Unis** (m. pl.), the United States
l'**étang** (m.), pond, marsh
l'**été** (m.), summer
vous **êtes** (see **être**), you are
l'**étoile** (f.), star
étranger (m.), **étrangère** (f.), foreign
être, to be
l'**étudiant** (m.), **étudiante** (f.), student

l'**Europe** (f.), Europe
européen (m.), **européenne** (f.), European
l'**évènement** (m.), event
évidemment, obviously, of course
exact (m.), **exacte** (f.), correct, exact
exactement, exactly
excellent (m.), **excellente** (f.), excellent
l'**excursion** (f.), excursion, trip
excuser, to excuse, forgive
expliquer, to explain
l'**exposant** (m.), l'**exposante** (f.), exhibitor

en face (de), opposite
facile, easy
faire, to do, make
    faire des achats, to shop, go shopping
    faire chaud, to be warm, hot
    faire du cheval, to go horse-riding
    faire doux, to be mild
    faire frais, to be cool, chilly, fresh
    faire de la planche à voile, to go windsurfing
    faire le pont, to take a couple of extra days off work in order to join a public holiday to the weekend
    faire une réservation, to make a reservation
    faire sec, to be dry
    faire du shopping, to go shopping
    faire du ski nautique, to go water-skiing
    faire du sport, to play sport
    faire du vélo tout terrain, to go mountain-biking
je **fais** (see **faire**), I do, make
    il **fait**, he does, makes
    il **fait beau**, it's fine weather
    vous **faites**, you do, make
falloir, to be necessary, to have to
fameux (m.), **fameuse** (f.), first-rate, first class; famous
fatigant (m.), **fatigante** (f.), tiring, annoying
il **faut** (see **falloir**), he has to, it is necessary to
le **fax**, fax
la **femme**, woman, wife
il **fera** (see **faire**), he will do, will make
férié (see **jour férié**)
fermé (m.), **fermée** (f.) (**de . . . à**), closed (from . . . to)
fermer, to close

GLOSSARY

la fête, feast, party, feast day
    la fête du travail, Labour Day
    la fête nationale, national feast day
le feu, fire; light
    le feu rouge, **les feux**, traffic lights
février, February
la fiche, form
    la fiche de réservation, reservation form
    la fiche d'inscription, registration form
    la fiche téléphonique, telephone message
la fièvre typhoïde, typhoid, typhoid fever
la fin, end
finalement, finally, in the end
finlandais (m.), **finlandaise** (f.), Finnish
la Finlande, Finland
la fleur séchée, dried flower
le fleuve, river
Florence, Florence
la foire, trade fair
folklorique, folk
au **fond**, at the end, down, at the bottom
la fontaine, fountain
le foot(ball), football, soccer
le forfait, set price, fixed rate
fort (m.), **forte** (f.), strong
fortifié (m.), **fortifiée** (f.), fortified, strengthened
le foulard, scarf
frais (m.), **fraîche** (f.), fresh, cool
le franc, franc
français (m.), **française** (f.), French
la France, France
froid (m.), **froide** (f.), cold
le fruit, fruit
fumer, to smoke
futur (m.), **future** (f.), future

la galerie, gallery
    la galerie des spectateurs, viewing gallery
    la Galerie Nationale, the National Gallery
gallo-romain (m.), **gallo-romaine** (f.), Gallo-Roman
garanti (m.), **garantie** (f.), guaranteed
la gare, station
    la gare maritime, ferry terminal
    la gare routière, bus station
    la gare SNCF, railway station (in France)

gastronomique, gastronomic
la gauche, left, left-hand side
    à gauche, on the left, to the left
en **général**, in general, generally, usually
Genève, Geneva
le genre, type, sort, kind
le gilet de sauvetage, life jacket
le gîte, gite, self-catering cottage
le golf, golf, golf course
les gorges (f. pl.), canyons
grand (m.), **grande** (f.), big, tall, high; great
    la Grande-Bretagne, Great Britain
    les grandes vacances (f.pl.), summer holidays
gratuit (m.), **gratuite** (f.), free
grec (m.), **grecque** (f.), Greek
la Grèce, Greece
gros (m.), **grosse** (f.), big, large, heavy
la grotte, cave
le groupe, group
la guêpe, wasp
le guide, guide
    le guide accompagnateur, tour guide, courier
    la guide accompagnatrice, tour guide, courier
guider, to guide

habiter, to live
le hand, (Olympic) handball
haut (m.), **haute** (f.), high, tall
    la haute ville, upper part of the city/town
l'hébergement (m.), accommodation
l'herbe (f.), herb, grass
l'heure (f.), hour
    l'heure d'arrivée, arrival time
    l'heure de départ, departure time
    l'heure locale, local time
    l'heure d'ouverture, opening time
    une heure, one hour, one o'clock
    une heure et demie, an hour and a half
hier, yesterday
hippique, horse, equestrian
l'histoire (f.), history
l'hiver (m.), winter
hollandais (m.), **hollandaise** (f.), Dutch
la Hollande, Holland

GLOSSARY

l'**homme** (m.), man
l'**hôpital** (m.), **hôpitaux** (pl.), hospital(s)
l'**horaire** (m.), timetable, schedule
hors service, out of order
hors taxes, duty-free
l'**hôtel** (m.), hotel
l'**hôtel de ville** (m.), town hall
l'**hôtellerie** (f.), hotel business/industry
l'**hôtesse d'accueil** (f.), conference assistant
l'**huile d'olive** (f.), olive oil
huit, eight
    huit cents, eight hundred
    huitième, eighth
l'**hydrospeed** (m.), jet skiing

ici, here
idéal (m.), **idéale** (f.), ideal
l'**idéal** (m.), the ideal (thing)
l'**idée** (f.), idea
il, he, it
l'**île** (f.), island
ils (m. pl.), they
il y a, there is, are; ago
immense (m. or f.), immense, vast
important (m.), **importante** (f.), important, significant
impressionnant (m.), **impressionnante** (f.), impressive
l'**information** (f.), information
    des **informations** (**sur**), information (about)
informer, to inform
s'**inquiéter**, to worry
l'**inscription** (f.), registration, enrolment
l'**instant** (m.), moment, instant
interdire (**à quelqu'un**), to forbid (someone)
interdit (m.), **interdite** (f.), forbidden
    il est **interdit de** . . ., it is forbidden to . . . ,
      . . . is forbidden
intéressant (m.), **intéressante** (f.), interesting
intéresser, to interest
international (m.), **internationale** (f.), international
irlandais, (m.), **irlandaise** (f.), Irish
l'**Irlande** (f.), Ireland
l'**Italie** (f.), Italy
italien (m.), **italienne** (f.), Italian
l'**itinéraire** (m.), route, itinerary

le **jacuzzi**, jacuzzi
janvier, January
le **Japon**, Japan
le **jardin botanique**, botanic gardens
je, I
le **jeu**, **jeux** (pl.), game(s)
jeudi, Thursday
joli (m.), **jolie** (f.), pretty
jouer, to play
    jouer au football, to play football
    jouer au golf, to play golf
    jouer au tennis, to play tennis
le **jouet**, toy
le **jour**, day
    jour férié, public holiday
    Jour de l'An, New Year's Day
    jour d'ouverture, opening day
la **journée**, day
    bonne journée! have a good day!
    les **journées grand public**, days open to the public
    les **journées réservées aux professionnels**, trade only days
juillet, July
juin, June
jusqu'à, until, as far as
juste, just

le **kilomètre**, kilometre
le **kiosque à journaux**, newspaper kiosk

la (f. sg.), the
laisser, to leave
la **lavande**, lavender
laver, to wash
le (m. sg.), the
la **légende**, key
le **lendemain**, following day, next day
lequel, who, whom, which
les (m. or f. pl.), the
la **liberté**, freedom
la **librairie**, bookshop
le **lieu**, **lieux** (pl.), place(s), location(s)
    avoir lieu, to take place
la **ligne**, line
Lisbonne, Lisbon

GLOSSARY

la **liste**, list
la **livre**, pound
le **livre**, book
local (m.), **locale** (f.), local
la **location**, hiring, renting
loger, to put up, accommodate
loin, far, a long way
les **loisirs** (m. pl.), leisure, spare-time activities
long (m.), **longue** (f.), long
lors de, at the time of
louer, to hire, rent
lui, him, it, to him
la **lumière**, light
lundi, Monday
le **Luxembourg**, Luxembourg
la **luge**, tobogganing

ma (f. sg.), my
la **machine**, machine
    la **machine à laver**, washing machine
Madame (f. sg.), Madam, Mrs, **Mesdames** (f.pl.), ladies, mesdames
Mademoiselle (f.sg.), Miss, **Mesdemoiselles** (f.pl.), (young) ladies
le **magasin**, shop
magnifique, magnificient, marvellous, great
mai, May
la **main**, hand
maintenant, now
le **maire**, mayor
mais, but
la **maison**, house
    la **maison de la culture**, cultural centre
mal, bad; badly
la **maladie**, illness, sickness, disease
la **malaria**, malaria
manger, to eat
manquer, to miss
    à ne pas manquer, not to be missed
le **manteau**, overcoat
le **marché**, market
mardi, Tuesday
le **mari**, husband
le **Maroc**, Morocco
mars, March
le **matin**, morning

mauvais (m.), **mauvaise** (f.), bad
maximum, maximum
me, me, to me
le **médecin**, doctor
médical (m.), **médicale** (f.), medical
médiéval (m.), **médiévale** (f.), medieval
meilleur (m.), **meilleure** (f.), better
    le **meilleur**, best
même, same; even
la **mer**, sea
merci, thank you
    merci beaucoup, thank you very much
    merci bien, thank you very much
mercredi, Wednesday
mes (m. or f. pl.), my
Mesdames (see **Madame**)
Mesdemoiselles (see **Mademoiselle**)
le **message**, message
Messieurs (see **Monsieur**)
la **météo**, weather forecast
le **mètre**, metre
le **métro**, underground, metro
mettre, to put
les **meubles** (m. pl.), furniture
le **Mexique**, Mexico
midi, midday
mille, one thousand
miniature, miniature
le **minitel**, minitel
minuit, midnight
la **minute**, minute
la **mise en forme**, keep-fit
moi, me
moins, less
    moins cher, cheaper
le **mois**, month
mon (m. sg.), my
le **monastère**, monastery
le **monde**, world
mondial (m.), **mondiale** (f.), world, worldwide
le **moniteur**, supervisor, instructor
Monsieur (m.sg.), **Messieurs** (pl.), Mr, Sir(s)
le **montant**, total, total amount
Montréal, Montreal
la **mouche**, fly
le **moule à gâteaux**, cake tin

GLOSSARY

le **moustique**, mosquito
moyen (m.), **moyenne** (f.), average
municipal (m.), **municipale** (f.), municipal, local
le **musée**, museum
la **musique**, music
    la **musique classique**, classical music

la **natation**, swimming
national (m.), **nationale** (f.), national
la **nationalité**, nationality
naturel (m.), **naturelle** (f.), natural
la **navette**, shuttle bus
nécessaire, necessary
la **neige**, snow
le **Népal**, Nepal
n'est-ce pas, isn't that so, don't you?
neuf, nine
    neuf cents, nine hundred
    neuvième, ninth
le **nez**, nose
Noël (m.), Christmas
le **nom**, name; surname
le **nombre**, number
nombreux (m.), **nombreuse** (f.), numerous
non, no
nonante, ninety (Belgian and Swiss French only)
le **nord**, north
le **nord-est**, north east
la **Norvège**, Norway
norvégien (m.), **norvégienne** (f.), Norwegian
notamment, in particular, particularly, notably
notre (m. or f. sg.), our
nous, we, us, to us
nouveau (m.), **nouvelle** (f.), new
novembre, November
le **nuage**, cloud
la **nuit**, night
le **numéro**, number
    le **numéro de fax**, fax number
    le **numéro de téléphone**, telephone number
obligatoire, compulsory, obligatory
obtenir, to obtain, get
occupé (m.), **occupée** (f.), engaged, busy
octante, eighty (Belgian and Swiss French only)
octobre, October
l'**office du tourisme** (m.), tourist (information) office

on, one, we, you
onze, eleven
    onzième, eleventh
l'**orage** (m.), thunderstorm, storm
l'**ordre** (m.), order
organiser, to organise, host
l'**organisme** (m.), organisation
original (m.), **originale** (f.), original
ou, or
où, where
    où est-il? where is he?
    où se trouve ……? where is……? where do you find ……?
oublier, to forget
l'**ouest** (m.), west
oui, yes
ouvert (m.), **ouverte** (f.), (**de . . . à**), open (from . . . to)
l'**ouverture** (f.), opening
ouvrir, to open

la **paire**, pair
le **palais des congrès**, conference centre
le **panier en osier**, wicker basket
le **panneau, panneaux** (pl.), notice(s), sign(s)
le **panorama**, panorama, view, viewpoint
le **pansement**, dressing, bandage, plaster
le **pantalon**, trousers
la **papeterie**, paper mill
Pâques (f. pl.), Easter
le **paquet**, packet, parcel
    le **paquet cadeau**, gift-wrapped
par, by, via, per
    par carte de crédit, by credit card
    par personne, per person
    par contre, on the other hand
le **parapente**, parachute gliding
le **parapluie**, umbrella
le **parc**, park
    le **parc nautique**, water park
parce que, because
le **parcours**, distance, journey, route, course
    le **parcours de golf**, golf course
pardon, excuse me
pareil (m.), **pareille** (f.), the same, similar, alike
par exemple, for example
parfait (m.), **parfaite** (f.), perfect

GLOSSARY

parfois, sometimes, occasionally, at times
le **parfum**, perfume, scent
la **parfumerie**, perfumery
le **parking**, car park
parler (de), to talk, speak (about)
de la **part de**, from
le **participant**, participant, member
participer (à), to participate, take part (in)
particulier (m.), **particulière** (f.), particular, specific
partir (à) (de), to leave (at) (from)
à **partir de**, from
partout, everywhere
ne . . . pas, not
pas de . . . , no . . .
passer (par), to pass, go (through); to give/hand something over; to spend (time)
le **pastis**, pastis
patienter, to wait
la **pause-café**, coffee break
payer, to pay (for)
    vous payez comment? how do you want to pay?
le **pays**, country
les **Pays-Bas** (m. pl.), the Netherlands
la **pêche**, fishing
la **peinture**, painting
    la **peinture sur verre**, glass painting
penser, to think
en **pension complète**, full board
la **Pentecôte**, Whit
la **période**, period
le **périphérique**, ring road
la **personne**, person
petit (m.), **petite** (f.), little
    le **petit déjeuner**, breakfast
peu, little, not much
il **peut** (see **pouvoir**), he can, is able to
peut-être, perhaps
ils **peuvent** (see **pouvoir**), they can, are able to
je **peux** (see **pouvoir**), I can, am able to
la **pharmacie**, chemist's (shop), pharmacy
la **pièce d'identité**, I.D., identity paper, proof of identity
le **pied**, foot
    à **pied**, on foot
la **piqûre**, injection; sting

la **piscine**, swimming pool
    la **piscine couverte**, indoor swimming pool
    la **piscine découverte**, open-air swimming pool
pittoresque, picturesque
la **pizza**, pizza
la **place**, square; place, seat
la **plage**, beach
la **plaisance**, pleasure (in the context of leisure as in '**bateau de plaisance**', pleasure boat)
le **plaisir**, pleasure
    avec plaisir, with pleasure, certainly
le **plan**, plan, map
la **planche à voile**, windsurfing; sailboard
il **pleut** (see **pleuvoir**), it's raining
    pleuvoir, to rain
la **plongée**, diving
    la **plongée avec bouteille**, scuba diving
    la **plongée libre**, snorkelling
    la **plongée sous-marine**, under-water diving
la **pluie**, rain
plus, more
    le **plus**, the most
    en plus, extra
plusieurs, several
plutôt, rather, instead
le **poisson**, fish
le **pollen**, pollen
la **Pologne**, Poland
la **pommade**, ointment, cream
le **pont** (see also **faire le pont**), bridge
le **port**, harbour, port
    le **port de plaisance**, marina
la **porte**, door
portugais (m.), **portugaise** (f.), Portuguese
le **Portugal**, Portugal
poser, to put down, set down, hang up
la **possibilité**, possibility
possible, possible
la **poste**, post office
le **poste**, extension (telephone)
la **poterie**, pottery
la **poupée**, doll
pour, for, in order to
je **pourrais** (see **pouvoir**), I could, would be able to
pouvoir, can, may, to be allowed to

GLOSSARY

préférable, preferable, better
préférer, to prefer
premier (m.), **première** (f.), first
prendre, to take
    vous **prenez** (see **prendre**), you take (sg. & pl.)
le **prénom,** first name
préparer, to prepare
près (de), near(by), close(by) (to)
    tout **près,** very near
la **présentation (sur),** presentation, display (on)
préserver, to preserve, protect
prier, to invite, ask, request
    je vous en **prie,** please do, of course, you're welcome
le **printemps,** spring
privé (m.), **privée** (f.), private
le **prix,** price, cost
le **problème,** problem
le **produit d'artisanat,** hand-made craft
le **professeur,** teacher
la **profession,** profession, occupation
professionnel (m.), **professionnelle** (f.), professional
profond (m.), **profonde** (f.), deep
le **programme,** programme
la **promenade,** walk, stroll, drive
proposer, to suggest, propose, offer
la **provenance,** origin, source, provenance
    en **provenance de,** coming from
à proximité de, near, close to
public (m.), **publique** (f.), public
puis, then, next
puis-je? (see **pouvoir**), may I, can I?
le **pull,** pullover, sweater

le **quai,** quay, platform
quand, when
quarante, forty
    quarante-deux, forty-two
    quarante-et-un, forty-one
le **quart,** quarter
    une heure et **quart,** a quarter past one
le **quartier,** district, area, neighbourhood
avoir **quartier libre,** to have a few hours off
quatorze, fourteen
    quatorzième, fourteenth

quatre, four
    quatre-vingt, eighty
    quatrième, fourth
que, what, that
    que signifie . . . ? what does . . . mean?
le **Québec,** Quebec
quel (m.), **quelle** (f.), what
    quel est votre nom? what is your name?
    quelle est votre adresse? what is your address?
    quelle heure est-il? what time is it?
quelque (sg.), **quelques** (pl.), some, a few
    quelque chose, something
qu'est-ce que . . . ? What . . ?
    qu'est-ce que ça veut dire? what does that mean?
    qu'est-ce que c'est? what is it?
la **question,** question
qui, who
    qui est-ce? who is it?
quinze, fifteen
    quinzième, fifteenth
quitter, to leave
    ne quittez pas, hold on
quoi, what

la **radio,** radio
le **rafting,** rafting
la **raison,** reason
    avoir **raison,** to be right
la **randonnée à cheval,** pony trek
    la **randonnée à pied,** walk, ramble
    la **randonnée à vélo,** bike ride
    la **randonnée pédestre,** walk, ramble
rapide, fast, quick, rapid
rappeler, to remind, recall
le **rapport,** relationship
    par **rapport à,** in relation to
la **raquette,** racket
la **réception,** reception; reception desk
recommander (à), to recommend (to)
la **réduction,** reduction, discount
réfléchir (à/sur), to think (about), reflect on
la **région,** region
régional (m.), **régionale** (m.), **régionaux** (m. pl.), regional

GLOSSARY

regretter, to be sorry
régulier (m.), **régulière** (f.), regular
remercier, to thank
le **rendez-vous,** appointment, date; meeting place
renommé (m.), **renommée** (f.), celebrated, renowned, famous
le **renseignement, renseignements** (pl.), information, directory enquiries
rentrer, to come back, return
répéter, to repeat
répondre, to reply
représenter, to represent
RER (le **Réseau Express Régional**), high-speed suburban branch of Paris metro
la **réservation,** reservation
réserver, to reserve
la **résidence universitaire,** university (hall of) residence
le **restaurant,** restaurant
la **restauration,** catering
rester, to stay
le **retour,** journey back; return ticket
    au retour, coming back
retourner, to return, go back
la **réunion,** meeting
réveiller (quelqu'un), to wake (somebody) up
le **rez-de-chaussée,** ground floor
rien, nothing
    de rien, you're welcome
la **rivière,** river
le **rosé,** rosé (wine)
rouge, red
    le **rouge,** red wine
la **roulotte,** caravan
la **route,** road, way
    la **route nationale,** main road
la **rue,** street
rural (m.), **rurale** (f.), **ruraux** (m.pl.), rural, country
la **Russie,** Russia
russe (m. or f.), Russian

sa (f. sg.), his, her, its
sacré (m.), **sacrée** (f.), sacred
je **sais** (see **savoir**), I know
la **saison,** season

la **salle,** room
    la **salle de bains,** bathroom
    la **salle de conférences,** conference hall
    la **salle de gymnastique,** gymnasium
    la **salle de musculation,** weights room
    la **salle de sport,** hall (sport)
    la **salle de réunions,** meeting room
le **salon,** trade fair
    le **salon de l'automobile,** car show
    le **salon de l'informatique,** computer exhibition
    le **salon du meuble,** furniture exhibition
    le **salon du tourisme,** travel fair
    le **salon mondial du tourisme et des voyages,** world tourism and travel fair
samedi, Saturday
sans, without
la **santé,** health
sauf, except
le **sauna,** sauna
savoir, to know
le **savon,** soap
la **sculpture sur pierre,** stone sculpture
se, oneself, himself, herself, itself
la **séance,** session
    la **séance d'ouverture,** opening (session)
    la **séance plénière,** plenary session
le **secours,** help
    les **premiers secours,** first aid
seize, sixteen
le **séjour,** stay
la **semaine,** week
le **Sénégal,** Senegal
sept, seven
    sept cents, seven hundred
    septième, seventh
septante, seventy (Belgian and Swiss French only)
septembre, September
il **sera** (see **être**), he will be
servir, to serve, be of service to
à votre **service,** at your service
ses (m. or f. pl.), his, her
seul (m.), **seule** (f.), alone
seulement, only
le **shopping,** shopping

GLOSSARY

si, if; yes
le **siècle,** century
signaler, to indicate, to point out
signifier, to mean
s'il vous plaît, please
simple, simple, straightforward
sinon, if not
le **site archéologique,** archeological site
situé (m.), **située** (f.), situated
six, six
    sixième, sixth
le **ski,** skiing
    le **ski nautique,** water-skiing
social (m.), **sociale** (f.), social
le **soir,** evening
la **soirée,** evening
soit . . . soit, either . . . or
soixante, sixty
    soixante-deux, sixty-two
    soixante-dix, seventy
le **soleil,** sun
nous **sommes** (see **être**), we are
son (m. sg.), his
le **son,** sound
    son et lumière, light and sound (show)
elles **sont** (f. pl.), ils **sont** (m. pl.) (see **être**), they are
la **sortie,** exit
    la **sortie de secours,** emergency exit
sortir (de), to leave, go out (of, from)
souhaiter, to wish (as in greet)
sous-marin (m.), **sous-marine** (f.), underwater
le **souvenir,** souvenir, memento
spécial (m.), **spéciale** (f.), special
spécialement, especially, particularly
la **spécialité,** speciality
    les **spécialités gastronomiques** (f.pl.), food specialities
le **spectacle,** sight; show
la **spéléologie,** pot-holing
le **sport,** sport
    les **sports nautiques** (m. pl.), water sports
sportif (m.), **sportive** (f.), sports, competitive, athletic
le **squash,** squash
le **stade,** stadium
    le **stade Olympique,** Olympic stadium

le **stand,** stand, stall
le **standard de l'hôtel,** hotel switchboard
la **station,** station
la **station thermale,** spa
le **style,** style
le **succès,** success
le **sud,** south
la **Suède,** Sweden
suédois (m.), **suédoise** (f.), Swedish
je **suis** (see **être**), I am
la **Suisse,** Switzerland
suisse (m. or f.), Swiss
suivant (m.), **suivante** (f.), following
suivre, to follow
le **sujet,** topic, subject
le **supermarché,** supermarket
supplémentaire, additional, extra
sur, on; about
les **surfaces louées** (f. pl.), total surface area let
le **surfing,** surfing
le **syndicat d'initiative,** local tourist office

le **tabac,** tobacco shop, newsagents
le **tableau, tableaux** (pl.), painting(s)
la **Tahiti,** Tahiti
le **tarif,** fare; tariff, rate(s)
    le **tarif apex,** apex fare
la **tarte,** tart
    la **tarte au fromage,** cheese cake
    la **tarte au kirch,** cherry tart
    la **tarte aux fruits,** fruit tart
    la **tarte aux pommes,** apple tart
    la **tarte flambée,** fruit pie flambé
    la **tarte tatin,** apple upside down tart
le **taxi,** taxi
la **télécarte,** phone card, callcard
le **téléphone,** telephone
    le **téléphone domicile,** home telephone number
    le **téléphone travail,** work telephone number
téléphoner, to telephone
la **télévision,** television
la **température,** temperature
le **temps,** weather, time
    quel temps fait-il? what is the weather like?
tenir, to take, keep, hold

GLOSSARY

le **tennis**, tennis
tenter, to tempt
terminer, to finish, end
le **terminus**, terminus
le **terrain de squash**, squash court
la **terre**, earth, ground; world
le **tétanos**, tetanus, lockjaw
la **tête**, head
le **TGV** (le **Train à Grande Vitesse**), high-speed train
la **Thaïlande**, Thailand
le **théâtre**, theatre
le **ticket**, ticket
le **timbre**, stamp
le **tir à l'arc**, archery
le **tissu**, material, fabric, cloth
les **toilettes** (f. pl.), toilets
    les **toilettes-dames**, ladies' (toilets)
    les **toilettes-messieurs**, gents' (toilets)
le **total**, total
toujours, always, still
le **tour**, trip, outing; tower
le **tourisme**, tourism
    le **tourisme d'affaires**, business tourism
    le **tourisme vert**, agri-tourism
tourner, to turn
le **tournoi, tournois** (pl.), tournament(s)
tous, (m. pl.), **toutes** (f. pl.), all, every
    tous les jours, everyday
Toussaint, All Saints' Day
tout, everything
    tout droit, straight ahead
    tout le monde, everyone
    tout près (de), very near (to)
traditionnel (m.), **traditionnelle** (f.), traditional
le **train**, train
    le **train-couchettes**, train with couchettes
    le **train auto-couchettes**, train with couchettes that carries cars
le **trajet**, route, journey
tranquille, quiet, tranquil, peaceful
le **travail**, work
travailler, to work
la **traversée**, crossing
traverser, to cross
treize, thirteen

treizième, thirteenth
trente, thirty
    trente-deux, thirty-two
    trente-et-un, thirty-one
très, very
    très bien, very well, good
trois, three
    trois cents, three hundred
    troisième, third
trop, too
le **trou, trous** (pl.), hole(s)
trouver, to find
se **trouver (à) (dans)**, to be found (at) (in)
la **Tunisie**, Tunisia
tunisien (m.), **tunisienne** (f.), Tunisian
turc (m.), **turque** (f.), Turkish
la **Turquie**, Turkey
le **type**, type
typique, typical

un (m.), **une** (f.), a, one
l'**Union européenne**, European Union
l'**université** (f.), university
utiliser, to use

il **va** (see **aller**), he goes, is going
les **vacances** (f. pl.), holiday(s)
le **vaccin**, vaccination, inoculation
    le **vaccin anti-malaria**, anti-malaria vaccination
    le **vaccin anti-poliomyélitique**, anti-polio vaccination
    le **vaccin anti-tétanique**, anti-tetanus vaccination
vacciner, to vaccinate, inoculate
je **vais** (see **aller**), I go
la **vallée**, valley
variable, variable, changeable, unsettled
varié (m.), **variée** (f.), varied, varying
Varsovie, Warsaw
le **vélo tout terrain** (or **VTT**), mountain bike
vendredi, Friday
venir (de), to come (from)
le **vent**, wind
venu (m.), **venue** (f.), (see **venir**), came
vérifier, to check, verify

GLOSSARY

le **verre,** glass
vers, towards, to, around
vert (m.), **verte** (f.), green
le **vestiaire,** cloakroom, changing room
    le **vestiaire des équipes,** team changing room
il **veut** (see **vouloir**), he wants
je **veux** (see **vouloir**), I want
ils **viennent** (see **venir**), they come, are coming
vieux (m.), **vieille** (f.), old
le **village,** village
la **ville,** town, city
le **vin,** wine
    le **vin blanc,** white wine
    le **vin rouge,** red wine
vingt, twenty
    vingt-deux, twenty-two
    vingt-et-un, twenty-one
la **virgule,** comma
visiter, to visit
le **visiteur,** visitor
    les **visiteurs attendus,** expected number of visitors
la **vodka,** vodka
voici, here is, here are, this is, these are
la **voie,** platform
voilà, there is, there are, that is, those are
la **voile,** sailing
voir, to see
la **voiture,** car
le **vol,** flight
    le **vol régulier,** scheduled flight
le **volley(ball),** volleyball
vos (m. or f. pl.), your
votre (m. or f. sg.), your
je **voudrais** (see **vouloir**), I would like
vous **voulez** (see **vouloir**), you want
vouloir, to want
    vouloir dire, to mean
vous, you, to you, yourself
le **voyage,** journey, trip
    le **voyage d'affaires,** business trip
    le **voyage organisé,** organised trip
    le **voyage de stimulation,** incentive business trip
voyager, to travel

vous **voyez** (see **voir**), you see
vraiment, really, truly
la **vue,** sight

le **wagon-restaurant,** restaurant car
le **wagon-lit,** sleeping car
les **W.C.** (m. pl.), toilets
le **week-end,** weekend
le **whisky,** whisk(e)y

y, there
Yaoundé, Yaounde
le **yen,** yen
les **yeux,** eyes

le **zoo,** zoo

ANSWER KEYS

UNIT 1

Listening 1:

(a)
1: Chantal Dupont
2: Philippe Durand
3: Bernard Martin
4: Madame Garnier
5: Claire Arnoux
6: Paul Dupuis
7: Isabelle Hugot
8: Hervé Lancel
9: Brigitte Fournet
10: Jean-Louis Palu

(b)
Bonjour 8; bienvenue 3; quel est votre nom 4; comment vous appelez-vous 3; s'il vous plaît 9.

Listening 3:

(a)
1. P-I-C-A-R-D
2. P-A-S-Q-U-A-L-I-N-I
3. V-A-C-H-E-R
4. M-U-R-P-H-Y
5. F-I-S-C-H-E-R

(b)
Countries: Belgique, Italie, France, Irlande, Allemagne
Cities: Bruxelles, Rome, Lyon, Dublin, Berlin

Listening 5:

2 - 5 - 13 - 18 - 20 - 27 - 31 - 39 - 43 - 46

Listening 6:

1.E;   2.D;   3.A;   4.B;   5.C.

Listening 7:

1.5;   2.20;   3.17;   4.7;   5.8.

Listening 8:

1.A;   2.E;   3.B;   4.C;   5.D.

ANSWER KEYS

Exercise 1:

1. DURAND
2. PIGOT
3. BONNEL
4. LEMARCHAND
5. PARON
6. BARON

Exercise 2:

Bonjour	*Hello*
Bonsoir	*Good evening*
Bienvenue	*Welcome*
Au revoir	*Goodbye*
Être	*To be*
S'appeler	*To be called*
Venir de	*To come from*
Habiter	*To live*
Voilà	*There is*
Merci	*Thank you*
S'il vous plaît	*Please*

Exercise 3:

1. Je m'appelle André Leclerc.
   Oui, L-E-C-L-E-R-C.
   Je suis français.
   J'habite 12 rue du Figuier, Paris.
   C'est le 43 25 16 32.
   Je suis agent de voyages.

2. Je m'appelle Anne Trigano.
   Oui, T-R-I-G-A-N-O.
   Je suis française.
   J'habite 30 rue Saint Blaise, Lyon.
   C'est le 35 24 46 13.
   Je suis animatrice.

ANSWER KEYS

Exercise 4:

Receptionist	*Bonjour Madame.*
Guest	Bonjour Madame.
Receptionist	*Comment vous appelez-vous s'il vous plaît?*
Guest	Madame Martin.
Receptionist	*Quelle est votre adresse s'il vous plaît?*
Guest	18 avenue Parmentier, Paris.
Receptionist	*Quelle est votre nationalité s'il vous plaît?*
Guest	Je suis française.
Receptionist	*Merci Madame.*

UNIT 2

Listening 2:

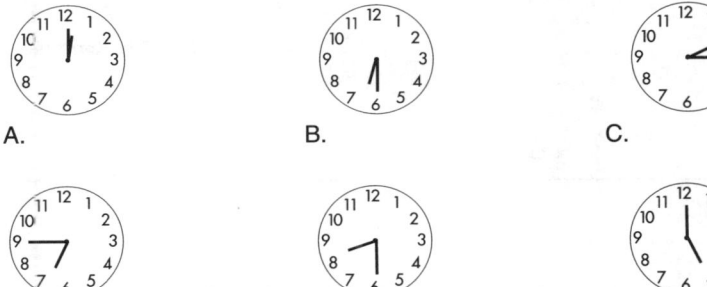

Listening 3:

A. 10h00
B. 6h00
C. 7h15
D. 6h30
E. 7h45
F. minuit

ANSWER KEYS

Listening 4:

(a) Excursion Provence-Côte d'Azur

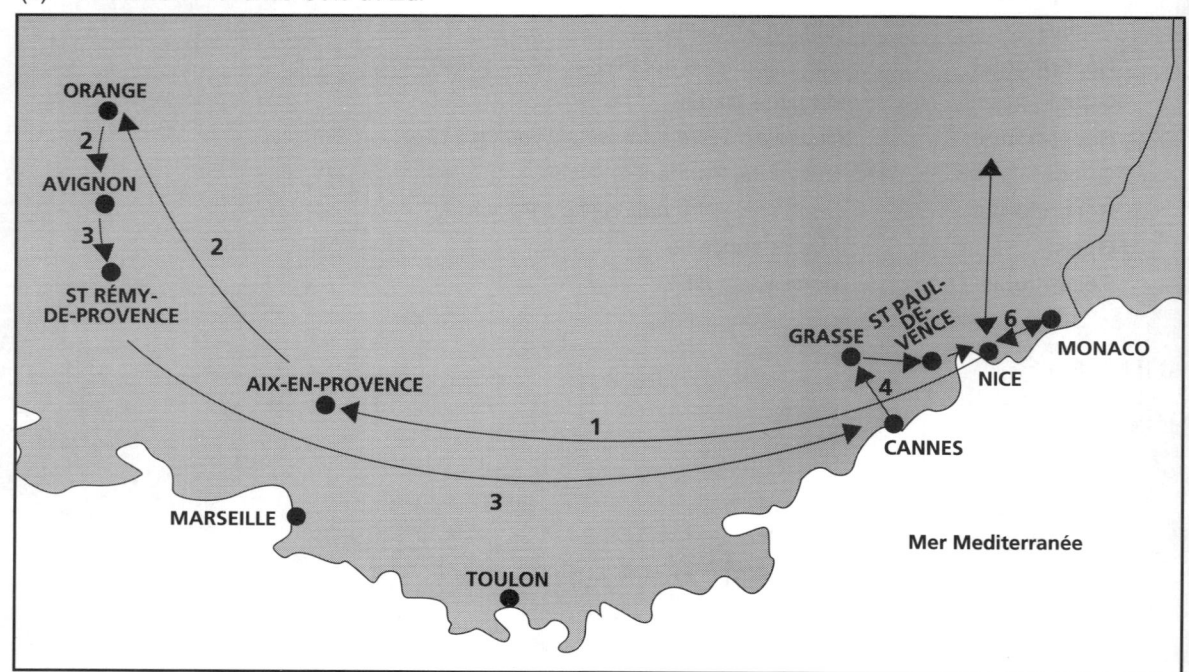

(b)

	matin	après-midi	soir
lundi	Nice	(Nice)	(Nice)
mardi	Aix-en-Provence	(Aix)	(Aix)
mercredi	Orange	Avignon	(Avignon)
jeudi	St Rémy	(St Rémy)	Cannes
vendredi	Grasse	St Paul	Nice
samedi	(Nice)	(Nice)	(Nice)
dimanche	Monaco	(Monaco)	Nice

ANSWER KEYS

Listening 5:

1. f;   2. l;   3. e;   4. b;   5. k;   6. i;
7. h;   8. c;   9. a;   10. j;   11. d;   12. g.

Listening 6:

1. **Banque**
- Ouverte de 9h30 à 12h45 / Open from to
- et de 14h à 17h30 / and from to
- Fermée le samedi et dimanche / Closed

2. **Poste**
- Ouverte de 8h à 18h00 / Open from to
- Fermée le samedi après-midi et dimanche / Closed

3. **Château**
- Ouvert de 10h à 19h / Open from to
- Fermé le lundi / Closed

4. **Musée**
- Ouvert de 9h30 à 18h30 / Open from to
- Fermé le mardi / Closed

Listening 8:

1. $300   2. £150   3. DM270
4. SF 1000   5. ¥3890   6. BF5630

Listening 9:

(a)
a. 98,00F   b. 177,00F   c. 102,00F
d. 245,00F   e. 8,00F   f. 126,00F

ANSWER KEYS

(b)

	whisky / whiskey	chocolats / chocolates	vodka / vodka	parfum / perfume	cigarettes / cigarettes	champagne / champagne
en espèces / in cash	✓		✓			
par chèque / by cheque					✓	✓
par carte de crédit / by credit card		✓		✓		

Exercise 1:

Mots trouvés dans la grille :
- AVRIL
- DECEMBRE
- JUILLET
- LUNDI
- JUIN
- FEVRIER
- VENDREDI
- MARDI
- SAMEDI
- DIMANCHE
- OCTOBRE
- MARS
- NOVEMBRE
- JANVIER
- AOUT
- MERCREDI
- JEUDI
- SEPTEMBRE

212

ANSWER KEYS

Exercise 2:

(a) 1. Le musée national est ouvert de dix heures à dix-sept heures. Il est fermé le mardi.
2. L'Hôtel International est ouvert de mars à novembre. Il est fermé en décembre, janvier, février.
3. La banque est ouverte de neuf heures à douze heures trente et de quatorze heures à dix-sept heures trente. Elle est fermée le samedi.
4. Le jardin botanique est ouvert de dix heures à dix-huit heures. Il est fermé en décembre.

(b) 1. Le jardin botanique ouvre à 10h.
2. Oui, le musée est ouvert le lundi.
3. La banque ferme à 17h30.
4. Non, la banque est fermée à 13h. Elle est fermée de 12h30 à 14h.
5. Non, l'Hôtel International est fermé en janvier.
6. Le musée ouvre à 10h.
7. Non, la banque est fermée le samedi.
8. Non, le musée est fermé le mardi.
9. Le jardin ferme à 18h.
10. Non, le jardin est fermé en décembre.

Exercise 3:

a. Ça coûte deux cents francs.
b. Ça coûte trois cent cinquante francs.
c. Ça coûte quarante-cinq francs.
d. Ça coûte quinze francs.
e. Ça coûte cent trente francs.
f. Ça coûte sept cent vingt-cinq francs.
g. Ça coûte vingt-trois francs.
h. Ça coûte soixante-treize francs.

Exercise 4:

Visitor	Bonjour
Assistant	*Bonjour, Monsieur. Je peux vous aider?*
Visitor	Est-ce que le musée est ouvert aujourd'hui, s'il vous plaît?
Assistant	*Non, je suis désolé, le musée est fermé aujourd'hui.*
Visitor	Il est ouvert quand?
Assistant	*Il est ouvert du mardi au dimanche de dix heures à dix-sept heures.*
Visitor	Avez-vous un guide pour le musée?
Assistant	*Oui, Monsieur. Ça coûte deux livres.*
Visitor	Je vais en prendre un. Voilà.
Assistant	*Merci bien, Monsieur.*
Visitor	Merci bien.
Assistant	*Au revoir, Monsieur.*

ANSWER KEYS

UNIT 3

Listening 1:

(b)

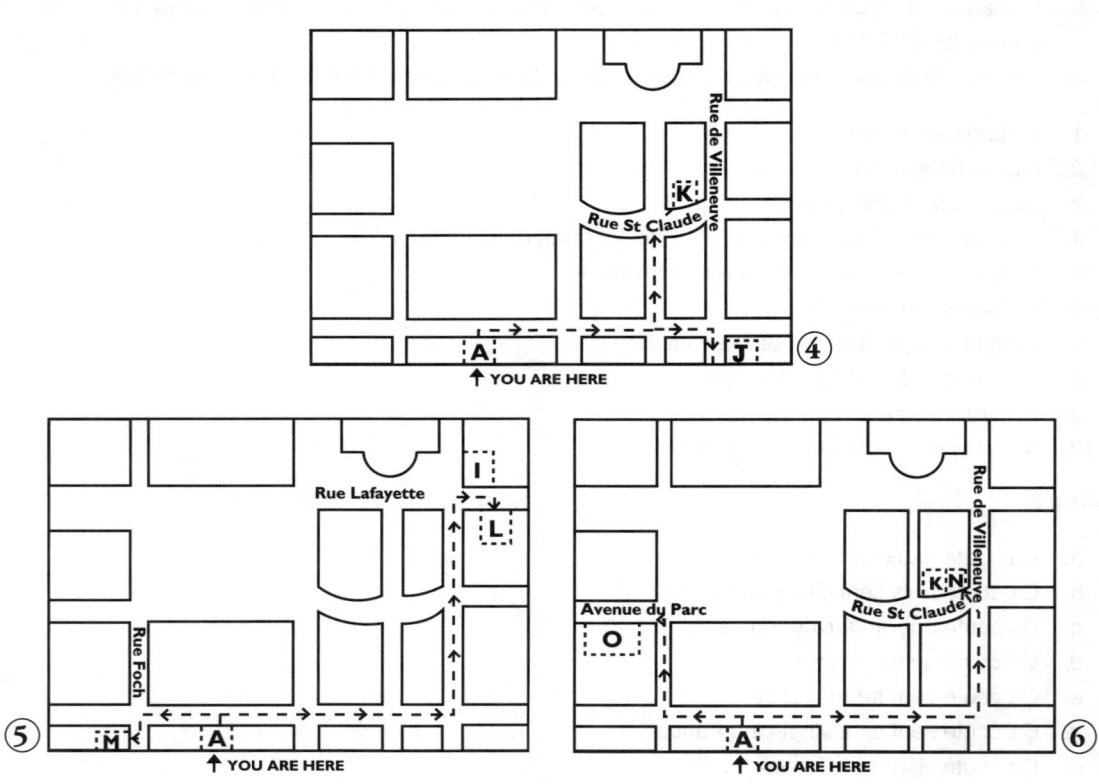

Listening 2:

les toilettes: 2;   la cafétéria: 8;   le vestiaire: 1;
la boutique: 3;   les escaliers: 4;   les ascenseurs: 6;
le restaurant: 7;   la librairie: 5.

ANSWER KEYS

Listening 3:

	À pied	Métro	Autobus/Bus	Train	Taxi	Voiture/Auto
Notre-Dame	✓					
La Sorbonne	✓	✓	✓			
Le Sacré-Coeur		✓	✓		✓	
La Tour Eiffel		✓	✓			
Les Champs-Élysées		✓	✓		✓	
Le Château de Versailles				✓		✓

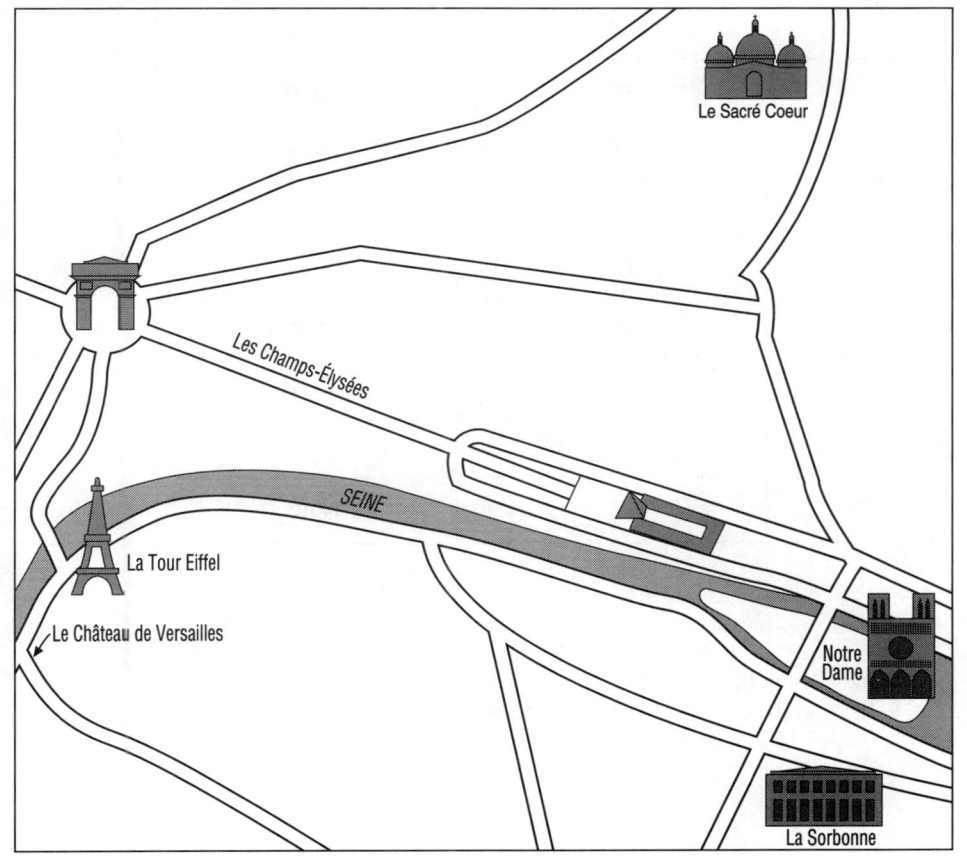

ANSWER KEYS

Listening 4:

	Distance: km	Direction
Châteaux:		
Chenonceaux (example)	30	Est
Montrichard	40	Est
Villandry	13	Sud
Ussé	42	Ouest
Chinon	60	Ouest
Villes/Towns:		
Angers	100	Ouest
Le Mans	65	Nord-est
Poitiers	70	Sud
Camping/Campsite:		
Municipal	7	Nord

Listening 5:

1. c;   2. e;   3. a;   4. b;   5. d;   6. f;
7. j;   8. g;   9. h;   10. i;   11. k;   12. n;
13. l;   14. m.

ANSWER KEYS

Listening 6:

(b)

 1.    2.    3.

 4.    5.   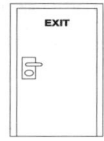 6.

Exercise 1:

1. La banque est rue Leclerc. Prenez à droite en sortant et à gauche sur la place de la Libération. Allez tout droit jusqu'à la rue Leclerc. La banque est sur votre droite.
2. Le cinéma est rue de Villeneuve. En sortant tournez à gauche. Prenez la première rue à droite, c'est la rue de Villeneuve. Allez tout droit jusqu'au cinéma. Le cinéma est sur votre gauche.
3. L'église est rue St Claude. En sortant de la gare, prenez juste en face - l'église est dans la première rue à gauche.
4. La pharmacie est sur la place de la Libération. Tournez à droite en sortant. Allez jusqu'à la place. La pharmacie est sur votre gauche, après l'hôtel.
5. La piscine est juste à côté de la gare. Prenez à gauche en sortant.

Exercise 2:

(a) 1. la poste;   2. la boulangerie;   3. le restaurant;   4. la banque;   5. le café.

(b)
1. Le restaurant est à côté du cinéma.
2. Le supermarché est à droite de la boulangerie.
3. La pharmacie est à gauche de la boulangerie.
4. L'église est à côté du café, à gauche.
5. La poste est à côté du café, à droite.

Exercise 3:

1. Il y a des toilettes à gauche près de l'entrée.
   Il y a aussi des toilettes au premier et au deuxième étages.
2. La boutique est à gauche, à côté des escaliers.
3. Les ascenseurs sont au fond.
4. La cafétéria est au deuxième étage.

ANSWER KEYS

Exercise 4:

1. Bruxelles est à neuf cent quatre-vingt-dix (990) kilomètres.
2. Amsterdam est à mille deux cents (1200) kilomètres.
3. Paris est à sept cents (700) kilomètres.
4. Marseille est à quatre cent quatre-vingts (480) kilomètres.
5. Grenoble est à cent soixante (160) kilomètres.
6. Genève est à cent quarante-cinq (145) kilomètres.
7. Lyon est à deux cent trente-cinq (235) kilomètres.
8. Turin est à cent quatre-vingts (180) kilomètres.

Exercise 5:

1. Ça veut dire 'Interdit de fumer'.
2. Ça veut dire 'Toilettes dames'.
3. Ça veut dire 'Vestiaire'.
4. Ça veut dire 'Sortie de Secours'.

Exercise 6:

Visitor	Bonjour.
Attendant	*Bonjour, Monsieur. Est-ce que je peux vous aider?*
Visitor	Est-ce qu'il y a une piscine dans le centre?
Attendant	*Oui, Monsieur. La piscine est ouverte toute la journée.*
Visitor	Où est-elle?
Attendant	*Vous allez jusqu'au bout du couloir et vous tournez à droite.*
Visitor	Est-ce qu'il faut un bonnet de bain?
Attendant	*Oui, il faut un bonnet de bain. Les douches sont à côté des cabines.*
Visitor	Où sont les cabines, s'il vous plaît?
Attendant	*Les cabines hommes sont à gauche de la piscine.*
Visitor	Merci beaucoup.
Attendant	*Au revoir, Monsieur.*

ANSWER KEYS

UNIT 4

Listening 1:

1. b, d, a, c.
2. c, a, e, b, d.
3. b, c, a.
4. b, d, c, a.

Listening 2:

1.
Hôtel Norotel

Call for: Mademoiselle Robinat
Room number: 25

2.
Hôtel Bonsaï

Call for: Madame Dupré
Room number: 212

3.
Hôtel Neptune

Call for: Monsieur Parillon
Room number: 315

4.
Hôtel de la Poste

Call for: Madame Lacoste
Room number: 12

Listening 3:

(a)
1. b;   2. c;   3. c;   4. b;   5. Lafont;   6. 33 45 58 91;   7. because the line is very bad.

(b)

Fiche Téléphonique
Telephone Message

Pour: *Michelle*
To:

De: *Monsieur Lafont*
From:

Téléphone: 33 45 58 91
Telephone:

a téléphoné / phoned	✓	prière de rappeler / please call back	✓
rappellera / will phone back			

219

ANSWER KEYS

Listening 4:

(a)
1. b;
2. d;
3. a;
4. c.

(b)

Salon Trade Fair	De From	Pour To	Contact établi Contact made	Message Message
Tourisme	–	poste 32	non	non
Automobile	M. Vacher	Mme Ricard	oui	non
Meuble	–	poste 21	non	rappellera
Informatique	M. Dufour	M. Martin	non	oui 43 55 75 80

Exercise 1:

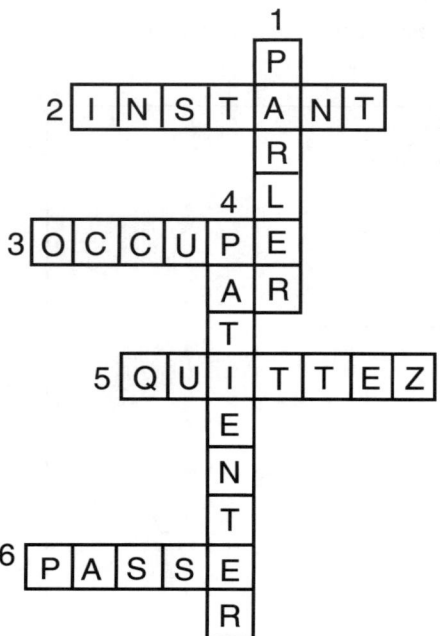

ANSWER KEYS

Exercise 2:

Model answer only

1. Je voudrais parler à Monsieur Durand.
   Un instant, je vous le passe.
2. Monsieur Lemarchand, s'il vous plaît.
   Un instant, je vous le passe.
3. Le poste 197, s'il vous plaît.
   Un instant, je vous le passe.
4. Pourrais-je parler à Madame Legris?
   Ne quittez pas, je vous la passe.
5. Madame Caron, s'il vous plaît.
   Ne quittez pas, je vous la passe.
6. La chambre 215, s'il vous plaît.
   Ne quittez pas, je vous la passe.

Exercise 3:

3 - 8 - 1 - 4 - 6 - 2 - 5 - 7.

Exercise 4:

Model answer only

Caller	Allô, Boomerang Voyages?	
Operator	*Oui, Boomerang Voyages, bonjour!*	
Caller	Bonjour, j'aimerais avoir des informations sur les voyages organisés sur la Côte d'Azur, s'il vous plaît.	
Operator	*Je ne comprends pas, vous pouvez répéter plus lentement, s'il vous plaît?*	
Caller	Oui, je voudrais des informations sur les voyages organisés sur la Côte d'Azur.	
Operator	*Je regrette, je ne comprends pas.*	
Caller	Je pourrais parler au directeur, s'il vous plaît?	
Operator	*Oui, ne quittez pas... Ça ne répond pas, vous voulez laisser un message?*	
Caller	Oui, dites-lui de me rappeler.	
Operator	*Oui, quel est votre nom, s'il vous plaît?*	
Caller	Je m'appelle Monsieur Durand.	
Operator	*Et votre numéro de téléphone?*	
Caller	C'est le 43 25 32 56.	
Operator	*Merci Monsieur Durand, au revoir.*	
Caller	Au revoir.	

ANSWER KEYS

TEST YOUR COMPETENCE 1

Exercise 1:

1. DURAND;   2. PETEL;   3. DELORS;   4. QUEDEC;   5. FOURNET.

Exercise 2:

1. 82   2. 98   3. 147
4. 297   5. 495   6. 570

Exercise 3:

Guest	Room Number	Call Time
1	55	6h30
2	213	7h45
3	21	5h45
4	315	7h15

Exercise 4:

1. 7h30 - 9h30   2. 11h00   3. 12h00 - 16h30
4. 12h30 - 14h30   5. 2 heures du matin 6. 23h30

Exercise 5:

(a) 1. cent soixante francs (160F)
    2. deux cent dix-huit francs (218F)
    3. trois cent soixante-dix francs (370F)
    4. quatre cent quatre-vingts francs (480F)
    5. quatre cent cinquante francs (450F)
    6. quatre cent quarante francs (440F)

(b) 1. Le weekend   à Luxembourg coûte mille quatre cent quatre-vingt-cinq francs (1485F).
    2. ....   à Amsterdam coûte mille six cent quatre-vingt-quinze francs (1695F).
    3. ....   à Vienne coûte mille sept cent soixante-quinze francs (1775F).
    4. ....   à Rome coûte deux mille trois cent quinze francs (2315F).
    5. ....   à Budapest coûte deux mille huit cent dix francs (2810F).
    6. ....   à Genève coûte mille cent quatre-vingt-deux francs (1182F).

ANSWER KEYS

Exercise 6:

1. The Carnot Museum = Q
2. The Opera House = P
3. The Post Office = N

Exercise 7:

1. Pardon, Madame, pouvez-vous me dire où est la banque?
   Tournez à gauche en sortant, puis tournez à droite. La banque est un peu plus loin sur votre droite, Monsieur.
2. Pardon, Madame, pouvez-vous me dire où se trouve le casino?
   Tournez à droite en sortant, puis tournez à gauche, puis prenez la deuxième rue à droite. Le casino est sur votre droite, Monsieur.
3. Pardon, Madame, où se trouve le bureau de poste?
   Prenez la rue en face en sortant, puis prenez la première rue à gauche. Le bureau de poste est tout de suite sur votre droite, Monsieur.
4. Excusez-moi, Madame, où se trouve le stade?
   Tournez à droite en sortant, puis tournez à gauche, puis prenez la deuxième rue à droite, et ensuite la rue à gauche. Le stade est sur votre gauche, Monsieur.
5. Excusez-moi, Madame, pouvez-vous me dire où se trouve le centre commercial?
   Tournez à gauche en sortant, puis tournez à droite, puis prenez la première rue à gauche. Le centre commercial est sur votre gauche, Monsieur.
6. Pardon, Madame, la mairie, c'est où?
   Prenez la rue en face en sortant, puis prenez la première rue à droite. La mairie est sur votre droite, Monsieur.
7. Pardon, Madame, où est l'église?
   Tournez à droite en sortant, puis tournez à gauche, puis prenez la première rue à droite. L'église est sur votre gauche, Monsieur.
8. Excusez-moi, Madame, je cherche le commissariat de police.
   Tournez à gauche en sortant, puis tournez à droite, puis prenez la première rue à gauche. Le commissariat de police est sur votre droite, Monsieur.

Exercise 8:

1. Lift
2. Squash court
3. Ladies' Cloakroom
4. Meeting room
5. Showers
6. Viewing gallery

ANSWER KEYS

Exercise 9:

1. f;   2. d;   3. a;   4. e;   5. c;   6. b.

Exercise 10:

	Date	Départ	Arrivée	Tarif en francs (aller-retour)
1. Paris-Londres	11 octobre (11/10)	7h40	7h50	920F
2. Paris-Luxembourg	9 juin (9/6)	17h10	18h10	860F
3. Paris-Venise	8 septembre (8/9)	10h10	11h50	2350F
4. Paris-Nice	13 avril (13/4)	18h05	19h35	770F

Exercise 11:

1. Vous prenez la rue en face jusqu'à la place au Blé. Ensuite, vous prenez la rue à gauche, rue de la Jarretière, jusqu'au bout. Vous arrivez derrière la cathédrale.
2. En sortant de la cathédrale vous prenez la rue à droite, elle s'appelle rue de la Rovère, jusqu'à la place de la Préfecture. Ensuite, vous prenez la deuxième rue à droite, la rue de la Liberté et tournez à gauche. Le musée est juste là, au coin de la rue.
3. En sortant du musée, vous prenez à droite, la rue de la Liberté, jusqu'à la place de la Préfecture. Ensuite, vous prenez la rue en face à droite, c'est la rue Notre-Dame; puis la première rue à gauche, la rue Monestier. La fontaine est juste là à droite.
4. Pour le pont Notre-Dame, vous prenez la rue à droite de la fontaine, la rue Notre-Dame, jusqu'à une place, ensuite vous prenez la rue en face à droite, c'est la rue des Bains. Vous allez jusqu'au boulevard et vous tournez à droite, le pont Notre-Dame est un peu plus loin à gauche.
5. Pour l'hôtel de ville, vous prenez le boulevard Lucien Arnault sur la gauche, en direction de Langogne. Vous allez tout droit jusqu'à la place d'Angiran. L'hôtel de ville est là, en face.
6. Pour le camping, vous prenez le boulevard Britexte à droite de l'hôtel de ville, en direction de Langogne.

ANSWER KEYS

UNIT 5

Listening 1:

Le château, la piscine, l'étang, le golf, le club de squash, le tennis, l'église, le musée, le centre équestre.

Listening 2:

1. La Camargue: 35 km
   Arles: 40 km
   Aix-en-Provence: 40 km
   Marseille: 50 km

2. Aux Deux Toques
   Lou Camargue

3. A map

4. No

Listening 3:

(a) 1. b;   2. c;   3. d;   4. a.

(b)

	jours d'ouverture opening days	heures d'ouverture opening hours
Église	tous les jours every day	jusqu'à 20h00 to 8.00 p.m.
Musée	tous les jours sauf mardi every day except Tuesday	jusqu'à 19h00 samedi à midi to 7.00 p.m. Saturday to noon
Château	tous les jours sauf mardi every day except Tuesday	14h00-19h00 2.00 p.m.- 7.00 p.m.
Site archéologique	tous les jours sauf mardi every day except Tuesday	9h00-19h00 9.00 a.m. - 7.00 p.m.

ANSWER KEYS

Listening 4:

(a) Cristal, chocolats, bijoux, cardigans, cigares.

(b) 1. False; 2. True; 3. False; 4. False; 5. True.

Listening 5:

(a)

Fiche de réservation	
Hôtel:	Le Hérel, Granville
Nombre de personnes:	2
Nombre de nuits:	1
Type de chambre:	Double avec salle de bains
Nom du client:	Madame Justal

(b) 1. c; 2. No; 3. **; 4. Breakfast.

Listening 6:

(a) 1. False; 2. True; 3. False; 4. True; 5. True; 6. False.

(b)

Name of customer:	Monsieur Eymard
Date for booking:	Friday 25 June
Amount paid:	1,187.50 francs
Method of payment:	Cheque

Exercise 1:

(a) 1.d; 2.e; 3.b; 4.c; 5.a.

ANSWER KEYS

(b)

free (example)	gratuit
every day	tous les jours
a brochure	une brochure
a street map/floor plan	un plan
a bedroom	une chambre
very beautiful	très belle
a discount	une réduction
a map	une carte
with bath	avec salle de bains
identification	une pièce d'identité
a leaflet	un dépliant
a show	un spectacle

Exercise 2:

1. L´église est de style roman.
2. Le château est impressionnant.
3. Les chambres sont confortables.
4. Le restaurant est bien situé.
5. Le foulard est en coton.

Exercise 3:

Il y a un centre équestre.
Il y a un tennis.
Il y a un golf.
Il y a une plage.
Il y a une rivière.
Il y a des jeux pour enfants.
Il y a un bar.
Il y a un restaurant.
Il y a des machines à laver.

ANSWER KEYS

Exercise 4:

L'hôtel du Bon Vieux Temps est un hôtel deux étoiles. Il y a un restaurant, un parking et le téléphone et la télévision dans les chambres. Les chambres coûtent 112F et 197F. Les animaux sont admis. L'hôtel est ouvert toute l'année.

Exercise 5:

Visitor	Bonjour.	
TI Officer	*Bonjour, je peux vous aider?*	
Visitor	Vous avez un plan de la ville, s'il vous plaît?	
TI Officer	*Oui, voilà, c'est gratuit.*	
Visitor	Merci, je suis ici pour trois jours. Qu'est-ce qu'il y a à faire d'intéressant?	
TI Officer	*Il y a une visite de la ville tous les matins à 10h00. Il y a aussi des excursions au monastère de Glendalough et à la ville médiévale de Kilkenny.*	
Visitor	Oui, combien coûte l'excursion à Glendalough?	
TI Officer	*L'excursion à Glendalough coûte onze livres. Vous voulez faire une réservation?*	
Visitor	Oui, j'aimerais deux billets, s'il vous plaît.	
TI Officer	*Oui, deux billets, ça fait vingt-deux livres. Quand voulez-vous faire l'excursion?*	
Visitor	Demain, si c'est possible.	
TI Officer	*Oui, voilà les billets Monsieur. Bonne journée.*	

ANSWER KEYS

UNIT 6

Listening 1:

(a)

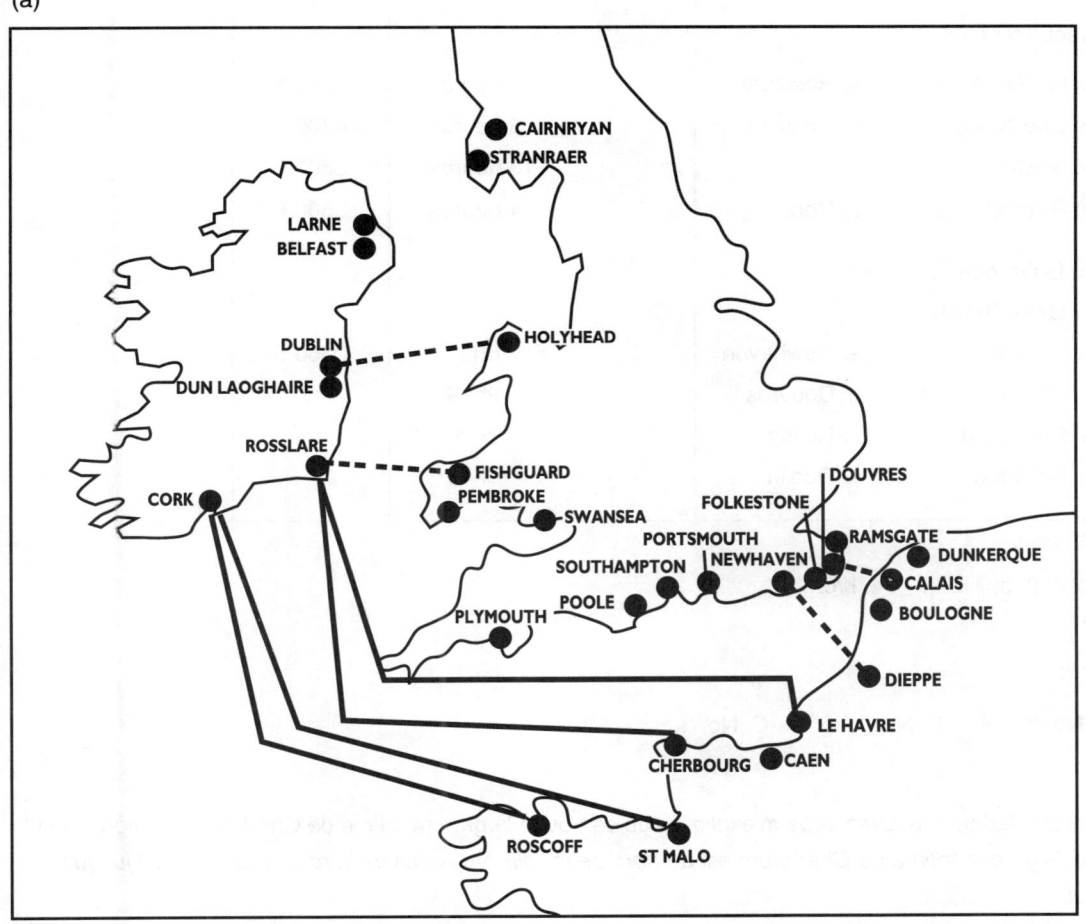

ANSWER KEYS

(b)

Trajets Routes		Durée de la traversée Duration of crossing	Prix Price
Direct/direct			
1. de: Le Havre	à: Rosslare	21 heures	4700 F
2. de: Cherbourg	à: Rosslare	18 heures	4700 F
3. de: St Malo	à: Cork	18 heures	3500 F
4. de: Roscoff	à: Cork	14 heures	3500 F
Par la Grande Bretagne Via Great Britain			
1. de: Dieppe	à: Newhaven	6h	2350 F
2. de: Calais	à: Douvres	2h15	
3. de: Fishguard	à: Rosslare	3h30	
4. de: Holyhead	à: Dublin	1h45	

(c) 1. b; 2. b; 3. a; 4. b/c.

Listening 2:

(a) A: No. 2; B: No. 1; C: No. 3.

(b)

1. Pardon Madame, pouvez-vous m'expliquer où se trouve la gare maritime de Cherbourg, s'il vous plaît?
    Oui, la gare maritime de Cherbourg est au nord de la ville. Vous suivez la route nationale 13 jusqu'au bout.
    Merci Madame.
    Je vous en prie.
2. Pardon, Madame, où se trouve la gare routière de Nice?
    La gare routière se trouve dans le centre, juste à côté de la place Masséna.
    D'accord. Et la gare SNCF?
    La gare SNCF est dans un autre quartier. Toujours à partir de la place Masséna, vous prenez l'avenue Jean Médecin vers le nord, et continuez tout droit jusqu'à la gare. Celle-ci est sur le côté gauche de l'avenue.
    Merci bien.
    Je vous en prie.

ANSWER KEYS

3. Pardon, le plus simple pour aller à l'aéroport Charles-de-Gaulle à partir du centre de Paris, s'il vous plaît?
   Le plus simple pour aller à l'aéroport Roissy-Charles-de-Gaulle est de prendre le RER ligne B. Ça s'appelle ROISSY-RAIL. Ça prend seulement 35 minutes. En arrivant à la station de RER de l'aéroport, vous prenez une navette qui vous conduit à l'aérogare 1 ou 2.

Listening 3:

De Paris à:	en car/by coach durée/duration	en train/by train durée/duration	en avion/by plane durée/duration
1. Rome	24h	15h	2h
2. Londres	8h	5h40	1h
3. Amsterdam	8h	6h	1h

Listening 4:

(a) 1. 22h22 - 14h44 : aller;   19h10 - 10h07 : retour
    2. 08h20 - 08h30 : aller;   18h45 - 20h50 : retour
    3. 22h30 - 07h00 : aller;   22h30 - 07h00 : retour

(b)
1.

SNCF		Billet		Classe: 2	
ALLER		Heures	RETOUR		Heures
Départ: PARIS – Gare-de-Lyon		22h22	Départ: ROMA - Termini		19h10
Arrivée: ROMA - Termini		14h44	Arrivée: PARIS–Gare-de-Lyon		10h07
Date: 23/6			Date: 17/7		
Réservation couchettes:		Aller	No. 22		PRIX
		Retour	No. 56		1440,00 F

ANSWER KEYS

2.

AIR FRANCE				
Nom:	VIOLET			
Prénom:	Catherine			
		Dates	Heures	
			Départ	Arrivée
De:	PARIS - Charles-de-Gaulle	27/05	08.20	08.30
À:	LONDRES Heathrow	30/05	18.45	20.50
À:	PARIS - Charles-de-Gaulle			
TARIF:	980,00 F			

3.

EUROCARS			
Nom:	VERDIER		
Prénom:	Jean-Paul		
		Aller	Retour
		Heures	
De:	PARIS-Charenton	22.30	07.00
À:	AMSTERDAM	07.00	22.30
		Dates:	
		24/10 - 27/10	
Prix:	320,00 F		

Listening 5:

(b)

1. b;   2. False;   3. a, b, c.   4. lunch
5. No; 6. c;   7. True;   8. c.

ANSWER KEYS

Listening 6:

```
                    NOUVELLES FRONTIÈRES
                    FICHE D'INSCRIPTION
```

Voyage
Destination: TUNISIE
Ville de départ: PARIS
Date de départ: 17 AVRIL   **Date de retour:** 24 avril

Circuit: DECOUVERTE DE LA TUNISIE

Participants

Nom	Prénom	Date de Naissance	Nationalité	Profession
BONNEL	Anne	26 juin 1950	Française	Dentiste
BONNEL	Paul	2 octobre 1952	Français	Professeur

Adresse: 34 Place de la République, Paris
Téléphone domicile: 45 42 43 06
Téléphone travail: 48 56 72 25
Montant à payer: 8160 F

☐ par chèque   ✓ par carte de crédit   ☐ en espèces

Exercise 1:

(a)

1. *Vous pouvez aller en Norvège en train ou en avion.*
   Et en voiture, c'est aussi possible?
   Oui, c'est possible. Et même en bateau si vous préférez.
2. *Vous préférez visiter la vallée de la Loire en autocar ou en voiture de location?*
   Non, je préfère visiter à bicyclette, à pied ou à cheval.
   Alors, bon voyage!

ANSWER KEYS

(b)
1. Vous allez en Espagne en avion?
   Non, en train.
2. Vous visitez la région en voiture?
   Non, en autocar.
3. Vous préférez voyager en voiture?
   Non, à bicyclette ou à pied.
4. Vous allez en Afrique en bateau?
   Non, en avion.

Exercise 2:

(a)
1. en Suisse   2. en Russie   3. au Portugal   4. au Cameroun   5. en Chine

(b)
1. à Genève, en Suisse?
2. à Copenhague, au Danemark?
3. à Athènes, en Grèce?
4. à Varsovie, en Pologne?
5. à Florence, en Italie?
6. à Yaoundé, au Cameroun?

Exercise 4:

1. a. golf   b. one week   c. half-board
   d. yes   e. high season - double room with bath and tv

2. a. By hired car
   b. Yes - 4
   c. Yes
   d. High season and only 2 people sharing car and hotel

3. a. 80
   b. Montpellier
   c. Swimming (beaches and swimming pool), fitness, tennis.
   d. Breakfast
   e. One meal

ANSWER KEYS

Exercise 5:

Visitor	Bonjour	
Assistant	*Bonjour, Madame. Je peux vous aider?*	
Visitor	Je voudrais aller à Paris le 18 (dix-huit) décembre, s'il vous plaît.	
Assistant	*Vous voulez voyager en train, en avion ou en car?*	
Visitor	Je ne sais pas. Quels sont les prix d'un aller-retour en train, en avion et en car, s'il vous plaît?	
Assistant	*En train, ça coûte £132 (cent trente-deux livres), en avion £215 (deux cent quinze livres) et en car £106 (cent six livres).*	
Visitor	Combien de temps dure le voyage en train, en avion, en car?	
Assistant	*En train, ça dure 19h (dix-neuf heures), en avion 1h30 (une heure trente) et en car 23h (vingt-trois heures).*	
Visitor	Est-ce qu'il y a un vol le 18 décembre?	
Assistant	*Oui, il y a des vols tous les jours.*	
Visitor	Quelle est l'heure de départ et l'heure d'arrivée?	
Assistant	*L'avion part à 13h14 (treize heures quatorze) et il arrive à Paris à 14h42 (quatorze heures quarante-deux).*	
Visitor	Où se trouve l'aéroport?	
Assistant	*L'aéroport est à 5 km au nord de la ville. Il y a un car spécial aéroport qui part de la gare routière. La gare routière est située en face de l'église Sainte Marie. Cela coûte £5.35 (cinq livres trente-cinq).*	
Visitor	Je voudrais réserver un aller-retour en avion pour le 18 décembre.	
Assistant	*À quel nom, s'il vous plaît?*	
Visitor	Isabelle Leclerc, L-E-C-L-E-R-C.	

ANSWER KEYS

UNIT 7

Listening 1:

(a) : Piscine découverte, voile, tennis, parcours de golf, tir à l'arc, musculation, mise en forme, planche à voile, arts appliqués.

(b) : 1. False;   2. False;   3. True;   4. True;   5. True;   6. False.

Listening 2:

1. Le bonnet de bain est obligatoire.
2. Les enfants de moins de 15 ans ne sont pas admis.
3. Le sauna et le jacuzzi sont interdits aux enfants.
4. Il faut réserver.
5. Il est interdit de fumer dans le club.

Listening 3:

(a) Matin: canoë-kayak.
    Après-midi: randonnée à vélo.
    22h30:   soirée de danses irlandaises.

(b) 1. planche à voile   2. canoë-kayak
    3. plongée sous-marine   4. randonnée à pied
    5. randonnée à vélo   6. golf
    7. danses irlandaises

Listening 4:

(a) 1. d/e;   2. c;   3. a/c;   4. f;   5. b;   6. b/c;   7. b/c;   8. b.

(b) 1. yes;   2. yes;   3. yes;   4. no;   5. yes;   6. yes;   7. no.

Listening 5:

   1. b;   2. c;   3. b;   4. b;   5. b;   6. a/c.

Listening 6:

(a) A. 3;   B. 5;   C. 2;   D. 1;   E. 6;   F. 4.

ANSWER KEYS

(b) 1. e;   2. a;   3. f;   4. c;   5. b;   6. d.

Exercise 1:

a. voile
   planche à voile
   plongée libre
   canoë-kayak
   tennis
   basketball
   parcours de golf
   tir à l'arc
   musculation

b. planche à voile
   voile
   ski nautique
   plongée libre
   plongée avec bouteille
   tennis

Exercise 2:

1. *Vous pouvez faire du ski nautique.*
2. *Vous pouvez faire de la plongée libre.*
3. *Vous pouvez faire du vélo tout terrain.*
4. *Vous pouvez faire de l'escalade.*
5. *Vous pouvez faire de la planche à voile.*
6. *Vous pouvez faire du canoë-kayak.*
7. *Vous pouvez jouer au tennis.*
8. *Vous pouvez jouer au golf.*
9. *Vous pouvez jouer au squash.*
10. *Vous pouvez jouer au football.*

Exercise 3:

1. Club des 4 vents.
2. Cycling, horse riding, social and cultural activities.
3. Westport.

ANSWER KEYS

4. Golf, tennis, canoeing, cycling, caravanning, fishing, horse riding, painting.
5. Guesthouse.
6. No.
7. No, summer only.
8. Cycling, walking, sea-kayaking, surfing.

Exercise 4:

Model answer

Bonjour et bienvenue au centre de Delphi. Ici vous pouvez pratiquer un grand nombre de sports.
Vous pouvez faire de l'escalade, du tir à l'arc, du VTT ou du vélo, vous pouvez aussi faire des randonnées à cheval. Pour les sports nautiques, vous pouvez pratiquer le surfing, la planche à voile, le rafting, le canoë-kayak, le ski nautique.
Dans la région, vous pouvez faire du golf.

Exercise 5:

Model answers

Bonjour.
Bonjour, je peux vous aider?
Quelles sont les activités auxquelles je peux participer ce matin?
Vous pouvez aller à la piscine couverte, faire de l'aérobic ou de la planche à voile.
Le bonnet de bain est obligatoire dans la piscine?
Oui, mais vous pouvez en louer un à la piscine.
Et cet après-midi, qu'est-ce que vous me conseillez?
Cet après-midi, il y a une randonnée VTT organisée, ou vous pouvez faire du cheval ou du tir à l'arc.
Il faut réserver pour la randonnée VTT?
Oui, il faut réserver.
Et ce soir, quel est le programme?
Il y a un spectacle son et lumière organisé à 22h00 mais il faut réserver les billets avant 16h00.
Les billets coûtent combien pour le spectacle?
Les billets coûtent £8.
D'accord. Au fait, ma femme a très mal à la tête. Est-ce que vous avez quelque chose?
Oui, voilà de l'aspirine.
Merci beaucoup.
Je vous en prie, au revoir et bonne journée.

ANSWER KEYS

UNIT 8

Listening 1:

(a) 1. a;   2. b;   3. b;   4. c;   5. b.

(b)

> Bonjour, Madame, pouvez-vous nous dire quelles sont les visites intéressantes dans les environs, s'il vous plaît?
> *Oui, bien sûr. Vous êtes en voiture?*
> Oui, et nous sommes dans la région pour trois jours.
> *D'accord. Et avez-vous une carte de la région?*
> Oui, la voici.
> *Bon, alors il y a beaucoup de choses à voir dans les environs. Vous voyez, vous avez plusieurs circuits possibles. Vous pouvez par exemple faire un circuit entre Cahors et Figeac, c'est un circuit très agréable d'une journée. Il fait environ 50 (cinquante) kilomètres.*
> *Vous pouvez aussi aller à Rocamadour, c'est à seulement 30 (trente) kilomètres au nord de Cahors. En deux jours, vous pouvez faire un circuit très varié avec des châteaux, des villages pittoresques et bien sûr, vous avez la visite des grottes à ne pas manquer. Ce circuit au départ de Rocamadour fait environ 65 (soixante-cinq) kilomètres.*
> Ces grottes sont importantes?
> *Oui, ce sont les grottes de Padirac. Elles sont immenses; la visite se fait en bateau et dure deux heures.*
> Ça a l'air intéressant. Vous pouvez nous décrire les differents circuits, s'il vous plaît?

Listening 2:

(a) Château: 5 times; village: 6 times; église: twice; grottes: 3 times; gorges: once; panorama: 3 times; station thermale: once; marché: once; baignade: once; pêche: once.

ANSWER KEYS

(b)

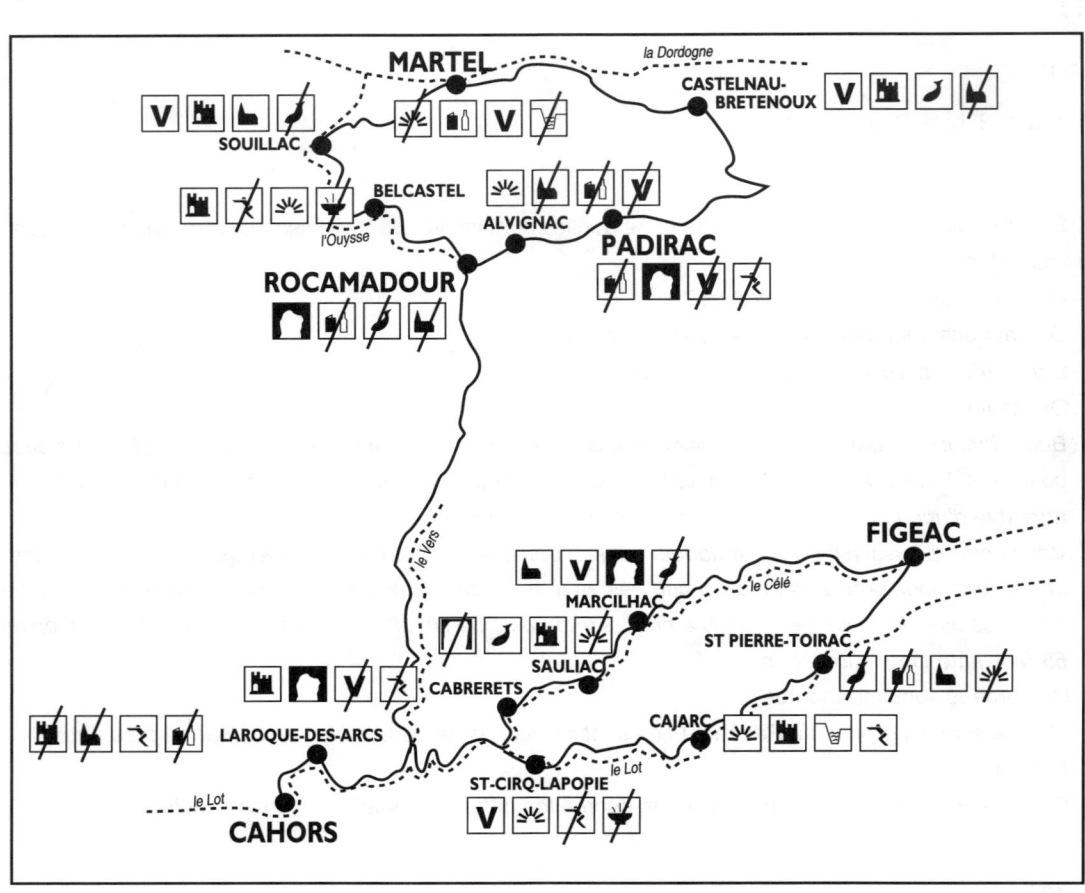

(c)
Avec plaisir. Alors, pour le premier, la balade entre Cahors et Figeac, vous suivez d'abord la vallée du Lot, puis la vallée du Célé au retour. C'est très agréable. Il y a plusieurs châteaux intéressants à voir, notamment à Cajarc, Sauliac et Cabrerets. Vous avez aussi plusieurs petits villages avec de vieilles maisons typiques de la région, par exemple à St Cirq-Lapopie et Marcilhac.

À St Cirq-Lapopie, il y a un très beau panorama sur la vallée du Lot; et à Cajarc, il y a aussi un panorama magnifique et des gorges impressionnantes. Si cela vous intéresse, il y a également des églises anciennes dans plusieurs villages, notamment à St Pierre-Toirac et Marcilhac. Vous pouvez aussi visiter de petites grottes sur ce circuit, à Marcilhac et Cabrerets. Finalement, si cela vous tente, il y a aussi des possibilités de baignade dans la rivière à Cajarc et Laroque-des-Arcs. Vous voyez, c'est un circuit très varié.

Oui, ce doit être très joli. Et qu'est-ce qu'il y a d'intéressant à faire du côté de Rocamadour?

Eh bien, il y a aussi beaucoup de sites intéressants à visiter à partir de Rocamadour. Vous avez l'embarras du choix. D'abord il y a plusieurs grands châteaux et de jolis églises très bien préservées. Au nord-est de Rocamadour vous avez le château de Belcastel avec un panorama magnifique sur la vallée de la Dordogne.

ANSWER KEYS

À Souillac, vous trouvez un village très animé avec un château et une église du 12e (douzième) siècle. Ensuite, vous allez au village médiéval de Martel, lui aussi très bien préservé. À Martel, vous avez un marché avec des spécialités gastronomiques de la région. Vous suivez la vallée de la Dordogne jusqu'à Castelnau-Bretenoux où il y a un village pittoresque et un très grand château du 11e (onzième) siècle. Au retour vous passez par la station thermale d'Alvignac.
Et où se trouvent les grottes?
Il y a beaucoup de grottes dans la région. Les plus importantes sont à Rocamadour et Padirac.
Et où est-ce que l'on peut aller à la pêche dans la région?
Il y a beaucoup de possibilités dans les environs de Sauliac et Castelnau-Bretenoux en particulier.
Merci. Vous avez quelques dépliants?
Oui. Voici des dépliants sur la région. Ils sont gratuits. Au revoir et bon séjour.

Listening 3:

(a)

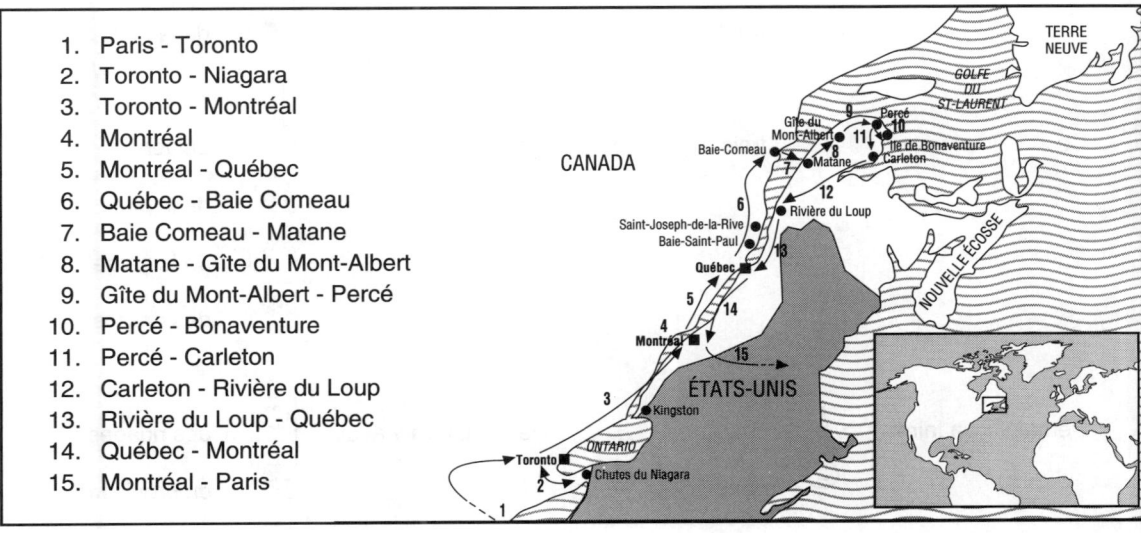

1. Paris - Toronto
2. Toronto - Niagara
3. Toronto - Montréal
4. Montréal
5. Montréal - Québec
6. Québec - Baie Comeau
7. Baie Comeau - Matane
8. Matane - Gîte du Mont-Albert
9. Gîte du Mont-Albert - Percé
10. Percé - Bonaventure
11. Percé - Carleton
12. Carleton - Rivière du Loup
13. Rivière du Loup - Québec
14. Québec - Montréal
15. Montréal - Paris

(b) 1. c; 2. a; 3. c; 4. b; 5. c; 6. b; 7. c;
     8. b; 9. b; 10. b; 11. c; 12. b; 13. c; 14. c; 15. a.

Listening 4:

(a) (4) un grand restaurant renommé, (2) concert de musique classique, (5) un petit restaurant pas cher, (8) une promenade tranquille.

(b) A (4); B (6); C (7); D (2); E (5).

(c) 1. 20h; 2. 21h; 3. 21h30.

ANSWER KEYS

Listening 5:

(a) 1. L'artisanat, la poterie, la peinture sur verres, les articles en bois, c'est très original.
2. La tarte flambée, c'est délicieux.
3. Les poteries miniatures, c'est joli, pas cher et original.
4. Les poupées folkloriques, c'est vraiment typique; c'est un beau souvenir. Les petits meubles en bois, c'est plus cher; c'est très apprécié.

(c) À proximité de la cathédrale (3); le marché sur la place (1) (3); le quartier de l'Europe (1); à côté du musée d'Alsace (2); tout près de l'hôtel (1); la vieille ville (3); un peu partout (4).

Listening 6:

a. Ce matin, il fait ☺ beau   Ce matin, il y a ☀ du soleil
                    🌡 froid   🌧 de la pluie

b. Ce soir, il va faire 🌤 frais   Ce soir il va y avoir 💨 du vent
                                                            🌧 de la pluie
                                                            ❄ de la neige
                                                            ⚡ des orages

c. Demain, il va faire 🌡 chaud   Demain, il va y avoir ☁ des nuages
                       😐 doux   🌫 du brouillard

d. Bruxelles ☺, Amsterdam 🌧, Berlin 🌫, Genève ☀,
   Rome ☀, Madrid ⚡, Londres 💨, Dublin ☁.

ANSWER KEYS

Listening 7:

(a)

Destination Destination	Temps/Weather					Températures/Temperatures		
	🌡	🌡	☼	☁	⚡	Moyenne Average	Min	Max
1. Pologne	✓				✓	32	–	–
2. Norvège			✓			22	–	–
3. Inde	✓			✓		30	–	–
4. Cuba	✓		✓	✓		–	25	30
5. Mexique				✓	✓	–	19	23
6. Australie		✓				14	–	–
7. Tahiti				✓		24	–	–
8. Turquie	✓		✓			25	–	–

(b) 1. Pologne: printemps, hiver; 2. Norvège: été; 3. Inde: hiver; 4. Mexique: automne

Exercise 1:

1. un village très animé;
2. village médiéval;
3. les visites intéressantes;
4. maisons typiques;
5. un circuit très varié;
6. un circuit très agréable;
7. des gorges impressionnantes;
8. châteaux intéressants;
9. spécialités gastronomiques;
10. grands châteaux;
11. des villages pittoresques;
12. petits villages;
13. panorama magnifique;
14. jolies églises.

Exercise 2:

Example: À St Germain-en-Laye   vous avez...
                                 il y a ....
                                 vous pouvez   visiter ....
                                               voir ....

Exercise 3:

(a) Aujourd'hui, dans le sud de l'Europe, il fait beau et chaud. Les températures sont entre 26 et 32 degrés. À Lisbonne, il y a des nuages.

ANSWER KEYS

À Paris, Munich et Genève, il fait beau. Les températures sont entre 24 et 26 degrés.
Dans le nord, il y a des nuages ou de la pluie. Il pleut à Dublin, Copenhague et Londres. Il y a des nuages à Amsterdam, Bruxelles et Berlin.

Exercise 4:

1. La Vie de Château
2. boat, your car, 'châteaux-hôtels'
3. No
4. No
5. a, c, d.

Exercise 5:

Visitor 1	Qu'est-ce qu'on peut faire à Dublin le soir?	
Guide	*Il y a beaucoup de choses à faire. Qu'est-ce qui vous intéresse?*	
Visitor 1	J'aimerais trouver un petit restaurant pas cher et ensuite écouter de la musique irlandaise.	
Guide	*Il y a beaucoup de bons restaurants pas chers à proximité de Grafton Street et il y a beaucoup de pubs avec de la musique irlandaise près de l'hôtel.*	
Visitor 1	Merci. Et à quelle heure ferment les pubs?	
Guide	*Les pubs ferment à onze heures et demie (11h30).*	
Visitor 1	D'accord. Merci.	
Guide	*Je vous en prie. Bonne soirée!*	
Visitor 2	Je voudrais faire des achats demain. Que me conseillez-vous?	
Guide	*Il y a cinq magasins près de l'hôtel. Je recommande les poteries, les pulls d'Aran et le cristal de Waterford.*	
Visitor 2	J'aimerais trouver quelque chose d'original et pas cher.	
Guide	*Je vous suggère d'acheter une cassette de musique irlandaise.*	
Visitor 2	C'est une excellente idée. Merci.	
Guide	*Je vous en prie.*	

ANSWER KEYS

UNIT 9

Listening 1:

A. 1. a, c;   2. c;
B. 1. c;   2. a.
C. 1. e;   2. c;   3. c.
D. 1. b, d.
E. 1. b;   2. c.
F. 1. b;   2. d.

Listening 2:

(a) 1. Sports complex   2. Bar   3. Students' shop
    4. Bank   5. Library   6. Residence office
    7. Restaurant

(b)

Sports Complex	
Opening hours:	8.00 a.m. - 10.00 p.m.
Fee for each visit:	£1

Bar	
Opening hours:	10.30 a.m. - 11.30 p.m.
Closed:	Sundays

Students' Shop	
Opening hours:	9.00 a.m. - 5.00 p.m.
Closed:	Saturdays and Sundays

Bank	
Opening hours:	10.30 a.m. - 12.30 p.m.
	1.30 p.m. - 2.30 p.m.
Closed:	Saturdays and Sundays
Location:	Henry Grattan building (ground floor)

Library	
Opening hours:	Monday - Thursday: 9.30 a.m. - 5.00 p.m.
	Friday: 9.45 a.m. - 4.45 p.m.
Closed:	Saturdays and Sundays
Location:	Next to Henry Grattan Building

Residence Office	
Opening hours:	7.30 a.m. - 10.00 p.m.
Telephone number:	704 5736
Fax number:	704 5777

Restaurant	
Breakfast served from:	8.30 a.m.

ANSWER KEYS

Listening 3:

Name	Temple Bar Hotel	Student Residences	Extra Nights	Accompanying Persons	Amount Paid £	Amount Due £
International Conference for Tourism Studies June 24–25–26, 1994						
BRAULT Alice		✓	~~0~~ *1*	1	370	*39*
JOUBERT Martine	✓		0	0	236	*0*
JOUVAL André		✓	0	~~2~~ *1*	185	*185*
LEBLANC Marcel	✓		0	0	185	*51*
SEBILLE Christine	✓		2	~~0~~ *1*	308	*308*
TISSOT Gabriel		✓	0	0	185	*0*

ANSWER KEYS

Listening 4:

	International Conference For Tourism Studies June 24–25–26, 1994 **Programme/Programme of Events**	
Date et heures Date and time	Activités/Activity	Emplacement/Location
Jeudi 24 juin **Thursday 24 June**		
09.00–09.30	Inscription/Registration	Réception/Reception
09.30–11.00	Séance plénière/Plenary session Accueil et ouverture/Welcome and opening	Amphithéâtre Larkin/ Larkin Lecture Theatre
11.00–11.30 11.30–13.00	Pause-café/Coffee Ateliers A à D/Workshops A to D	~~S255~~ *S254* A: S217 B: S219 C: S220 ~~D: S218~~ *D: S216*
13.00–14.30	Déjeuner/Lunch	Restaurant
14.30–15.30	Ateliers E à H/Workshops E to H	E: S217 F: S219 G: S218 H: S220
15.30–16.00	Pause-café/Coffee	~~S255~~ *S254*
16.00–17.30	Ateliers I à L/Workshops I to L	~~I: S122~~ *I: S120* J: S122 K: S121 L: S123
~~18.00~~ *18.30*	Bus pour le centre ville/ Buses to city centre	Parking/ Car park
~~18.30~~ *19.00*	Réception organisée par le Maire Reception hosted by Lord Mayor	Mansion House

ANSWER KEYS

Listening 5:

20e Salon Mondial du Tourisme et des Voyages
20th World Tourism and Travel Fair

Lieu/Location:	PARIS
Dates/Dates:	16 - 22 février
Journées réservées aux professionnels/Trade only days:	16 - 17 février
Heures d'ouverture/Opening hours:	09h - 20 h
Journées grand public/Open to the public:	18 - 22 février
Heures d'ouverture/Opening hours:	10h - 19h
Exposants/Exhibitors:	1125
Étrangers/Foreign:	310
Français/French:	815
Surfaces louées/Total surface area let:	21 560 m^2
Visiteurs attendus/Expected number of visitors:	140 000

Renseignements/Information:

Numéro de téléphone/Telephone number:	43 49 60 85
Numéro de Fax/Fax number:	46 35 78 22

ANSWER KEYS

Listening 6:

20ᵉ SALON MONDIAL DU TOURISME ET DES VOYAGES

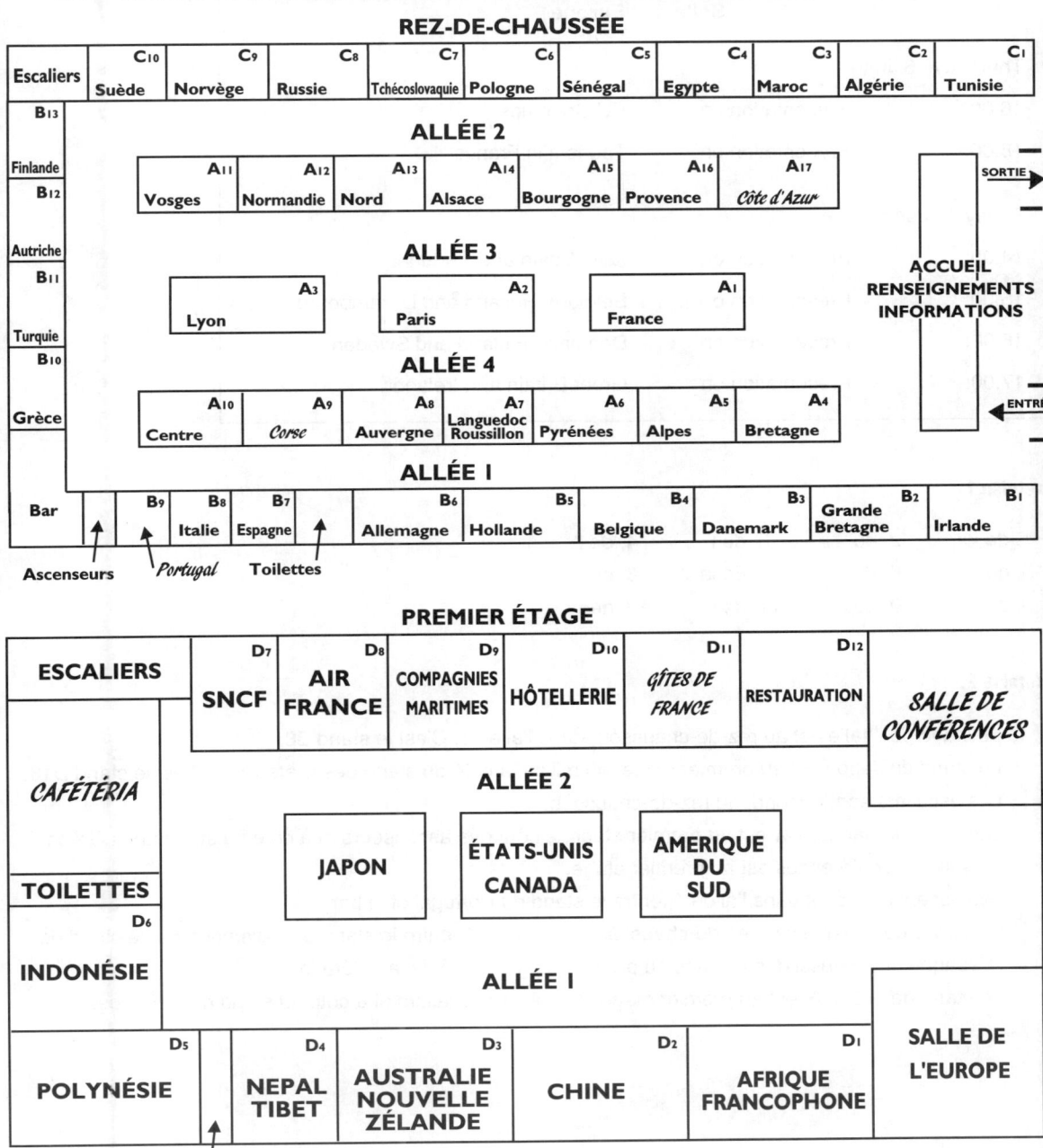

ANSWER KEYS

Listening 7:

Salle de l'Europe
Thursday 16 June
16.00:   Presentation on   EU Countries
18.00:   Presentation on   Tourism in France
Friday 17 June
14.00:   Presentation on   Italy, Spain and Portugal
15.00:   Presentation on   Belgium, Holland and Luxembourg
16.00:   Presentation on   Denmark, Finland and Sweden
17.00:   Presentation on   Great Britain and Ireland

Exercise 1:

1. de la   2. du   3. de l'   4. de l'
5. du   6. du   7. de la   8. du
9. des   10. des   11. de l'   12. des

Exercise 2:

1. Le stand de l'Italie est au rez-de-chaussée, dans l'allée 1. C'est le stand B8.
2. Le stand du Japon est au premier étage, au milieu, à côté du stand des États-Unis. C'est le stand D13.
3. Les escaliers sont au fond, au rez-de-chaussée.
4. Oui, il y a un bar. Le bar est au premier étage, à côté des ascenseurs et à côté du stand de la Grèce.
5. La salle de conférences est au premier étage.
6. Les ascenseurs sont dans l'allée 1, entre le stand du Portugal et le bar.
7. Oui, il y a des toilettes au rez-de-chaussée dans l'allée 1, entre le stand de l'Allemagne et le stand de l'Espagne. Il y a aussi des toilettes au premier étage à côté de la cafétéria.
8. Le stand de la SNCF est au premier étage, à côté des escaliers et à côté du stand d'Air France.

ANSWER KEYS

Exercise 3:

International Conference for Tourism Studies
June 24–25–26, 1994

Date: Vendredi 25 juin/Friday 25 June

Heures/Time	Activités/Activity	Emplacement/Location
09.30–11.00	Séance plénière/Plenary session	Amphithéâtre Larkin Larkin Lecture Theatre
11.00–11.30	Coffee	S254
11.30–13.00	Workshops	N: S217
		O: S219
		P: S218
		Q: S220
13.00–14.30	Lunch	Restaurant
14.30–16.00	Workshops	R: S217
		S: S218
		T: S220
16.00–16.30	Coffee	S254
16.30–17.30	Plenary Session	Larkin Lecture Theatre
18.00	Bus pour la réception au château Buses to the Castle for reception	Car park

Exercise 4:

Participant	Bonjour.	
Assistant	*Bonjour, Madame. Vous participez à la conférence sur le tourisme?*	
Participant	Oui, Monsieur.	
Assistant	*Quel est votre nom, s'il vous plaît, et quel est le nom de votre entreprise?*	
Participant	Je m'appelle Valérie Petit et je travaille pour Eurovoyages. Quels sont les sujets des conférences, à quelle heure est-ce que cela commence et dans quelle salle?	
Assistant	*Voilà le programme des conférences:* *lundi, aujourd'hui, à 10 heures - conférence sur les agences de voyages.* *mardi à 9 heures et demie - conférence sur le tourisme rural.* *mercredi à 11 heures - conférence sur le tourisme des affaires.* *jeudi à 10 heures et demie - conférence sur les centres de loisirs.* *Toutes les conférences finissent à 16 heures trente et elles ont lieu dans la salle des conférences au rez-de-chaussée, au fond du couloir à gauche.*	
Participant	Est-ce qu'il y a un restaurant sur place?	
Assistant	*Non, je suis désolé, il n'y a pas de restaurant dans le centre mais il y a un restaurant à 50 mètres en face de la gare.*	
Participant	Est-ce que vous pouvez me dire où se trouvent les toilettes et le vestiaire?	
Assistant	*Les toilettes dames sont à droite à côté des ascenseurs. Le vestiaire est à côté de la réception.*	
Participant	Je vous remercie.	
Assistant	*Je vous en prie. Bonne journée!*	

ANSWER KEYS

TEST YOUR COMPETENCE 2

Exercise 1:

(a) 1. originale   2. ancienne   3. pittoresque   4. magnifique   5. allemande

(b) 1. agréables   2. immenses   3. irlandais   4. françaises   5. variés

Exercise 2:

(a)
1. il est fermé le mardi
2. il est espagnol
3. il part à 18h15
4. elle est magnifique
5. elle est à gauche
6. elle est belge

(b)
1. elles sont impressionnantes
2. ils sont à l'hôtel Concorde
3. ils ont une piscine
4. elles sont en réunion
5. elles sont au fond du couloir
6. ils sont à votre gauche

Exercise 3:

(a)
1. vous devez aller à la gare
2. vous devez tourner à gauche
3. vous devez prendre une douche
4. vous devez payer à la caisse
5. vous devez passer par Paris
6. vous devez faire attention

(b)
1. Téléphonez à Madame Richet.
2. Achetez une carte postale.
3. Visitez la Tour Eiffel.
4. Choisissez un restaurant.
5. Sortez par la porte B.
6. Partez le samedi.

Exercise 4:

1. Ce matin, Marc va faire du tennis.
2. L'avion va arriver dans vingt minutes.
3. Elle va visiter les Antilles.
4. Il va pleuvoir.
5. Il va faire beau.
6. Il va y avoir du vent.

Exercise 5:

(a)
1. Le musée n'est pas ouvert le lundi.
2. Le restaurant n'est pas fermé en décembre.
3. Le gîte n'est pas situé à St Jean.

ANSWER KEYS

4. La visite n'est pas gratuite.
5. L'avion n'arrive pas à 18 heures.
6. Paul ne fait pas de la plongée sous-marine.

(b)
1. Il n'y a pas de poste sur la place.
2. Il n'y a pas de bus pour Avignon.
3. Il n'y a pas de chambre libre.
4. Il n'y a pas de cinéma en ville.
5. Il n'y a pas de concert ce soir.
6. Il n'y a pas de boutique de souvenirs.

Exercise 6:

1. Voulez-vous un dépliant?
   Est-ce que vous voulez un dépliant?

2. Allez-vous en Irlande en bateau?
   Est-ce que vous allez en Irlande en bateau?

3. Désirez-vous le menu?
   Est-ce que vous désirez le menu?

4. Prenez-vous le train ou l'avion?
   Est-ce que vous prenez le train ou l'avion?

5. Acceptez-vous les cartes de crédit?
   Est-ce que vous acceptez les cartes de crédit?

6. Passez-vous par la Suisse ou l'Italie?
   Est-ce que vous passez par la Suisse ou par l'Italie?

Exercise 7:

1. c;   2. e;   3. No;   4. b;   5. c, d;   6. Yes.

Exercise 8:

1. La Tour de James Joyce est à huit miles de Dublin, environ douze kilomètres.
   Pour aller à la Tour, vous pouvez prendre le bus No. 8 ou le train DART.
   La tour est ouverte du lundi au vendredi de 10 heures à 17 heures d'avril à octobre.
   De mai à septembre, elle est ouverte de 10 heures à 17 heures du lundi au samedi.
   Le dimanche et les jours fériés, elle est ouverte de 14 heures à 18 heures.
   Elle est fermée de 13 heures à 14 heures pour le déjeuner pendant la semaine.

ANSWER KEYS

L'entrée coûte une livre soixante-quinze (£1.75) pour les adultes.
Pour les adultes en groupe, ça coûte une livre vingt-cinq (£1.25).
Pour les cartes Vermeil et les étudiants de 12 à 17 ans ça coûte une livre quarante (£1.40) et une livre dix (£1.10) en groupe.
Pour les enfants, ça coûte quatre-vingt-dix pence (£0.90) et soixante-dix pence de 3 à 11 ans (£0.70) en groupe.
Il y a aussi un billet famille. Il coûte cinq livres (£5.00).
C'est pour deux adultes et trois ou quatre enfants.
Il y a une librairie sur place.

2. La maison de George Bernard Shaw est à Dublin. Elle est ouverte de mai à septembre, du lundi au samedi de 10 heures à 17 heures.
Le dimanche et les jours fériés, elle est ouverte de 14 heures à 18 heures.
L'entrée coûte £1.75 pour les adultes et £1.25 pour les adultes en groupe.
Pour les cartes Vermeil et les étudiants de 12 à 17 ans, ça coûte £1.40 et £1.10 en groupe.
Pour les enfants de 3 à 11 ans, ça coûte £0.90p et £0.70p en groupe.
Il y a aussi un billet famille.
Il coûte £5.
C'est pour deux adultes et trois ou quatre enfants.
Il y a une librairie sur place.

Exercise 9:

1. c;   2. a, b, d;   3. c;   4. a, b, c, e;   5. b;   6. No.

Exercise 10:

Il y a trois îles Aran - Inishmore, Inishmaan et Inishere.

Pour aller à Inishmore, vous pouvez prendre le bateau ou l'avion. Il y a trois traversées par jour à partir de Galway. Le retour est à 5 heures.

Il y a trois ou quatre traversées par jour à partir de Rossaveal, à trente-huit kilomètres à l'ouest de Galway.

Il y a plusieurs vols par jour. L'avion part de l'aéroport de Galway. L'aéroport est à Carnmore, à huit kilomètres à l'est de Galway.

Pour aller à Inishmaan, vous pouvez prendre le bateau ou l'avion.

Il y a trois traversées par jour de juin au 9 septembre. Le bateau part de Spiddal, à dix-huit kilomètres à l'ouest de Galway. Il y a une navette de la gare de Galway à Spiddal.

Il y a plusieurs vols par jour entre Inishmaan et Galway et entre Inishmaan et Inishmore et Inishere. La compagnie aérienne est Aer Arann.

ANSWER KEYS

Pour aller à Inishere, vous pouvez prendre le bateau ou l'avion.

Il y a douze traversées aller-retour par jour, entre Doolin et Inishere. Le bateau quitte Doolin à l'heure et rentre à la demi-heure. La traversée prend de vingt-cinq à trente minutes.

Il y a trois traversées par jour de juin au 9 septembre entre Spiddal et Inishere.

Il y a plusieurs vols par jour entre Inishere et Galway et entre Inishmaan et Inishmore.

Exercise 11:

1. Côte d'Azur;   2. d;   3. c;   4. b, c, d, f, g, h, j, l;
5. sailing; tennis;   6. dolphins.

Exercise 12:

Le centre Eilí Bay est dans l'ouest de l'Irlande, dans le comté Mayo.

Un weekend coûte soixante livres ou soixante-treize livres. Cela comprend la nourriture (les repas), le voyage et l'hébergement. Vous pouvez aller à Eilí Bay en autocar (£60) ou en train (£73). Vous pouvez faire (pratiquer) beaucoup d'activités: le canoë, la planche à voile, la voile, la randonnée pédestre, le vélo, la natation et le golf. C'est très varié.

Exercise 13:

1. d,   2. a,   3. e,   4. c,   5. b.

Exercise 14:

Le dimanche, vous avez trois possibilités:

- La visite de Glendalough et du panorama de Wicklow. Elle commence à 10h30 et finit à 17h45. C'est du 30 mars au 26 septembre. Ça coûte douze livres (£12) pour un adulte et six livres (£6) pour un enfant.

- La visite de la 'Boyne Valley' avec une visite à Newgrange part à 10 heures et finit à 17h45. C'est du 12 mai au 27 septembre. Ça coûte douze livres (£12) pour un adulte et cinq livres (£5) pour un enfant.

- La visite des jardins de Powerscourt et du 'Pine Forest' commence à 14h15 et finit à 18h. C'est du 3 mai au 13 septembre. Ça coûte dix livres (£10) pour un adulte et cinq livres (£5) pour un enfant.

Le vendredi, vous avez deux possibilités:

- La visite de Dublin. Elle commence à 11h15 et finit à 15h. C'est du 4 mai au 26 septembre. Ça coûte neuf livres (£9) pour un adulte et quatre livres cinquante (£4.50) pour un enfant.

- La visite de Avondale, Glendalough et les collines du Wicklow. Elle commence à 09h30 et finit à 16h30.

ANSWER KEYS

C'est du 5 juin au 18 septembre. Ça coûte douze livres (£12) pour un adulte et six livres (£6) pour un enfant.

Exercise 15:

1. c; 2. car; taxi; coach; train; 3. under the esplanade; 4. No; 5. No; 6. yes; 7. Métro Express Regional; 8. c; 9. 1: (c); 2: (i); 3: (k); 4: (g); 5: (l); 6: (e); 7: (d); 8: (f); 9: (h); 10: (b); 11: (a); 12: (j).

Exercise 16:

Le salon 'National Catering Exhibition' aura lieu à Dublin à R.D.S. du 15 au 18 février.

Le R.D.S. se trouve à Ballsbridge. Pour aller du centre ville au R.D.S., vous pouvez prendre les bus Nos 7, 7A ou 8 ou le train DART.

Le salon est ouvert de 11 heures à 20 heures le lundi 15, mardi 16 et mercredi 17. Le jeudi 18, il est ouvert de 11 heures à 17h30. C'est un salon pour les professionnels. L'entrée coûte cinq livres (£5). Il faut avoir seize ans ou plus pour entrer.